ODE TO DIDCOT POWER STATION

KIT WRIGHT

BLOODAXE BOOKS

ISBN: 978 1 78037 106 1

First published in 2014 by
Bloodaxe Books Ltd,
Eastburn,
South Park,
Hexham,
Northumberland NE46 1BS,

Second impression 2015.

www.bloodaxebooks.com
For further information about Bloodaxe titles
please visit our website or write to
the above address for a catalogue.

Cover design: Neil Astley & Pamela Robertson-Pearce.

Printed in Great Britain by Bell & Bain Limited, Glasgow, Scotland, on acid-free paper sourced from mills with FSC chain of custody certification.

CONTENTS

ACKNOWLEDGEMENTS

A number of these poems first appeared in *The Oldie* when I was its resident poet, others in *The Guardian*, *Folio*, *The Spectator, The Times Literary Supplement*, *The Wisden Cricketer* and the anthologies *A Mutual Friend: Poems for Charles Dickens* (Two Rivers Press, 2011) and *Jubilee Lines: 60 Poets for 60 Years* (Faber & Faber, 2012). *Talking to the Weeds* was first published as a limited edition pamphlet by Happy Dragons Press and *A Lisbon Sheaf* by Kings Lynn Poetry Festival.

For Marianne

Metal

A steelmill town, a ridge of pine,
   The taste of snow upon the tongue,
Meant all the world was black and white
   At Christmastime when he was young.

In softened angle, muted line,
   The harshnesses became oblique.
The keening lathes were pacified:
   All quiet on the frozen creek.

And it was Christmas when he died
   Far off, no place on earth to go,
But fresh as in his childhood came
   The scent of metal and of snow.

That Was the Summer

That was the summer as I recall,
the man next door and I began
to call each other Sir,
in a kind of roguish formality or
mock-combative collusion. Why,
I cannot say, but keep it up
we somehow did for some little time;
for as long, you might almost say, as it took.
'Are you all right, sir?' 'Quite all right, sir.
You all right, sir?' 'Sir, I'm well.'
Nor did we fail to operate
attendant quasi-theatrical business:
the stiff half-turn; the ritual bow;
the planted stare of profound regard,
as we met on our doorsteps, housekeys poised...
or bellowed across the howling High Road
'ARE YOU ALL RIGHT, SIR?' 'QUITE ALL RIGHT, SIR!'
as though in loyal defence of a principle
both were prepared to die for, soon.
But the ending seemed as inexplicable
as the beginning: the disappearance,
ambulance sirens, police, old pressmen
hogging the bar at the Horse and Artichoke,
cats gone skinny, the haunted dog.
And of course I know no more than anyone
else as I walk these streets at midnight,
hoping to coax from neon or starlight
a final reflexive *Sir, I'm well.*

A Word from a Small Figure in a Strict Drawing

In Architects' Impressions,
How fair they are to see:
The gleaming towers like perfect teeth,
The patterned courtyards underneath;
The beds of well-instructed flowers
Baptised at birth, improved by showers;
The walkways beaming in the sun;
The project luminously one
Where Art and Function shake hands and agree…

And purposefully striding,
Decisive, bold and free,
Look, it's the little people
Pretending to be.

That's us! Attendant folk, we're charmed to play
Our small part in rehearsals for the day
The dream's made concrete. We shall not reveal
The fat backhander that secured the deal,
Nor prophesy what seems to lie beyond:
Brute decibels, the condom in the pond,
The terrorising gangs, the shit-writ wall,
The rule of drugs and death and, oh, 'respect',
Which we would recommend but can't detect.

Lament for Stinie Morrison
(Convicted 1911)

These are the canyons of Ukraine
from which he came
to take the name,
to take the name
of Stinie.

These are the sharp and hungry streets
of black Whitechapel, that pulled as tight
as fiddle-strings round the lying throat
of Stinie.

This is the Yiddish theatre played
by flickering candles, penny gaffs
with songs and poems and fiddle tunes
for Stinie.

These are the *spielers* and shebeens,
the bouncing brothels, the gambling holes
with rat and cockroach working a living
inside them just
like Stinie.

This is the man they smashed to death
on Clapham Common, his ankles crossed,
with fiddle-holes cut in his shrouded face,
and smack in the frame
was Stinie.

This is the fence and this the gold,
the jemmy, the knife, the Browning gun,
and this is Whitechapel and it's done
for Stinie.

The Plague Horses

When people began to bring out their dead, the dead-
Cart drivers at first seemed blessed with a strange immunity.
They piled the items high on the buckboard bed
And trotted them off to the limepits with impunity.

But when they began to die themselves, their horses,
Burdened with husbands and daughters and sons and wives,
And a corpse at the reins, were ruled by eccentric forces,
Ambling and shambling and tacking about the community,

Wondering what to do with the rest of their lives.

A Travelling Song for Sam Johnson

If I had no duties, and no reference to futurity, I would spend my life in driving briskly in a post-chaise with a pretty woman.

Briskly in a post-chaise
  I'd go driving down the lanes,
With a pretty woman sitting by my side...
And our hearts would beat like hoofbeats
  To the jingle of the reins,
And we'd never head for home till eventide!

Gaily in a post-chaise,
  How I'd bid all care adieu,
How I'd leave my weary labours far behind...
And with a pretty woman
  Such as you, or you, or you,
Out of sight would put all duties out of mind!

Posterity? Futurity?
Each noun is an impurity
  That blights the present tense.
Futurity? Posterity?
I'd ditch them with celerity,
  For instantaneous pleasure
  Is a treasure
    More immense!

Blithely in a post-chaise,
  We'd go lilting on our way,
All sorrow and all guilt would be undone...
And with a pretty woman
  My companion for the day,
Felicity would light me like the sun!

Littlebredy

At the top of the hill the twisted thorns
Were crouching out of the way of the wind
That raced in over the miles of shivering furze.
The valley air
Was sweet with the honey of yellow-beaked flowers
And across the lake the house
Stared at itself in the olive water.

What had been remembered
By the folk intelligence of the path
That chose that way of all ways through the trees?
Why had the dreaming ice
In the slumbering glacier warmed toward this shape,
Beyond all others,
To hollow out its inclination?

Everything there knew why,
However,
The white-robed cricketers
Had made their way down into the valley
To do their dance of stillness,
To do their courtly dance of almost stillness,
Dancing upon their graves before they died.

Ode to Didcot Power Station

What vasty thighs outspread to give thee birth,
DIDCOT, thou marvel of the plain?
Colossal funnels of the steamship EARTH,
Thy consummate immensity
Enshrines the rare propensity
Of fumes to form eternal acid rain!
While, in their pious hosts, Romano-Celtic ghosts
Are knelt to worship thy
All-belching *amphorae*,
And shadows of thy sacrificial breathing fill the sky!

DIDCOT, thou bugger!
Thou teaser of the mind
And recollection-tugger! Thee I find
To replicate the days when I was small
What time my mother, sweet and kind,
The fragrant Friar's Balsam did infuse.
She therewithal
A towel placed upon my head
And loving care did use
That pulmonary perils might not wake me with the dead.

DIDCOT! To one more
Soft eidolon thou steam'st ope mem'ry's door...
For in thy hanging shrouds I view return
Far other blue-grey clouds;
My father's pipe-smoke I in thee discern,
Companion true,
That followed him all days
And ways he ventured through this singing maze,
To take that turn
All entrants in their bafflement and grace may not eschew.

What links of tenderness are forged by thee,
DIDCOT, thou ever-burning core!
Insensate lover of the loves that flee!
Thou glade of past felicity,
Thy sap of electricity
Complicit in our veins for evermore!
Struggling anent the storm, thy children ghost the form
Of all our quickenings may ever be...
DIDCOT, thy billows pour,
Connatural, contiguous, familial as the sea!

Animula

(the Emperor Hadrian dying)

animula vagula blandula
hospes comesque corporis
quae nunc abibis in loca
pallidula rigida nudula
nec ut soles dabis iocos

Little wanderer, gentle soul of mine,
My body's guest, my body's friend as well,
  Wherever will you go to now,
  Pale and naked, cold and stiff,
  With no more jokes to tell?

Oratory

(Fulvia: wife of Mark Antony)

The silver tongue of Cicero
  Had not a match in Latin.
The nemesis of Cataline,
  Corrosive and as harsh as brine,
    It yet was smooth as satin.

The silver tongue of Cicero,
  His head cut off, turned black.
Then Fulvia wrenched it from its root
And it became her fond pursuit
  To stab it with a hairpin… so!
  The silver tongue of Cicero,
    That could not answer back.

Watching the Wireless

Way back down in the fifties,
Deep back dark back down in the fifties,
When the dockers were always on strike
Except for Sir Bernard and Lady Docker
Who plated their cars with gold
And were deemed ineffable...

When, shall we say, Jack Hawkins played
The Detective Superintendent,
Said 'Wait, I've got an idea!'
And raised his trilby hat on a stick
Over the warehouse wall,
The better to draw the villain's fire
And determine his position –
HE'S OVER THERE! –
Well, round about then...

That's way back down in the fifties,
Boom back zoom back down to the fifties,
The family watched the wireless,
Niched like an icon in the tied
Flat with a school kitchen
Four floors down below,
And it spoke to them.
As from a ship
On the night sea with its lit and steadfast
Foreign cabin windows...
Or it hung there like a sybil
In the cave of its own sound,
And in the singing cage of the room
High in the windy trees,
They watched the wireless to see what it would say.

There Was a Ship, Quoth He

When I was on the rolling main in 1969,
From Montreal to Liverpool bound on the dear old CP line,
No finer liner took the flood than ours of the *Empress* class,
But everyone knew, ourselves and the crew, sea-travel was on its arse.

So a sort of pall hung over the decks, a doomy sense of loss,
The kind you get when somebody's died or bagged an albatross,
And on and on, till it made you want to plunge into the sea,
A Scouse ship's band played *Lily the Pink* in the ballroom *(nbg)*.

At least, I say it was *nbg*. Perhaps it was OK,
For superhumanly we contrived to dance the night away,
Nor did I neglect to attend by day those mariners in their prime
At the fixed and normative, highly informative *Nautical Question Time*,

Well, once I made it. For most of the time, I concede that I was drunk
And nearly killed myself by falling backwards out of my bunk.
But also I was sweetly involved where sweetness shouldn't have been,
Which I regret though almost forty summers intervene,

So maybe it tastes like vinegar and maybe it tastes like wine,
That time upon the rolling main in 1969.

The Year Nijinsky Won the Triple Crown

Oshawa-foaled in the boundless Dominion of Canada –
Great
Scott!

Was he the mightiest thoroughbred ever conceived –
Or
What?

Northern Dancer his sire
And Flaming Page his dam,
This matchless colt
Like a thunderbolt
Whizzed out of the bunch and WHAM!

Horse of the Twentieth Century!
All time King of the Flat!
No one had seen
An equine machine
Accelerate like that!

The 2000 Guineas, the Derby and then the St Leger –
Ker-
ripes!
And up was the greatest jockey ever in silks
Or
Stripes:

The Long Fellow, Lester Piggott,
Beating the whole field down
Like a wave that's tidal –
On bit and bridle
Taking the Triple Crown!

Then peacefully put out to stud,
This superhorse was fecund,
Retired from that Annus Mirabilis
(By all sound judges reckoned):

The eighteenth year of Her Majesty
Queen Elizabeth the Second!

A Man of Mynton

Widely regarded
As Mynton Parish Church's

Most talented sidesman
Of the post-war period,

Eric Arthur Upton
Has handed in his plate.

Sombre and scrotal now
Hangs his collection bag,

Dark in the Vestry
In abandoned state.

Sad are the aisles
That were graced by the advent

Of his soft-shoe shuffle,
Alert yet sedate:

Mournful the heads
Of the pews where benignly

And with seamless discretion
He would stand in wait.

Highly regarded
As Mynton Parish Church's

Most finished servant
As of even date,

Eric Arthur Upton,
Boxed as a rarity,

Pauses with honour
In his own lych-gate.

Ornamental Waters

A ride ran down to the Ornamental Waters
Where islands were planted and here was a heronry
And there was a shoulder-of-mutton-shaped lake.

What was it drew her, wandering in Wanstead,
Taking the mist where the Tudor and Palladian
Mansions had once ruled geometric gardens

And yelling boarhounds were gored in the brake?

Maybe a mirror for her loss and bewilderment,
Maybe an echo of her own estrangement,
Lakeland and woodland made in her heart:

Where the queen's favourites lay with their favourites,
Dragon-mouthed grottoes were ports for the marsh birds,
Leaves were of perilous, brittle weaving

And the boar in the thicket was dragged apart.

Birthday Poem for Vernon Scannell

They seem to like each other, years.
One year won't mind another
Supplanting it, however fast
It witlessly becomes the past.
Each seems to each a brother.
For them it is no cause for tears;
They snuggle, close and matey,
As they go whizzing on their way.
For us, not so. But still I say,
I can't believe you're eighty!

When I was unsweet seventeen,
I met you first, in Surrey.
And you were kind enough to read
What I thought very good indeed,
My adolescent slurry.
Naïve my verse, jejune and green,
And neither wise nor weighty.
Quite talentless. But you somehow
Encouraged kindly then. And now,
I can't believe you're eighty!

From there the film of you and me
Grows slightly more erratic.
Round sudden zooms and strange dissolves
The lurching narrative revolves,
The sound-track rent with static.
Yet all locations seem to be,
If plaster, brick, or slatey,
Uncannily, some kind of bar.
What can this mean? I'm glad you are,
I'm very glad you're eighty!

My dear old friend, I think your art
        Is cause for love and wonder.
Of grief, of tenderness and truth
It speaks to me as in my youth.
        Let no man put asunder
Such marriage of the mind and heart.
        Not Papa Doc in Haiti
Could blackly magic it from view.
For being brave, for being you,
        God bless you now you're eighty!

Birthday Poem for Posy Simmonds

At the birth of gifted Posy,
Edmund Heep was also born,
Did he know it, and his rosy
Cheeks appeared the self-same dawn:
Features of that fond buffoon
Which by dint of deep carousing
Later shed their trouser housing,
Mooning at the August moon.

In the wings her own inventions,
Like the shades in Plato's cave,
Hovered, waiting her intentions,
All the ways that she would pave.
There, about to be begun,
George and Wendy, angst-tormented,
Stanhope, all lust unrepented,
And the fat Bear in the Sun.

Teddy Bear of Picnic Teddies!
Lord and leader of the rest!
K. Penwallet, squeezing readies
From the grockles in the West.
By her cot the Baker's Cat
Slept on guard and in his keeping
Safe she lay, and in her sleeping
Dreamed his story's tit-for-tat.

Lulu and the Flying Babies
Watched the baby lying there.
Possibilities and maybes
Danced on the enchanted air.

Every drawing, every plot.
   Hilaire Belloc smiled benignly,
Knowing her to be so finely
   Realised, his fibbing tot.

Emma countermanded sadness,
   Seeing who would tell her tale,
And the Webers danced for gladness!
   Edmund, though beyond the pale,
Chuffed to wet the baby's head,
   Had a noggin for the natal
Day – just one should not prove fatal –
   Though it proved a score instead.

Posy, your inspired creations,
   Motive by your hand and eye,
Join us in these celebrations,
   Lighting up the fictive sky
In eudemonistic mood!
   Beautiful and kind and clever,
For the strength of your endeavour
   You've our love and gratitude.

Birthday Poem for Gerda

We sometimes get away with murder,
        Flat of foot and dull of wit,
Muses flightless or in Purdah,
        Dead as ducks upon a spit.
Then we lack the art of Gerda,
That true wizard wonder-worder,
        For the highest laurels fit!

Gerda Mayer, Gerda Mayer,
What a bright poetic player
        You have been
        For all these years!
What a player, what a stayer,
What a quizzical truth-sayer,
        Close to laughter
        And to tears!

Personal, your maker's mark –
Dark in light and light in dark –
        Please accept
        This birthday card:
Blessings to a true inspirer
From an unreserved admirer
        And an envious
        Fellow-bard!

TALKING TO THE WEEDS

Long Purples 1

Ophelia for Millais sang and died,
A drift of river crowfoot by each side,
And on the far bank those 'long purples' rose
He understood as loosestrife. We suppose
Him wrong. Yet how integral now they seem,
A smoky grief above the laden stream,
Although 'dog's bollocks' were the bard's intent:
Those early purple orchids Gertrude meant.

Long Purples 2

And early purple orchids, so they told
My mother as a child in Derbyshire,
Wore those dark blotches on their leaves because
They grew beneath the Cross and bore the stains
Of Christ's blood, so my mother told to me.

Oxford Ragwort

Senecio squalidus,
Or there again, dirty old man,
Is the handle of Oxford Ragwort,
Now seasonably at large.

And I certainly wish you a hearty
Welcome back, old man,
On behalf of all the other
Dirty old men in town…

For you're the urban vagrant,
Far from your country cousins
That give cirrhosis to cattle
And nourish imperilled moths…

And though I know you're game
For sticking around all winter
If days are mild enough
And the vitals to your liking,

It's now that you're out in force:
Busting from rumpled tarmac,
Yomping along the pavement,
Seeded in narrow cracks.

And though it's a fact you favour
Angles of punished brickwork,
Haunts of the lifted dog-leg,
How free a spirit you are!

Only the clumsy cut
Of your amateurishly drafted
Leaves, like Roman British
Mosaics, is less than lyrical.

Squalid you just are *not*
But fresh and apparently youthful
And all in all, old man,
Quite the golden boy.

Star of Bethlehem

And what did Leonardo make of you?
A whirlpool:

A Gorgon's head,
A nest of scourges,

Whip and seethe of narrow, white-striped leaves
Electrically kinetic:

As though the spiral-forging
Generator

Turned on the current for each six-point
Bright white inflorescence

To open in the woodland as a star.

Hedge Mustard

Here comes the wind to dance in your bony arms,
officially open your scarecrow convention,
set your antennae twisting for news,
whip your weathervanes, broadcast
your bitter stars.

Wiry Jack, how faithful you are!
The whole scrap metal stack of your ratcheted stems
is the rig of affections and beliefs
that's never entirely toppled,
however so often you're trashed and count for nothing.

Rosebay Willowherb

On the Docklands Light Railway I rumbled along,
   I swung round the flank of the Bank of Hong Kong,
My heart was so heavy the train nearly fell
   From the grey viaduct to the canyons of hell –

      But I found where the fireweed was growing
         At the edge of the Island again –
            The Isle of Dogs –
      At the edge of the Island again.

When I got out at Mudchute that old City Farm,
   With the lowing of livestock, was salve and was balm,
As I walked by the water my spirits arose
   With the mist in my eyes and the muck at my toes –

      For I'd found where the fireweed was blowing
         At the edge of the Island again –
            The Isle of Dogs –
      At the edge of the Island again.

So come all you hangdogs and listen to me,
   Go down where the river swings round for the sea,
Abandon your *angst* where those purple blooms are,
   Obligingly served by the old DLR –

      And you'll find where the fireweed is glowing
         At the edge of the Island again –
            The Isle of Dogs –
      At the edge of the Island again.

Ivy

Too strong, too dark, too smothering, too baleful,
   And all-pervasive like a graveyard cough,
The ivy ran a tight protection racket,
   So I resolved to run the hoodlum off.

And when I struggled out the stumpy root
   And yanked it free, it wrenched from me a groan
Which I heard echoed by that sensate thing
   That seemed to breathe a death-sigh of its own.

Large Bindweed

You'll make a trampoline of a garage roof,
Obliterate a fence in days
With twinings
Of that tapestry…

In which your leaves plaster the wire like tongues,
And the white bells of your flowers are strangely
Lustrous and serene
For a thing so objurgated.

X2, x5, x10 they might be had,
The humble fags that bore your rural name:
Wild Woodbine. And your image too
Adorned the pack

In a style on loan from William Morris.
We smoked them at fourteen
Illicitly in dripping underhangs
Of beech trees, in your presence.

Hop

Sun brings out the spider, fat as a crab in a rockpool,
Legging it over the rigging. And rain entertains the slug

That snogs the leaf with the whole of its body
On demolition contracts. Nothing

Could suffer so much from mite or kiss or blight
As the hop, which is shredded alive.

Males have the tendrilish catkins, females the sacred cones
That give the edge to that otherwise bland potation

I have so loyally consumed that I stand by the root and whisper:
You died that we might drink.

Honesty

So pure and still a purple
breathing at dusk from the tall mantles
ruined into paper coins
and helpless see-through tears of honesty…

Periwinkle

How beautiful are the five wide tapering rotas
that spin your milky
blue propeller
that turns through the sea of the air
and turns
the sea of the air
into something grateful.

Likewise how volatile is St Elmo's fire
that plays the mast
like burning blossom
(the straight line down the heart of your leaves)
and shapes within each one
a tree of flame.

Germander Speedwell

It's a poor heart that wouldn't rejoice
in the middle of Wanstead Flats
while taking the long diagonal
between the Baptist chapel and the pub
called the Golden Fleece

at meeting in that consummately
featureless terrain
(the flats are flat surrounded by blocks of flats)
with only ratstail plantains
and dandelions for company…
you: as often, a singleton,
as always, a small gift.

A gift I would say of collusion
or conductivity
for which we are inexplicably
created. An intrigue
in which we are all players perhaps
and the rules while everywhere evident
are just beyond us forever.

Or utterly beyond in the roaring dark.
Meanwhile you're here,
close to the earth on travelling stems,
an all but stoloniferous
mystery: *Jenny's blue e'en.*

Fat Hen

In prehistoric days you lined
The stomach of the victim
Of a sacrificial snuffing.

Now your grey blossoms peer
From rainy haze:
Mountains of sage
And onion stuffing.

A Likeness

The long campaign is over
  That ended in defeat.
The shields that flashed are darkened.
  The lines are in retreat.

Each soldier in that army
  Hangs down his ruined head:
A burnt-out field of sunflowers,
  The dying with the dead.

Alexanders

Marching mile after mile
Every step of the cliff road,

Massed in clump after clump
Of hulking brimstone umbellifers,

Imperial comestibles
Garrisoned by the Romans –

Raucous coastal cauliflowers
To boil in the roiling sea!

Cleavers

Tiny blossoms like sprinkled salt
Appear to be the reason

For bundles of stems to clamber
From low-life vegetation

To high-life aerial views…
Then dip back down on their switchback

Ride across anything going,
And cleave

To whatever might help their cause
Including

Hair and clothing and memory
With blurs and burrs of its own.

Notes to *Talking to the Weeds*

Long Purples 1 (34)

Hamlet IV. 7: The 'long purples' Gertrude includes in her description of Ophelia's death-garland were taken by John Everett Millais to be purple loosestrife and thus he painted them. But the 'grosser name' she says 'liberal shepherds' give to them is presumably 'dog-stones', which was actually the name of the early purple orchid, from the appearance of the root-tubers (*orchis* is Greek for testicle).

Star of Bethlehem (37)

Leonardo da Vinci's drawing of the plant, so titled.

Large Bindweed (41)

The cigarette packet in fact displayed honeysuckle, I think, but woodbine is a name for many climbers.

❧

The Spiritus Loci Has Provided *Vers Noir* in Your Room

The poisoned heart of this hotel,
   So shrewd and dark and small,
I know particularly well
   For I co-wrote them all:
The crisis in the corridor,
The body on the store-room floor,
   The outrage in the hall.

The worry beads of summer stars
   I ran between the trees;
The groaning sun beyond the bars
   I brought down to its knees.
Whoever codified but I
The ventilation system's sigh
   Of yearning to appease?

The ghost trapped in the trouser press
   I vocalised by night.
The artful dream that came to bless
   But horror put to flight;
The gurgle of the shower sump
Wherein the dead go on the stump,
   I dragged into the light.

The mutant heart of this hotel
   Was partially designed
By me and yet, the truth to tell,
   I could not do it blind.
No, I had need of expert aid,
And that's the contribution made
   By your collusive mind.

For you it was who underwrote
   The cheque drawn on despair,
Who hung your foggy overcoat
   Beneath the kitchen stair,
And made that curious guilt ascend,
Without a cause, without an end,
   Promiscuous as air.

So, welcome. Here you are once more.
   You fit us like a key!
You are the yawning of the door,
   The pen-chain swinging free.
You are the signing of the book
In rustling prose; you are the hook
   You shan't be let off: me.

Beak

To the clicking of kitting needles, I fell asleep on the train
And I dreamed of knitting, is this what they call woolgathering,
Dreamed of my mother purling and plaining to patterns
In *Woman's Own* and *Woman*. I woke to a woman
Whose long mauve thumbnail was sharpened into a spike
And she texted, texted, texted, with that pecking beak.

London Stars

They seem to resent the hours they have to shine,
Each one nailed to the sky like a *Keep Out* sign,
Their influence even-handedly malign.

On whose authority are they so mean and sparse?
Why are they made not of silver or gold but brass?
And why do they look like sorrow or a cat's arse?

The Walk of a Friend

'The walk of a friend, the line of a melody, the healthy throbbing of a motor, are known when they are seen or heard.'

SCOTT BUCHANAN: Poetry and Mathematics (1929)

And so they are; and so combined,
Are cause for celebration:
The motor and the melody
Of human ambulation!

The dude's roll and the chain-gang drag,
The foursquare-down-the-line,
The lyric 'clearance from the mist',
Are walks of friends of mine

In copyrighted variants –
For like a fingerprint,
A face, or voice, the human walk
Is from the human mint.

Laconic shrugging of the knees
The pigeon-toe, the splay,
The wagtail-pulled-out-on-a-string,
The combative, the fey;

The optimistic lope, the strudge,
The bustling rise-and-shine –
Exemplars of each honoured mode
I've counted friends of mine.

Man hands on mastery to man
Of prancing or prosaic
Gaits, in ribbons of design
Deoxyribonucleic.

And it's a small, redemptive grace
    That walks go walking on,
With little in their chromosomes
    Forgotten or forgone.

They're felt when they are seen, or missed,
    Beyond their journey's end:
A mantle in the memory,
    The known walk of a friend.

Cold Harbor

(On the night before the Battle of Cold Harbor in 1864, many of the doomed Federal soldiers wrote their names on slips of paper which they pinned to their backs, so that their families could be told of their deaths. One made a last diary entry, a line reproduced here.)

The hour my blood is to be spilled
I know. I therefore write it in:
June 3. Cold Harbor. I was killed.

Upon our backs our lives are billed,
Our names and numbers on a pin,
The hour my blood is to be spilled.

As though toward this ending willed,
I carve my tombstone for my kin:
June 3. Cold Harbor. I was killed.

For this dawn dying we were drilled,
A battle no known God can win
Nor stop the hour our blood is spilled,

Which cannot ever be distilled
As balm, but only re-begin:
June 3. Cold Harbor. I was killed.

So all our dreams flow unfulfilled
To death by this blind creek. Within
The hour my blood is to be spilled.
June 3. Cold Harbor. I was killed.

Cranes in the Middle Distance

To Homer their cries suggested
Echoing bugle calls
Of an advancing host.
In grosser banqueting halls
They meant a not-to-be-bested,
Status-proclaiming roast.

Their angular V formation
Prompted the alphabet.
All dancing owes a debt
To their fluttering courtship rite,
And they move in imagination
As Plato's shape of flight.

If what we have in lieu
Are outstretched necks of steel
Machines of inordinate strength,
Humanly charged they feel
As into expressionless blue
They measure their tensile length.

In beauty that soars and dips,
Delicate, riding, slow,
Upon the aerial flow
They pay their lines from the sky
And they seem high-masted ships
Round which the seagulls fly.

A Kite's Dinner

The heart is a small thing, but desireth great matters. It is not sufficient for a kite's dinner, yet the whole world is not sufficient for it.

FRANCIS QUARLES, Emblems

Shakespeare couldn't stick them, surely, *hell-kite* being the bird
That swooped on all the little ones of Macduff;
Goneril, her father's
Detested kite.

Wingers-away of filth and carrion, gangs of scavenger-pirates,
Once they operated in cities,
Valued and reviled.
Snatchers of hens and chicks from the green,
Their slow, dark, hoisted sail
Was execrated.

Yet the heart is so strange a creature
That almost gone, they were grieved, and now
They mesmerise.
A complicity
Locks our stare to the chestnut tan
That ripples over itself; to the deft turn of the cape;
To the wide, high, motionless set of the angled wings
In abrogation of all the sky
With all the time in the world.

Stabat Mater

Consider the young girl, who for homework or recreation,
Was drawing a tree that rose in soaring flight from the gardens
Behind the ground-floor flat. And these
Were dark with buildings in the daytime;
Pressed by walls of lichened brick and a grove of ash and plane.

But this was an evening of lemon September sunlight.
Her mother was taking the washing down from the line.
And the girl from her bedroom window, a sketchpad on her knees,
Looked and looked at the ash tree, saw

It move. It shouldn't have done that.
For this was no shivering of the leaves, or a branch dipping, it stepped
Forward on its own authority,
Made the decision. She screamed.

Her mother, with a clothes-peg in her mouth,
Looked up and saw the great tree like an animal
Considering her and manoeuvring. She hurled
Her body that dragged in dreamtime over the lawn,
Made the back door as it came down like the sky.
It had seemed to rise a shade and swivel,
Then crack like thunder in two along
Three garden walls of shattered masonry
And rubble. From its grave,
Lain where the woman had been standing,
Only the seething of the leaves.

Disbelieving in retribution or providence,
We recoup the moral: proof
That God has a sense of theatre? Salvation through Art?

But the woman and the child,
Crying and shaking in each other's arms,
Come back to me, and what broke cover there,
Still feels like the wind of an energy not then blind.

Carol: When Man Anthropomorphic

When Man Anthropomorphic
   Gave all the creatures speech,
And Music-makers Orphic
   Enchantment leant to each,
They made a game of magic
   Within their children's reach.

It seemed the human thing to do:
They never thought that it was true.

And when the catastrophic
   Descended on their days,
They shaped a philosophic
   Account for their *malaise*:
They harmonised the tragic
   In many different ways.

It seemed the human thing to do:
They never thought that it was true.

And when they sought exemption
   From Death's unswerving law,
As agent of redemption
   They laid a child in straw,
The son of their Oppressor,
   To cherish and adore.

It seemed the human thing to do:
They never thought that it was true.

But when the world about them
  Filled with such whopping lies
They could not fail to doubt them,
  They found, to their surprise,
The tale of their Redresser
  They viewed with different eyes.

Compared to all the other stuff,
The tale was more than true enough.

Between Bangs: A Jig

The principle that happenings, unhappily, aren't principled,
Was every time a shocking thing to find,
Despite so many, many shocks. Eternal and invincible,
Their outrage at the absence of a Providential Mind.

Or just about eternal. This was in the Old Futurity,
Before the Non Continuum came down,
Its transcendental Nescience as blinding in its purity
As on the night Reality hit town.

Blemish

After passing a miserable row of cottages, and forcing our way through a crowd of importunate beggars, we stopped to examine the rich architecture of the west front…

WILLIAM COXE 1801

…encumbered on every side with unpicturesque cottages and pigsties, rudely built with the consecrated stones of the violated ruin.

W.H. THOMAS 1839

Tintern Abbey tintinnabulations
Were stealing down the waters of the Wye,
  When romantics made excursions
  To the House of the Cistercians
In the wooded valley plunging from the sky.

The ruins drew the first domestic tourists,
Enamoured of the glamour of the spot,
  But the sketchers of the chasm,
  Home to moonlight and phantasm,
Looked less ardently upon the rustic cot.

To them the *mise en scène* was not quite perfect,
For beggars buggered up the picturesque,
  And the rhapsodising walkers
  Felt the peasants and their porkers
Were regrettably less gothic than grotesque.

The Roller in the Woods

Who would imagine a cricket ground
Had ever existed here,
Folded into a farm on the downland pasture,
Lapping the edge of the oakwood
And the buttercup-quilted rides?

For the Toll is returned to plough
After a century of combat,
Sown to a sea of blue-green waves
Beneath which it lies drowned.
And now,
Stick nor stone of the old pavilion,
Hook nor slat of the scoreboard left:
Never an echo of tumbling children,
Tattle of Edwardians,
Knocking their pipes out on the rough deal benches.

Foaming hawthorn and rhododendron
Have colonised the field-edge, spreading
Through copper beech and flowering chestnut
And adventitious saplings.
Where
Is the *camaraderie*
Of the side I played for so often here:

Their thunderous blows and heroical overs,
The days that flowed with sun and wind:
Stalemates in dismal drizzle,
And the finger of death uplifted in the dusk?

Where,
I might ask,
Are Nobby and Dave and the Colonel and Phil,
The two Pauls and the one and only
Moggy Worsfold and Arthur Spark?
I have failed to raise them
By staring out at the level meadow
As if I were Cadmus who had sown
The dragon's teeth and awaited
His armed men springing from the earth.

But I did untangle my way
Through the canopied darkness of what had been
The boundary. Among the laurel bushes
And snagging goose-grass and rabbit holes,
I found what I'd forgotten, hidden
Under a wide oak. For this

Was what they could not lightly move
In the rhythm of abandonment:
Here was the deep ground-bass and the solemn
Measure of constancy, foundry-born,
That had lasted so long.
                    And I laid
My arms across the surface, feeling
Under the rust and dust and pollen,
The summers that never seemed to move
And all the years gone by to the creak of iron.

The Song of the Old Club Bag

As though they found inside
An ancient batting glove an ancient hand,
Severed and mummified…

When you're down on your luck and feel common as muck
And degraded as deep river slime;
When you're up to your neck in a swampful of drek
And your life's without reason or rhyme;
When your heart's on its knees and each day's a disease
And Dame Fortune's a venomous hag –
You can bet your boots
You are in cahoots
With the soul of the Old Club Bag!

When you're bust at the seams and you're dead as your dreams
And there's no credit left on your slate;
When you haven't a clue what the hell you can do
And you're right roundly rogered by Fate;
When you're all out of tune as you howl at the moon
And you ripple the raspberry rag –
You can rest assured
You have struck a chord
With the soul of the Old Club Bag!

When you're wholly done in and you're ugly as sin
And the jaws of the chasm gape wide;
When you're plumb out of luck like a pig that's been stuck
Or like old Saint Sebastian's hide;
When you're dumped in a cell in the worst jail in hell
And you are its longest old lag –
You can take as writ
You're the living spit
Of the soul of the Old Club Bag!

As a Hiding Place from the Wind and a Covert from the Tempest

Rain is falling, time out of mind,
On this sad park, in this same city,
And running forever down the regulations
On a wooden notice,
Undersigned:

BY ORDER OF THE BOWLING CLUB COMMITTEE.

High ash trees in their lamentation
Career and weep in the riding rain
Over the roof of the Bowls Club Pavilion;
Likewise the streaming, bobble-hung plane
Guards the toy picket fence, sitting so pretty
By the formal and hopeless official ditty
With its stout refrain:

BY ORDER OF THE BOWLING CLUB COMMITTEE.

And Oh, to believe in the Committee's powers
As the rain keeps falling for unfathomable hours!
That none hereabouts may be stabbed or shot,
For the members of the Bowling Club Committee say not!
As the waters fountain down their holy mountain,
Cruelty and Treachery and Hate shall be demolished,
And Death shall be abolished
And replaced by Universal
Tenderness and Pity:

BY ORDER OF THE BOWLING CLUB,
HEAVEN'S HIGH-ROLLING CLUB,
BY ORDER OF THE BOWLING CLUB COMMITTEE.

In Memory of a Jeweller

Within the crescent of your jeweller's bench,
Nothing, of all the intricate things you made,
More beautiful than the shining
Necklace of your laughter,

Linking the days. Within the days,

Nothing of any rarer,
More precious metal than were you,
Loving and strong and brave
And capable and true.

Ricole

The first King of Essex was called Aescwine.
His son and successor Sledda…married Ricole…

DAVID WILLIAMSON: Kings and Queens of England

An Anglo-Saxon Queen of Essex
Was named Ricole – imagine that!
She wasn't Nicole, as she might have been –
RICOLE, RICOLE was the name of the Queen –
On the Essex throne she sat!

I'm honoured to live with an Essex girl,
Count others friends – hurray, hurrah –
And I'd declare to you, out of hand,
That the finest women on sea or land
Are Essex girls, by far!

Was she the child of Nicole and Ricky?
No, she wasn't! Her father's name
Was Ethelbert, an unmanly handle
For Essex, of course (who holds a candle
To them in the naming game?)

But there it is. And here we are
With a nominal archaeological find
Of sharp significance. Bless her soul,
That first and definitive Queen Ricole,
The template of her kind!

Ode to Colonel Hearne

Brother officers love to flirt
With Colonel Hearne in his dirndl skirt.

Martial but winsome, stern yet pert,
Is Colonel Hearne in his dirndl skirt.

Colonel, bird thou never wert,
With thy trim moustache so clipped and curt!

Thy brother officers all desert
The birds for thee in thy dirndl skirt,

Thee by thy dirndl skirt begirt,
That tents thy limbs like a Mongol yirt.

Thy brother officers all assert,
'He's a cert, he's a cert, you can put your shirt
On Colonel Hearne in his dirndl skirt!'

A Dedication Restored from 1860

Poems by Alfred Tennyson
Of 1859:
Blue, battered boards; indented gilt;
A loose and flapping spine.

The first day of the new-turned year,
She penned this *affidavit*,
A bright inscription that revives
The ghost of her who gave it:

A New Year's gift from a loving wife
to her fond and affectionate husband.

It's gone forever from the world,
That tender, measured kind
Of intimate formality,
Long fallen out of mind,
Long fallen out of mind.

And I know nothing of the man
And wife thus linked, or rather
Know just that when he died she gave
The book to my grandfather…

Who drowned beneath the Bay of Biscay
When my Dad was ten,
And therefore was a mystery
And is one, now as then.

So I am glad to find what lay
So long without detection:
A testament of ancient love,
And fondness, and affection.

Quilp Rock

So when, just over a century later,
  in 1948,
the Falkland Islands Dependencies
  surveyors first beheld
an isolated hump in Labeuf Fjord –
  a mile and a half North West
  of the island of Pourquoi Pas –
it seemed the natural thing to those Dickensians

  to name it after Daniel.
Perhaps the pitiless seas in which it rose
  gave them a hint for its christening.
Perhaps the slavering tumulus suggested
  his last appearance,
careening off the fogbound wharf till the river
  'carried a corpse away'.

Or maybe it simply seemed
  an exemplary dystopia:
  a feature of the planet
  with no redeeming ones.

Objectionable to us is the conception
of an evil dwarf, evil because a dwarf,
  irrevocably stigmatised
  and demonised by shape. But this
was the old monstrosity shop of horrors,
  noir and foundered fairy tale:
  road movie, oriental quest,
  tragic show-down, comedy *shtik*,
  and waxworks…

Yet didn't his author humanise him too
    with the weirdly loyal boy, Tom Scott,
who fought him and fought *for* him?
And with Daniel sleeping like a child
    on the table in the counting-house?

And didn't he make so distantly
reverberating a dark creation
    as to spring to the lips of scientists
bringing to book the Antarctic Peninsula?

A LISBON SHEAF

Ceremony

Off certain laconic squares,
or up an alley climbing between two streets,

you come from time to time on a mouth of darkness
blinder for the surrounding sunlight,

a high cavern of inexplicable secrecy.
It might be that an antique lift,

circa World War One, reposes
on a flight of steps in a corner there,

gateway to commerce or domesticity.
Neither is any business of yours

but you are nosy and relish
the micro-climate and mystery.

Off the Praca dos Restoradores,
I stepped into one. And blackout for a moment.

Abatement of engines and voices, replaced
by a rhythmic, swishing scuffle. When light

leaked into my brain, I began to see
the tableau. An elderly shoeshine man

plied his obeisant trade at the welts
of an elderly customer in a high-backed chair,

joined to two others; this troika fully occupied.
It might have been any time in the century.

Three thousand miles away they might have been singing
a barber shop quartet. I felt

a ripple of Lawrence with his snake,
and Theodore Roethke who'd violated

the sacrament of moss. I apologised
and retreated from the dignity

of this intimate convention. Strange,
how often you need to break things to know their worth.

The English Connection

1

The English Connection
   Is problematic,
Its meaning equivocal
   Over the years
Of a near millennium:
   Quite a chunk
Out of Atlantean
   Atlantic careers…

And to stand at the top
   Of the Edward VII
Park's geometric
   Knee-high hedge,
An almost unlimited
   Clinical vista,
A right-angled hymn
   To Order and Edge,

Is to wonder: quite how much
   Jubilation
Went into its naming?
   Gratitude
For helping to bash back
   Moors and Castilians
Might have a date,
   One might conclude.

2

The phrase, 'the lowest of the low',
Was coined, I think but do not know,

By clever Gordon Byron who
Happened to be passing through.

He wrote it of the Portuguese
Peasantry. Such expertise!

But let's suppose his judgment true –
Might he supply a reason too?

It's hard to rise, oppressed by hordes
Of shiny-booted passing Lords.

ram Lines

The city has a rhythm you seem to know.

A one-in-ten you laboured up,
As you come back down, appears to possess
Some braked momentum of its own,
Some ratcheted decelerant
Or stay of foot and eye.

For the hills of Lisbon constitute a house
Where you move without anguish
Between the rooms of distinct floors.

Or you might prefer the Lift:
A travelling oak saloon inside a meccano
Cathedral tower will shoehorn you high above
The terracotta cataracts
And the pastel cliffs,

With here a Cezanne and there
An aeronautical Lowry.

Best of all might be one of the oval
Doll's house trams with their brainy wands
To magic them, with a difficult magic,
Over and round and through the switchback course.

It is like a sometimes recalcitrant
Children's electric train set,
Needing a jog from time to time.

And the driver, working his live man's handle
360 degrees through twelve positions,

Is never without a civilian
Consultant at his elbow,

To chew the fat and roust out cars in his way.

Or there's the other
Big Bendy Wender of a tram
With it's double-concertina'd articulation,
Sashaying into a turn with rolling hips.

In any case,
You will want to be still
Under the olive trees on the battlements
Of the castle of St George
With the mare's tail grass and poppies and hawkweed and mallow…

And gaze out at the blazing wide blue Tejo,
The sea of straw; likewise
Foundation stone of the uncovered planet.

For Here Comes Everything,
With its lateen sail and its astrolabe,
Its octant, or its Manueline
Armillary sphere,

Gunning for the mouth
Of what might be known.

Here comes Africa,
Here comes India,
Here come the Americas.

They were not, of course, lost,
That they needed to be discovered,

But here comes Most of It,
And of course, one way and another,
Here comes McDonalds.

Two Children

1

From a square away
you hear an accordion playing.
When you find the source,
it is a boy of seven
cross-legged on the tiles,
rolling the big machine on his knees,
a money cap beside him,
his small, dark head weary
with so long a working life.

2

A child is playing at being a child
behind an ugly pane
of shattered glass.
She is intent
on making a theatre of herself
as she dances with her arms
to the angles of what's missing.

A Summit

In a jacket and tie sort of town,
in a second-hand bookshop sort of a town
with people of charm and courtesy,

I was strolling down the Avenida
when an old man coming towards me
spied my freakish height.

He stopped.

Between his teeth was a plastic mouthpiece
and in that mouthpiece a longish cigar.

Very, very slowly,
he elevated his head with this cargo,

checking me fully out from toe to head,
then slowly, slowly down from head to toe,
as it might be, a passing aeroplane
of passing interest.

On the other hand,
he seemed to be thus conducting with his cigar
some section of the music of the spheres
in the gentlest possible arrangement,
and I read his gesture as one of tolerance,

one of goodwill, even of World Peace!

Hero

I've known in Portugal those tableaux
of beggars, unmoving, silent,
holding their true poses
in the religious frame:

a father on one knee
with a sleeping child on his back,
around the man's neck that precious clasp,
that section of the eternity ring.

In such a take
the man is bowed in devotion,
his eyes fixed on the ground.

But this was nothing like that.
This was different again.

We turned a corner,
then washed up with a sunlit wave of the crowd
that runnelled past his pitch.

And there was his face, so terrible
we stared like children and then remembered our adulthood,

swallowed the horrified thrill
and shuffled past, eyes faking
interest in something on the horizon.

Pity would not begin to know where to begin.

I do not want to describe this public man.
Suffice it to mention by contrast
the shocking conventionality of his shoes.

But I want to remember him.

I want to locate his implacable
relevance in the chain of things,

the wholly stricken, heroically everyday,
standing there patiently manning the stall of himself
to teach us what life is like.

It wasn't until we'd returned to the *pensao*
that I realised we'd given him nothing, of course,
and when I went back the next day, he was gone.

On a Rood-Screen in Worstead, Norfolk

I sing a saint of Portugal,
   Her name is Saint Uncumber,
And heaven does not hold a more
   Resourceful little number.

She kept a snow virginity
   And when a satyr neared,
To foil his suit, became hirsute
   And grew herself a beard.

Homage to thee, Uncumber!
   Thy legend is seductive,
And pilgrims turning Worstead way
   Will find it most instructive.

A Song of Surfaces

You might wish to find the wrist-bones
Of Prince Henry the Navigator
In a casket of *lignum vitae*
Out at Belem…

Or take in a room that is furnished entirely in porcelain
And whisper at it through the grille.

You might, conceivably, feel the urge to dance
On the wide, calm inland seas of tesserae,
Under the palm trees and eucalyptus.

For here, there are many surfaces
Of many-styled remembrance.

You could almost imagine the ghost of the tidal waves
In a range of bad-tooth stucco, facades
Of wash upon wash, wrung rose
And leeched- out ochre.

But the medium of choice is the *azulejo*:
Ubiquitous cladding, civic crockery,
Garden of glaze and one-dimensional rockery
Down from the topmost hill to the banks of the Tejo.

A sympathetic, a human,
Somehow a humble form of art.
From the Copts it comes, to the Moors, to Spain, to Italy,
But quite without qualification,
Portugal has taken it to its heart.

Works there are of genius in the Museum
But also proof, and this makes me glad,
That it's possible to fashion a grotesque
That is, in itself, almost grotesquely bad.

Or so I think. But I love the fantastic animals,
Not least the middle-age cherubs with thyroid eyes
Among the brocades; the goat-legged Pans and Satyrs;
The unicorn, regarding old-fashioned wise

The raging dog it reproves. There's a Hunt
In full cry down a staircase; Alexander
Smiting the Persians; saints in huts
With more obdurate agenda.

Best of all perhaps, a satirical panel:
Begoggled baldy is driving a giant syringe
Into a prostrate buttock whose owner
Registers loud dismay:
Or is this possibly part
Of an *auto-da-fe*?

So the form has something for everyone,
So various is its style:
Pastoral, lyrical, epic, quotidian:
Versatile.

A Statue of Fernando Pessoa

Here sits Mr Person but there is
  More of him.
Here sits Mr Person, all
  Four of him.

I think his strategy ill-advised, none
  Iller.
I think the device, I'm sorry to say,
  A killer.

There's nothing enabling in it,
  Nor wise;
Better believe in a single
  Pair of eyes,

And a single imagination,
  However split,
For at least whatever you've written,
  That's you, that's it.

And heteronyms did not liberate tragic Person
  From whatever contained him.
On the contrary, they
  Enchained him.

'The Tobacconist', though, is certainly the business,
  By one of him
(Alvaro). He might have exploited more
  The fun of him.

But fun is not quite what you think of
  With Pessoa.
How shitty to make him a standby
  Partygoer,

A prop for tourist kisses and slobbered drinks,
  This private man:
Some good old pal of the scrunched-up
  Lager can.

Fado

What is it fills the canvas of this song?

For the ocean is in its bones
And longing and despair.
A hauling of ropes and a dragging back of the shingle
Are at its throat, and the stones
Of desolation have made
A harbour there.

What is it weaves the fabric of this song?

The optimistic lope of a walking bass
Attends
A Spanish guitar deployed
To complementary ends;
But the Portuguese one ripples and ascends
And cascades
Up and along and over
These barricades.

It is mandolin-ish,
But altogether a truer, more plangent sound
Whose notes don't
Self-diminish.

It is, I suppose, bland,
But over its gay, skip-dancing 2/4 trot,

There surfaces one enormous
Reef of grief
For what is not.

And I take burden of this
Saudade to be
The terrifying and absolute
Democracy of the sea:

Its wholly international
Deep reach,
Where nations lie down together
Devoid of speech:

And on this local quay
The fishwives of Lynn,
A marvel in their constancy,

Salt in their eyes, on their skin, on their tongues,
In every orifice,

Prayed and gutted,
Gutted and sang like this

To the echolalic sea:

My sailor boy,
My sailor boy,

Come home to me.

Notes to *A Lisbon Sheaf*

Ceremony (78)

Theodore Roethke (1908-64), author of 'Moss-Gathering' which describes his boyhood experience of collecting moss for lining cemetery baskets; his father and uncle had a nursery business. The poem concludes:

> And afterwards I always felt mean, jogging back over the logging road,
> As if I had broken the natural order of things in that swampland;
> Disturbed some rhythm, old and of vast importance,
> By pulling off flesh from the living planet;
> As if I had committed, against the whole scheme of life, a desecration.

The English Connection (81)

> Well doth the Spanish hind the difference know
> 'Twixt him and Lusian slave, the lowest of the low.
>
> *Childe Harold's Pilgrimage*, Canto 33

I haven't found the phrase anywhere earlier, nor been directed to a classical source, so this seems to be the origin. Byron is relentless in his disparagement of the Portuguese, something still resented.

On a Rood-Screen in Worstead, Norfolk (88)

A happy Norfolk–Portugal connection. The legendary St Uncumber or Wilgeforte is also shown in West Sussex and her effigy is in Henry VII's chapel in Westminster.

A Song of Surfaces (89)

Divine, municipal, domestic, the encaustic tile is Portugal's favoured visual medium. The latter part of the poem describes the Museu Nacional do Azulejo in Santa Apolónia.

A Statue of Fernando Pessoa (91)

This takes a different view of the extraordinary Fernando Pessoa (1888-1935), Portugal's most famous modern poet, who wrote as four distinct personae: himself, Alberto Caiero, Alvaro de Campos and Ricardo

Reis. Pessoa means person. He is regarded by an increasing number of people as one of the 20th century's great poets. See *Selected Poems* tr. Jonathan Griffin (Penguin) and *Fernando Pessoa: Voices of a Nomadic Soul* by Zbigniew Kotowicz (The Menard Press).

Outside a bar in the Bairro Alto is a table-seated statue of the poet and tourists by the million, in profound ignorance of anything about him, snap each other embracing him.

Fado (93)

Saudade: Nostalgia, homesickness, yearning, sorrow, melancholic fatalism, tribal grief. The prevailing spirit of *fado*: see, for instance, the songs of Amalia Rodriguez.

KT-198-909
STANDARD LOAN
UNLESS RECALLED BY ANOTHER READER
THIS ITEM MAY BE BORROWED FOR
FOUR WEEKS
To renew, telephone:
01243 816089 (Bishop Otter)
01243 812099 (Bognor Regis)
WITHDRAWN

The Education of Children with Physical and Neurological Disabilities

Third Edition

Simon H. Haskell
Foundation Dean, Faculty of Special Education and Disability Studies, Deakin University, Australia
and
Elizabeth K. Barrett
County Liaison Support Teacher for the Handicapped, Bucks., UK

CHAPMAN & HALL
London · Glasgow · New York · Tokyo · Melbourne · Madras

Published by Chapman & Hall, 2–6 Boundary Row, London SE1 8HN

Chapman & Hall, 2–6 Boundary Row, London SE1 8HN, UK

Blackie Academic & Professional, Wester Cleddens Road, Bishopbriggs, Glasgow G64 2NZ, UK

Chapman & Hall Inc., 29 West 35th Street, New York NY10001, USA

Chapman & Hall Japan, Thomson Publishing Japan, Hirakawacho Nemoto Building, 6F, 1–7–11 Hirakawa-cho, Chiyoda-ku, Tokyo 102, Japan

Chapman & Hall Australia, Thomas Nelson Australia, 102 Dodds Street, South Melbourne, Victoria 3205, Australia

Chapman & Hall India, R. Seshadri, 32 Second Main Road, CIT East, Madras 600 035, India

---

Distributed in the USA and Canada by Singular Publishing Group Inc., 4284 41st Street, San Diego, California 92105

First edition 1977, published by Croom Helm
Second edition 1989
Third edition 1993

Typeset in 10/12 Palatino by Mews Photosetting, Beckenham, Kent
Printed in Great Britain by St Edmundsbury Press, Bury St Edmunds

ISBN 0 412 47410 7 1 565 93062 2 (USA)

A catalogue record for this book is available from the British Library

Library of Congress Cataloging-in-Publication data available

Contents

Preface

The authors have attempted to explain and discuss four main aspects of physical and neurological disabilities in children, viz. medical, psychological, pedagogical and educational, briefly and simply, for the educated and interested non-specialist involved in the care and education of physically disabled children. We have described philosophical and educational theories and medical and psychological experiments which, though not perhaps immediately apparent in their relevance to the education of physical and neurologically disabled children, have much to offer in this respect. We have also referred to teaching practices which are based on sound pyschological principles.

We have tried to indicate where difficulties may arise when a child's normal reaction to the environment is incomplete, as it is with a physically impaired and neurologically disordered child. It is hoped that the reader will have been prompted and encouraged to think anew upon the predicament of the children for whose benefit this book has been written.

For the third edition the text has been revised, added to or brought up to date. In revising the book we have continued to adhere to the aims and principles of the first edition. We hope that the result will be of even greater assistance to those working with children with physical and neurological disabilities.

Acknowledgements

This book would not have been possible without the help of a great many friends and colleagues.

It is a pleasure to record our appreciation to Noel Blick for his careful reading and correction of the manuscript. We are greatly indebted to Mrs Val Blick for her cheerful and meticulous care in the preparation of the manuscript. Special thanks are offered to Mr and Mrs T.M. Barrett and Miss E.A. Taylor for their support and helpful suggestions.

Others have given valuable advice: these include Professor Neil Buchanan and Professor Herb Goldstein. Dr Mike Steer gave valuable assistance in the preparation of chapters on USA, Australia and Hungary.

Thanks are also due to Ms Barbara Riddick for kind permission to reproduce photographs from her book, *Toys and Play for the Handicapped Child* (1982): Croom Helm, London, pp. 121, 122 and 126.

Our warm thanks to Ms Theresa Cooper, Associate Editor (Health Science) for her unfailing patience and informed support throughout the period of preparation of the manuscript.

We are particularly grateful to Ms Gail Schumann, whose generous and skilled help in typing, editing and proof reading several drafts of the entire book has brought this third edition into publishable form.

About the authors

Dr Simon H. Haskell obtained his doctorate from the University of London, and trained as a psychologist at the Tavistock Clinic.

He began his career in London schools and later was appointed psychologist to Hertfordshire County Council. He became the first full-time educational psychologist to the British Spastics Society.

He was next appointed to the Institute of Education, University of London, as lecturer in the advanced course for teachers of physically handicapped children.

Since his arrival in Australia he has served as Dean of the Institute of Special Education, Melbourne, and is currently the Foundation Dean of the Faculty of Special Education and Disability Studies, Deakin University. Dr Haskell has lectured in his specialist field throughout Europe, North America, Africa and Asia. He has served as a consultant on services for the disabled to UNESCO, UNICEF and a variety of national and international agencies. His work has been published widely in scientific journals. Dr Haskell is the recipient of the Folke Bernadotte International Award for 'Outstanding Work in the Field of Cerebral Palsy', Sweden.

Elizabeth K. Barrett obtained her B.A. and M.A. degrees from the University of London. Her teaching qualification was gained at Cambridge University and the specialist qualifications in physical and visual handicap from London and Birmingham Universities.

She has had wide experience working with physically and visually impaired children, in both teaching and advisory capacities, in mainstream and special scools. She has served as head of the Hospital Special School at Taplow and at the Unit for Physically Handicapped Children in Aylesbury. At present she is Liaison Support Teacher for physically and visually impaired children in Buckinghamshire.

Elizabeth Barrett has lectured in institutions of higher education and to various professional groups in England, and she has been guest lecturer in Australia.

Part One

Medical issues

The aim of this section is to enable the reader to have some understanding of the medical aspects and background of a physically disabled child. We have included brief accounts of antenatal procedures, recently developed to diagnose abnormal development in the foetus. There are also descriptions of diagnostic tests used on young children. A brief description follows of the more common and seriously disabling congenital handicapping conditions. Disabilities acquired through trauma and diseases acquired during childhood are not included. Readers are referred to the Glossary at the end of the book for technical terms not explained in the text.

1

Normal child development and assessment procedures

From the first moments of life, a child is rated in terms of success or failure according to criteria adopted by the society into which it is born. In our own society those initial criteria are medical. The newborn child can be assessed in health terms by means of the Apgar test, which rates his physical condition on arrival into the world.

Even before this, throughout a woman's pregnancy, the health service has provided standard antenatal care at a hospital, clinic or from the local general practitioner to ensure, as far as possible, the normal development of the child from conception to birth. Monthly, and eventually weekly, examinations of the expectant mother are undertaken to monitor the baby's development and the mother's health. In particular, her blood pressure is checked to note early signs of toxaemia of pregnancy. Special care is recommended to avoid exposure to infectious diseases, for example rubella (German measles), which, if contracted, may damage the developing baby by causing mental retardation or other disabilities.

The maintenance of good health and adequate nutrition is important to the mother and her child. The family history of both parents is noted to check for any past physical or mental diseases, and history of previous pregnancies or miscarriages is recorded. Thus the baby who is 'at risk' from conception can be identified.

ANTENATAL DETECTION

As a result of new technological advancements there have been significant improvements in the diagnosis and treatment of genetic diseases, congenital malformations and neurological disorders. These tests are offered to mothers whose babies are 'at risk'.

Gene probes

This procedure provides genetic analyses of foetal abnormalities. It offers new and effective treatment in the prenatal screening of pregnant women.

Amniocentesis

Amniocentesis is used to diagnose such conditions as Down's syndrome or spina bifida. The test is generally offered to mothers who are over the age of 35 years. The procedure involves the insertion of a needle (administered under local anaesthesia) into the womb through the abdomen. A sample of the amniotic fluid surrounding the foetus is withdrawn and analysed. The test is not offered to mothers before the 16th week of pregnancy. The results are not usually available before three to four weeks. This test carries a small risk of miscarriage.

Chorionic villus sampling (CVS)

CVS is available to women over 37 years of age. It is used for detecting certain inherited disorders, especially Down's syndrome. This test is preferred by doctors to amniocentesis because it can be carried out earlier, at about eight weeks into the pregnancy. However, the procedure carries some slight risk of miscarriage.

The process involves taking a small sample of developing placenta either by extracting it through the cervix, or by inserting a small needle into the womb through the abdomen.

Ultrasound scans

This procedure involves passing sound waves through the mother's abdomen. A picture is created of the developing foetus. Doctors are able to detect any possible abnormalities of the baby. This techique is being further developed to identify 'biological markers' which reveal minute differences in the ultrasound scans of babies at risk. This test is considered safer than amniocentesis. At Guy's Hospital in London a team is using this method to screen babies at risk, as well as to initiate treatment of newborn infants at the earliest possible moment.

An ultrasound technique can be used to identify toxoplasmosis, a condition that can cause blindness and brain damage in infants. The disease can be transmitted though the soil, cat faeces and by digesting undercooked meat. If the disease has crossed the placenta and reached the foetus, an ultrasound will reveal the nature and degree of damage. Drugs can then help prevent further damage.

Cordeocentisis

This test is administered to a mother under local anaesthesia to detect rhesus babies who might need a blood transfusion in the womb rather than after birth. The procedure consists of inserting a needle into the womb and through the umbilical cord. Cordeocentisis is being offered in many of the major teaching hospitals of today.

Blood tests

A blood test has recently been made available to mothers who have already had a baby born with cystic fibrosis, a genetic disorder (see Chapter 2). Blood tests can also detect most carrier mothers of muscular dystrophy.

Alpha feto protein (AFP)

The AFP test was administered originally in order to screen mothers with a higher than average risk of giving birth to a baby with spina bifida. The test, however, has also proved invaluable in detecting infants with Down's syndrome. Some specialists claim that the AFP test might double the detection rate in the future. A notable feature of this test is that it is safe for both mother and infant. Early detection of Down's syndrome is strongly urged for older mothers. The risk of giving birth to a Down's syndrome baby increases from 1 in 1 500 for mothers of 25 years to 1 in 100 for mothers of 40 years of age.

CHILDBIRTH

In some Western countries mothers are administered anaesthetics and analgesics during childbirth. Some authorities point to potential risks to the newborn infant exposed to medication during the critical period of birth. Because the mother's blood pressure and oxygen intake may be reduced or high levels of toxins retained in the maternal system, these drugs could be passed on to their infants through the placenta. It is claimed that babies are affected in various ways. Affected babies may have anoxia, lack attention and, when compared with infants delivered by mothers who receive no medication, become less vigorous suckers, tend to have poorer vision and are slower in muscular and neural development.

POSTNATAL DEVELOPMENT

The Apgar test, administered within minutes of a baby's birth, assesses the heart rate, the respiratory effort (in terms of the cry) and muscle tone (in terms of the flexion of the limbs), the response of the baby's skin to stimulation (known as reflex irritability) and the colour of the baby, whether bluish or a healthy pink. The full score of ten shows the normal healthy baby.

The newborn baby's score on the Apgar test may well be affected by the process of birth, and the first response to life is a useful indication of what, if any, immediate treatment is necessary, and the likely subsequent progress. Any of the following factors might affect the Apgar test result:

1. the baby is premature;
2. labour has been long and difficult;
3. there was a multiple birth;
4. delivery was Caesarean, breach or required forceps;
5. there was any temporary cut-off in the oxygen supply to the baby;
6. drugs were used to aid delivery.

A low score can help to predict the probability of death or permanent cerebral damage in a child.

Following this test, in the next few days, a full medical examination of the baby will take place. The doctor assesses the baby's reflexes, weight, eyesight and abduction of the hips.

The primitive reflexes present in babies up to about the first six months, and which indicate a normal neurological condition, include:

1. the Moro reflex, in which the baby's arms and legs extend when its head is allowed to fall back;
2. the sucking and swallowing reflex;
3. the rooting reflex, whereby a touch at the side of the baby's mouth causes it to turn and seek the nipple;
4. the grasp reflex, that is, the fingers gripping an object placed in the baby's palm;
5. the placing reflex, where the baby's foot steps up on to the table if first held up against the table edge;
6. the stepping reflex, where the baby's feet 'walk' along the ground when placed on a surface; and
7. the asymmetric tonic reflex, in which the baby's right side limbs extend and the left flex, when the face is turned to the right, and vice versa.

From early life, therefore, the child's health and development are checked against an expected norm to obtain warning of developmental delays or more serious motor and neurological damage. This assessment is continued at infant welfare clinics throughout the first five years of life, under the supervision of the health visitor or child health personnel responsible for the area, who are assigned to every family from the birth of a new child, and the paediatrician who sees the child regularly at the clinic.

Development assessment is a part of preventive medicine designed to detect any problems in a child and chart progress in the early years of life. It is dependent for its success upon the cooperation of parents, the efficiency of health visitors and doctors and the accuracy and standardization of the procedures used.

The general procedure at developmental screening sessions includes:

1. discussion with the mother about any problems of feeding, sleeping or behaviour in the child;
2. any illnesses affecting mother or child;
3. any family or environmental changes, such as a change in the father's job or perhaps moving house.

The paediatrician usually has some equipment for testing the child, which is the next step in the proceedings. This includes things like tissue paper, a bell and a rattle for testing hearing, white balls of different sizes for testing visual acuity, cubes for stacking and grasping, and familiar toys for older infants to assess the level of language development. There is also a physical examination. By comparing with others of the same age and with their average performance, the baby's rate of development can be assessed and developmental potential predicted.

Routine developmental assessment usually takes place at six weeks, six months, ten months, eighteen months, two, three and four-and-a-half years. As children vary greatly in their development, the following 'milestones', as they are sometimes called, are only approximate, and the paediatrician would not be worried by a single delay in a child's progress. Rather, a 'cluster' of delays or abnormalities are looked for as a sign that all is not as it should be.

Neonatal period

In the first three to four months, the absence of the primitive reflexes referred to earlier, or their continuation beyond that period, may indicate cerebral damage or delay. Asymmetry in the Moro reflex or in 'walking', or tightly closed fists after two months are examples of what the doctor looks for.

From about the fourth to the seventh month, other responses occur in the normal baby. Examples are the rolling responses, where if the head is rotated the body follows it round, and various protective reactions such as the 'parachute' reflex in which the arms stretch forward if the baby is tilted towards the ground, or the head remains erect (balancing reaction) as the body changes position in space. This reaction is absent or partially present in children with cerebral palsy. Apart from the reflexes, the expected pattern of development in the six-week-old baby includes the presence of reasonable head control, responses to visual and auditory stimuli, and the beginning of smiling back and gazing at mother. Problems the doctor looks for are: difficulties in sucking or swallowing, undue sleepiness, irritability or crying, and any factors at home causing stress to mother or child. Prematurity or postnatal illness such as jaundice may delay these 'milestones', but more serious signs of abnormal development include restricted hip abduction, an unusually large or small head, asymmetry of movements, tone and reflexes, head lag or low/high muscle tone (the floppy/stiff baby).

Six months

By now the primitive reflexes have gone, the baby has good head control, is interested in the visual and auditory stimuli presented by the paediatrician, can almost sit unsupported, can raise head and chest off the couch when prone, can roll over, is socially responsive, fixates well visually, and smiles frequently. The baby has 'found' its own hands and begins to transfer objects between them; is able to chew, to vocalize, to show excitement at the approach of food, or protest at the removal of a toy; holds out its hands to be picked up, coughs to attract attention, and begins to imitate its parents.

Indications of cerebral damage, or delays, will show in various ways, namely the lack of alertness in the baby, visual defects, tightly closed hands, head lag and abnormal head size. It is also shown in the inability:

1. to support its weight on its feet, or
2. fix the gaze on a pellet, or
3. grasp a small wooden brick, or
4. hear tissue paper, the rattle of the spoon in a cup and turn to it.

Ten months

At about ten months the baby is usually mobile, able to roll, to crawl, and to pull up to standing. The index finger is used to explore objects, a pincer grasp (thumb and first finger) is present, and the baby follows falling objects, vocalizes widely and imitates well. The baby objects to strangers and is aware of the difference in individuals; can sit well, by now unsupported, and may walk holding on to furniture. Perhaps the baby can say 'Mummmm' or 'Dada', wave bye-bye, take a biscuit, chew solids and babble a lot in play.

There would be doubt as to whether the infant was developing normally if there had been any convulsions, it still had

had an abnormally sized head, could not bear its weight on its legs, showed low or high muscle tone; were backward in manipulating objects with its hands; had poor vision or hearing; failed to respond to vocalizing, and smiled or laughed very little. Unusually static limbs or ataxia (tremor) in reaching for objects would also indicate damage or delay.

Eighteen months

The child is now highly active; responds to objects all around it, and shows simple constructive abilities; has good verbal comprehension, says several familiar words, and begins to show some obstructive behaviour as independence is gained. The child usually makes its wants known by pointing and naming simple objects. From about thirteen months the child will have been walking; can feed itself and drink from a cup without spilling the contents; copies its mother's domestic activities, and is beginning to be toilet trained. Girls are usually more advanced than boys at this stage.

The paediatrician would consider referring the child to a specialist if, at this stage, it drools, casts down objects, is unsteady in gait, cannot build with bricks or cannot respond to simple commands or speak any words clearly.

Two years

Now extremely independent, the child walks, runs, climbs, attempts activities for itself but needs the support of adults, communicates well and expresses ideas of its own. Points to be checked are the presence of two-or-three word sentences, the understanding of instructions, the ability to play with a toy, the ability to feed and dress itself, and to note if the child is beginning to stay clean or dry. The paediatrician checks responsiveness to pictures in books, to the offer of a pencil, to the copying of a bridge of bricks, and to awareness of the parts of the body, and also ensures that hearing and sight are in order.

Three years

Now quicker in its movements, enthusiastic in jumping,

climbing, attempting to throw and catch a ball, the child has increased in security and can tolerate being left for short periods, but still needs familiar adult surroundings. The child plays imaginatively and enjoys playing in company with other children but sharing things with them is still difficult. Speech is well established. The paediatrician will assess the child's ability to stand on one foot, build a cube tower, copy a simple bridge construction, copy a circle, match colours and identify useful objects, and will also test the child's ability to recognize letters.

At this stage the paediatrician would be concerned by aimless over-activity on the part of the child, or failure to talk in sentences or indistinct speech.

Four-and-a-half years

The child can now skip, hop, ride a tricycle and play with other children; can understand ideas of sharing and taking turns, indulge in make-believe play and produce clear thinking speech in long sentences. The paediatrician will check for tremor, for the child's ability to dress itself, general alertness, relationships with others and behaviour when alone. The shape copying, mentioned earlier, will be repeated, together with the construction of a bridge. Vision and hearing are tested. A reasonable conversation between doctor and child is expected.

The school-age child

Once the child is of school age and has for any reason to be seen by a doctor, the information about it is extensive. Developmental history, as outlined above, has been recorded, and the examining doctor can also refer if necessary to any history of disease or ill health in the family. In addition, physical examinations of the vital systems are carried out (heart and peripheral circulation, the lungs and upper respiratory tracts). At the same time, the nose and throat are considered and a check of the ears is usually made (ear infections being commonly associated with upper respiratory tract infections).

Physical examination may reveal abnormality of stomach, alimentary system, spleen, liver, kidneys and genito-urinary system. Measurements of physical growth may also prove useful. If a disabling condition is suspected at any stage there are numerous procedures which the paediatrician can use to detect it. As well as the collection of historical information on the child and its family, and the observation of symptoms, mentioned above, sophisticated tests and equipment have been developed to aid diagnosis of abnormalities. Non-invasive techniques involving computers working in conjunction with X-rays enable a child's skull or spine to be 'scanned'. An example of such development is a computerized axial tomography (CAT) scan. This produces direct pictures of the brain safely and painlessly.

Electrophysiological investigations are another modern method of diagnosis. These include:

1. **Electroencephalography (EEG)**. This is the measurement of electrical waves in the brain, usually to identify the possibility of epilepsy.
2. **Electromyography**. This is a measurement of electrical activity from active muscle fibres. It can indicate disease either of nervous control of muscle activity or the muscle itself.

Other methods involve injection techniques. Lumbar puncture is one such method, used to take specimens of cerebrospinal fluid. It helps to diagnose meningitis and other neurological conditions. Procedures involving dyes are sometimes used.

1. **Angiography** (less often used now) is where a radio-opaque dye is injected into an artery to trace the course of blood vessels, and possible obstructions to the flow.
2. **Myelography** is a means of examining the spinal cord by introducing a dye into the subdural space around the cord so that possible abnormalities of shape and movement within the spinal column are demonstrated.
3. **Magnetic resonance imaging (MRI)** is a more recent and technologically advanced diagnostic instrument used for early detection of diseases. The patient is placed on a non-magnetic scanning table and placed into a large machine housing a giant magnet. The machine uses the magnet, radio waves and a computer to produce precise pictures of tissues in the body. The special feature of this machine is that several pictures may be obtained without repeatedly

moving the patient. The information gained by the machine is fed into a computer which creates images on a monitor and can be recorded on magnetic tape or film to create a permanent copy. Generally, the procedure takes from 30 to 90 minutes.

Disorders of the brain and nervous system, e.g. multiple sclerosis, tumours, hydrocephalus, cardiovascular disease, and organ diseases of the liver, spleen, pancreas and adrenal glands are accurately scanned by this sophisticated diagnostic instrument.

Some of the clear benefits of this procedure for patients are its greater accuracy, early detection and treatment, painless procedure and avoidance of X-rays when compared with other invasive and non-invasive techniques.

In conclusion, it should be emphasized that the most important aspects of a child's development are alertness, powers of concentration, determination and interest in its surroundings. These are functions the paedicatrician finds difficult to assess, but if a proper history is taken and the child is seen at regular intervals, a great deal in the way of prediction and prevention can be achieved.

2

Handicapping conditions

Once a child has been diagnosed as suffering from a particular disability, the parents, the child and the teachers involved need to understand the nature of the condition, its cause (if known), its treatment (if any), and any special education facilities needed. Most of the common continuing physically disabling conditions affecting the development and learning ability of children are briefly described. The strictly medical definition which this section employs, however, must be seen as only one aspect of the child. Furthermore, many children suffer from a number of conditions, and behavioural and psychiatric disorders may result from these in addition to the medically diagnosed disability. It is more realistic to assemble a full picture of a child with special needs based on medical, social, psychological and educational records, and to recognize the great degree of overlap between these aspects.

CEREBRAL PALSY

'Cerebral palsy (CP) is a disorder of movement and posture resulting from a permanent, non-progressive defect or lesion of the immature brain.' (Bax, 1964). The motor aspects of the disorder are often accompanied by defects of sight or hearing, speech and intellect. There is often lack of control of tongue and lips, visual perceptual disorders, loss of tactile discrimination, spatial disorders and seizures as well as abnormal behaviour patterns. Although the condition may be pre-natal (before birth), peri-natal (at or shortly after birth) or postnatal (after birth) or a combination of factors.

Pre-natal causes include inherited causes (rare), infections in the mother during pregnancy, lack of oxygen to the foetal brain, prematurity, and metabolic disorders (such as diabetes or toxaemia) in the mother. Another cause is Rhesus incompatibility (avoidable nowadays by immunization and exchange transfusion of the infant) in which the mother's immune system destroys the infant's red corpuscles. The resulting excess of bilirubin combined with lack of oxygen produces kernicterus which may result in brain damage. Some pre-natal causes of CP are unknown.

Peri-natal causes include birth injury (trauma) and anoxia (a reduction in the supply of oxygen to the baby's brain). In the postnatal period, infections of the brain such as meningitis, and encaphalitis may result in CP. Brain tumours and brain haemorrhages can cause brain damage leading to CP.

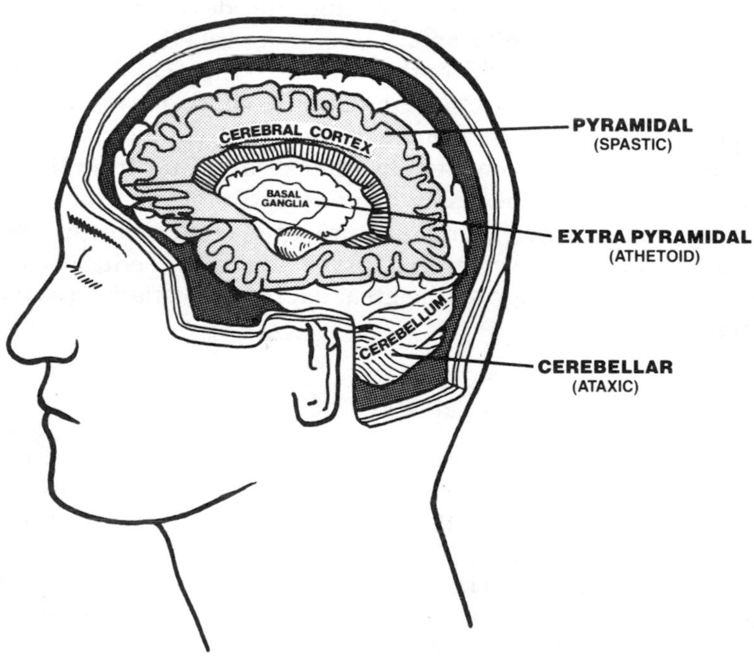

Figure 2.1 Areas of the brain, which, when damaged, cause the different forms of cerebral palsy.

The three major kinds of CP are classified as spasticity, athetosis and ataxia, although there may be mixed types. The incidence of CP has been estimated by various investigators in a number of countries and varies between 0.6 and 5.9 per 1000 births (Rutter *et al.*, 1970a; Hagberg *et al.*, 1975; Cruickshank, 1976; Lagergren, 1981; Hall, 1984).

Spasticity

Spasticity affects about 60% of the CP population and is the most common of the three types. It is due to damage in the pyramidal tracts. (The relevant neurons in the cerebral cortex, whose role is to initiate rapid movement, are shaped like a pyramid, hence their name.) These nerve cells in the motor cortex descend from the cerebral cortex via the spinal cord to the limb muscles. This area of the brain controls muscles of the face, limbs, trunk and extremities. Spasticity is diagnosed as an increase in muscle tone or hypertonicity. The limbs involved are stiff but weak and have a muscle imbalance. This means that one set of muscles is contracting too much, whereas the other corresponding set is too weak to withstand the contractions. The spastic child shows abnormal postures and reflex activity which is higher than normal. Limbs are affected variously by the disorder. Hemiplegia involves paralysis of two limbs on the same side of the body, the arm being more affected than the leg. The limbs on the affected side grow more slowly. Spastic hemiplegics are the largest group in the CP population.

A more detailed picture of the spastic hemiplegic would show the following pattern of development: delays in sitting, walking and talking at the infant stage and subsequently learning and perceptual disorders at school. Abnormal physical development would include the shortness of one leg, an inducted and internally rotated hip, a flexed elbow and wrist, and contracture and atrophy of the muscles due to non-use. Bony growth on one side would be less. The spastic hemiplegic child may have a multiplicity of handicaps, such as low intelligence, motor difficulties, tactile deficits, convulsions, speech difficulties, problems of vision and hearing, behaviour difficulties, respiratory difficulties and contractors. The child also has to cope with greater pressures of school and home life than would an able-bodied child.

Triplegia means that three limbs are affected and quadriplegia (tetraplegia) means the involvement of four limbs. Paraplegia is present when both legs are affected though the face and hands are normal, in which case speech is not affected, intelligence is often normal, and convulsions are rare. However, many children are found to have mild involvement of the upper limbs also, thus being strictly defined as diplegics. Diplegia is present when all four limbs are affected and the legs are worse than the arms. The two halves of the body are affected symmetrically, unlike double hemiplegia. Several intellectual disorders and convulsions are common in diplegia. Double hemiplegia affects all four limbs, the arms being more affected than the legs.

Athetosis

Athetosis, the second major kind of CP, is characterized by increased involuntary and uncoordinated movements, which may be slow and writhing or dramatically jerky. These movements do not occur in sleep or when the child is relaxed, but are always grossly exaggerated when a voluntary movement is initiated. Attempting to prevent this involuntary movement may also produce severe muscle tension in the child. The persistence of the primary reflexes, such as the asymmetrical tonic reflex and the Moro reflex, often accompany the disorder. Facial movements are often abnormal and can involve the tongue, lips and breath control. The muscles involving speech are often affected, producing a condition known as dysarthria. Intelligence, however, is usually normal. There may also be high-frequency deafness. Unlike spastic children, athetoid children are often thin, because of their excessive movements. The damage to the brain in the case of athetosis is in the extrapyramidal system and affects the cells found in the central part of the brain (basal ganglia), which co-ordinates posture and assists in movement control.

Ataxia

Ataxia affects only a small number of children. It is caused by damage to the cerebellum which refines the muscular movements controlled by the motor cortex. The ataxic child fails to integrate the information relevant to its position and balance in space. The condition affects the arms, preventing precise movements and giving the appearance of clumsiness, or it affects the legs, causing an unsteady trembling gait. Sometimes all four limbs are involved, the legs more so than the arms. Nystagmus and tremor may also be present.

Other terminology associated with CP includes:

1. **'hypotonia'**, (floppiness) which is often used in reference to athetoids and indicates a decrease in muscle tone;
2. **'hypertonia'**, mentioned earlier in connection with the spastic form of CP and referring to increased muscle tone;
3. **'rigidity'**, which is a term applied to hypertonia not of pyramidal origin involving a stiffness over all the muscles affected; and
4. **'tremor'**, rhythmic trembling of trunk or extremities, characterized by oscillating to and fro movements as a person attempts movement.

Any of the types of cerebral palsy may be found in one child at the same time. Observation in diagnosis is therefore of great importance as one type may obscure another, especially in a severely involved child.

The importance of early and accurate diagnosis cannot be too strongly emphasized, as treatment may be applied successfully and deformities of the limbs prevented. The clinical classification of a particular child's condition should also be made known in some detail to the responsible teachers. It has been found, for example, that approximately 25% of hemiplegics also have a loss of vision in either the left or right half of the visual fields of both eyes (Tizard *et al.*, 1954). This clearly may interfere with normal classroom learning. Tizard also showed that approximately 50% of hemiplegics have an associated tactile impairment of the involved side, so that the child is unable to recognize an object by touch, and has a diminished sense of light touch or pain. Such information may indicate the type of physiotherapy suitable for the child.

Treatment for CP may be of three kinds; surgical and non-surgical orthopaedic treatment, the use of drugs, and the treatment offered by the various therapists (physiotherapy, speech therapy and occupational therapy). Surgery, usually to relieve spasticity, includes correction of bony deformities, spinal abnormality, tendon and muscle releases and elongations and also neurectomies where the nerves causing spasticity are temporarily paralysed. Electromyographic (EMG) studies of involved muscles are now employed to ascertain which are the principal muscles involved and also after surgery to evaluate the surgical procedure. Non-surgical orthopaedic treatment includes bracing or, in the case of spasticity, the wearing of casts to prevent contractures.

The major form of treatment, however, is continuous physiotherapy from the time the condition is diagnosed. Whichever approach is adopted, the aim is to increase mobility, to enable the child to have as many of the normal explorative and locomotive experiences of the growing child as possible, and to vary muscle tone, increasing and decreasing it where necessary. The physiotherapist tries to improve posture and enable the child to walk with or without support; and also provides exercises to prevent contractures. The occupational therapist, and also the physiotherapist, in most cases, concentrate on manipulative skills relevant to everyday needs. Toileting, eating, dressing and undressing can thus become the child's responsibilty, and not another adult's. Therapy may extend into the classroom, where help in using a special typewriter may be given. Parental involvement and instruction is usually encouraged by the therapists, but discussion here of some of the types of physiotherapy treatment currently successfully in use cannot do justice to their methods. The Bobath approach is probably the most widely adopted, and the Peto system of conductive education is described elsewhere in this book in considerable detail. When a CP child has speech impairment, another important part of the treatment may involve the speech therapist, though severe damage to the muscles relevant to speech cannot be treated by formal speech therapy. For further details see Gilette (1969) and Levitt (1977).

As a postscript to the various treatments, the abnormal patterns of behaviour frequently associated with CP children, which are considered organic, must be mentioned. These include hyperactivity, emotional lability, attentional peculiarities (short attention span or perseveration), low frustration tolerance, impulsivity and distractability. These are discussed in greater detail elsewhere. Family counselling can help to stabilise these behaviours and the use of drugs may also be thought appropriate in some instances. Behaviour modification can also be employed to reduce or eliminate undesirable behaviour.

EPILEPSY

Epilepsy is a paroxysmal disturbance of the function of the brain, which develops suddenly, ceases spontaneously and has a tendency to recur. Epilepsy frequently occurs together with other disabilities, e.g. cerebral palsy and hydrocephalus. Its manifestations are a loss of concentration or even of consciousness, which may be accompanied by involuntary movements of the body. The excitation begins in a particular part of the brain and may remain localized there. This will produce a partial seizure, without loss of consciousness. On the other hand, the excitation may spread to involve the brain as a whole, producing a generalized seizure, with loss of consciousness. It is difficult to establish the precise incidence of epilepsy because of disagreements and problems relating to diagnoses and sampling procedures. However, estimates of the incidence vary between 0.3 and 18.6 per 1000 (Caveness, 1976; O'Donohoe, 1979).

Fits can be provoked by a number of factors. Disturbances of the body's homeostasis for whatever reason, e.g. fever, lower the convulsive threshold and increase the likelihood of seizures. Other precipitating factors are emotional distress or excitement, over-fatigue and inadequate administration of drugs to control the condition. With infants and children, maturation and the state of development of the nervous system also affect the susceptibility, form and frequency of attack.

There have been many attempts to classify epilepsy using different criteria:

1. according to the motor manifestations of the seizure;
2. by differentiating between general and partial seizures;
3. by dividing it according to its anatomical location;
4. by its aetiology, if known.

As a generalization, it can be said that epilepsy is due to a definable brain lesion which may have occurred during birth, due to a head injury, meningitis etc. If no cause can be defined, the epilepsy is said to be idiopathic (cause unknown). It is probable that in the idiopathic group there is a biochemical abnormality in the brain.

The following are the common ways of classifying the seizure disorders:

Febrile convulsions

These occur from three months to five years of age, last for a short period of time, and are associated with fever. Genetic factors play a large part in these convulsions. There is no means of distinguishing these fits from generalised seizures (tonic-clonic grand mal) except that by definition febrile convulsions occur with fever. Febrile convulsions, except when they lead to status epilepticus, are not associated with the development of subsequent epilepsy.

Generalized seizures

These involve the brain as a whole and are associated with a loss of consciousness.

1. **Tonic–clonic (grand mal) seizures** (the commonest seizure type)
   There are four stages in the attack: aura, tonic phase, clonic phase and stupor. Sometimes the child can anticipate the fit by the onset of a headache, a tired feeling or even a feeling of fear. The convulsion is commenced with loss of consciousness, the child may fall, the eyes roll upwards and respiration ceases momentarily. At this point rhythmic movements of the extremities and face occur, though the arms and legs remain rigid. This may last minutes or continue, in rare cases, for some hours. Finally, the child becomes relaxed, moans, and begins to move spontaneously. Sleep often follows. Incontinence of urine may occur in the attack. The tongue or lip may be bitten, but this is rare. During such an attack, the child should be turned on its side, anything tight around the neck loosened and any nearby dangerous objects removed. It

is impossible to swallow one's tongue, thus there is no need to try and insert anything in the mouth.

2. **Status epilepticus**
   This term is applied to a series of rapidly recurring tonic–clonic attacks without return of consciousness. This is a medical emergency and help should be sought urgently.
3. **Childhood absence epilepsy (petit mal)**
   This form of epilepsy occurs in children between the years of three and nine, and rarely after the age of fifteen and represents about 5% of childhood epilepsy. There is a momentary loss of consciousness without any convulsive movements, no aura and no after-effect. The child may stop talking, stare into space, his eyelids may flutter but he does not fall. He may lose colour briefly and sway a little, but then continue as though nothing has happened. Attacks can be brought on by hyperventilation (deep breathing) or by photic stimulation. During such absences the child is unconscious and as episodes may occur many times a day, this leads to inattention and learning problems.
4. **Myoclonus**
   There is a sudden spasm of a muscle or group of muscles, without loss of consciousness. This may occur alone or in patients with other seizure types.

Partial seizures

These seizures involve only part of the brain. Consciousness is not lost, although it is often impaired.

Complex partial seizures (temporal lobe epilepsy)

This form of epilepsy, which is common, begins with an abnormal discharge from the temporal lobe, which may produce hallucinations of smell and taste, with the child complaining of stomach discomfort or headache at the onset of the seizure. This is followed by unusual movements of the tongue, smacking of the lips or some repetitive motor movement. The child may be frightened and seek the comfort of someone near. During the few moments of the seizure, signs of perspiration, salivation, pallor, blushing and a rapid pulse may occur. In some of these children a lesion has been found in the temporal lobe, which may be due to scarring following birth trauma. Accompanying this condition is an abnormal pattern of behaviour where the child tends to be hyperkinetic, easily distracted, and has a short attention span. There are also rapid changes of mood, with aggressive tendencies or temper tantrums, and little sign of fear or shyness. Complex partial seizures are often quite difficult to diagnose and are less responsive to treatment than other seizure types.

Diagnosis

The diagnosis of epilepsy is based largely on the clinical history provided by relatives or onlookers. This may be assisted by a brain-wave test (electroencephalogram, EEG) and a sophisticated X-ray procedure of the brain (computerized axial tomography (CAT) scan).

Treatment

The treatment of epilepsy is predominantly with medication (anticonvulsants) although there is a limited place for surgery in people with temporal lobe epilepsy. About 70% of epileptics achieve good seizure control with anticonvulsants and a similar number of people with epilepsy can be controlled with one medication only.

All the anticonvulsants have the potential to produce side effects to a greater or lesser extent. Those with the least side-effects include carbamazepine, sodium valproate and clobazam. Phenytoin, the barbiturates and clonazepam usually have more side-effects. From an educational point of view the predominant side-effects include drowsiness, fatigue, poor concentration, diminished cognitive functioning and a deterioration in memory. Some of these effects may be because drug dosage is too high and needs to be reviewed.

Most children with epilepsy would continue to take anticonvulsants until they are seizure free for one to four years, after which gradual withdrawal of the drug(s) may be considered.

HYDROCEPHALUS

Hydrocephalus may occur in association with spina bifida or independently, and is present when there is too much cerebrospinal fluid in the ventricles of the brain. As the brain is soft, the ventricles enlarge with the pressure of fluid, the brain tissue becomes thin and stretched, and eventually permanent damage is caused.

In a small baby the bones at the top of the head are not joined together and the excess fluid pushes them apart, allowing the head to become much bigger. This symptom indicates the presence of hydrocephalus. The onset of the condition in older children or adults is likely to lead to a more severe disturbance of the brain because the bones of the head are no longer pliable.

A CAT scan can provide early detection of hydrocephalus and later associated problems.

The obstruction to the normal circulation of cerebrospinal fluid may be because:

1. the brain may have developed abnormally;
2. there has been a severe infection of the brain, such as meningitis, which causes changes in the cerebrospinal fluid pathways;
3. of a brain haemorrhage, at birth, or in the neonatal period or subsequently;
4. of the presence of a lump or cyst in the brain, which, according to its position, may cause an obstruction.

If the condition is mild, no treatment may be thought necessary, but the child must remain under observation to prevent deterioration. Any severe case requires some form of operation to direct the accumulating fluid away from the distended ventricles of the brain. It may be through a tube from the ventricles to the atrium of the heart (an operation known as a ventriculo–atrial shunt) where it is absorbed into the blood stream. The ventriculo–peritoneal shunt directs the fluid to the peritoneal cavity, which is the space surrounding the intestines, and works on the same kind of principle. A spino–peritoneal shunt directs the fluid from the ventricles of the brain to the space around the spinal cord and from there to the peritoneal cavity.

Once such an operation has been performed the child has to be reviewed medically, so that, with growth, the tube that has been inserted may be lengthened accordingly. On rare occasions, the pump which is attached to the tube may become blocked and require manipulating by hand. This can be detected by a CAT scan. There is also the risk of an infection occurring when a 'foreign body' such as the tube has been inserted. In this event, drugs or the temporary removal of the tube may be necessary. Most of the time, however, the child can be allowed to lead a normal life with no special attention necessary, and no restriction in activity because of the inserted tube.

The prognosis for this condition varies according to its severity when first treated. If the condition was mild in the first place, and no significant brain or associated disease followed, intelligence and physical development should be in the normal range. A large head and wide popping eyes, together with a rather happy, talkative disposition and facile behaviour may characterize the condition. If there is associated brain damage, spasticity or intellectual disorders may be present, despite the treatment here described.

NEURAL TUBE MALFORMATION

Neural tube malformations refer to a family of defects and include spina bifida (meningocele, myelomeningocele and spina bifida occulta), encephalocele, anencephaly and associated hydrocephalus.

There are striking national and racial differences in the reported incidence of neural tube disorders, with the highest frequency recorded from the UK (with the highest rates reported from Ireland and the mining valleys of Wales, and progressively lower prevalences in the western and eastern regions in England), Northern India, Cairo and Alexandria. Medium frequency was found in Europe and low incidence occurring among people of Mongolian and Afro-Carribean origins (Carter, 1974). The birth frequency in Australia shows higher rates for immigrants from UK than immigrants from other European countries and native born Australians (Hobbs *et al.*, 1974).

Spina bifida

The term 'spina bifida' means literally 'a spine which is split or divided'. In a baby with this condition, at one part of the

Table 2.1 Frequency of neural tube malformations (per 1000 total births) in cities in England, Hungary, Japan and Nigeria

City	*Total births*	*Spina bifida*	*Anencephaly*
Birmingham (Leck *et al.*, 1968)	94 474	2.5	2.0
Budapest (Czeizel *et al.*, 1970)	94 900	1.9	1.1
Hiroshima and Nagasaki, (Neel, 1958)	44 109	0.3	0.6
Lagos (Lesi, 1968)	16 720	0.2	0.8

(For references, see Carter, 1974)

spine one or more vertebrae are not completely formed. In normal vertebrae there is a 'canal' through the centre containing the spinal cord, which houses the nerves connecting the brain to various part of the body. When there is a split in the vertebrae this central canal is not complete at the level of the split, and it is, therefore, possible for the spinal cord and its coverings to protrude through the opening, causing a lump on the baby's back. The disruption and damage to the nerves at this point mean that the messages between the brain and the trunk and limbs are impaired, causing paralysis. Messages from the body to the brain indicating sensations of touch, pain and position are also blocked. The split in the vertebrae may occur at any point in the spine, although usually it is found at the lower end. There is a higher risk of the condition recurring in subsequent pregnancies following the birth of a spina bifida child. There is a greater incidence of anencephaly in the families of children with spina bifida than in the normal population. It is possible to test for spina bifida at an early stage of pregnancy (as by amniocentesis).

There are three major forms of spina bifida. The mildest form is known as **spina bifida occulta** in which the malformation in the vertebrae occurs in the lower portion of the spine. There is no protrusion of the spinal cord and the defect is covered with skin. It poses no major medical or educational problems.

The second most serious form is **meningocele** (cele means sack). With this the spinal cord coverings are exposed. There is a protruding meningocele which may or may not be covered with skin. The protrusion is between the vertebrae in the neck or upper back. The cord remains within the spinal canal. Generally this condition causes some loss of normal function in bladder, bowel and limbs. The most serious form is **myelocele** (myelomeningocele, meningomyelocele) which occurs in the lumbar region. The nerves in the spinal column are exposed. Apart from paralysis of the legs and loss of sensation, the nerve supply to the sphincters is affected, causing incontinence of bladder and bowel. The higher up the spine the lesion occurs, the greater the loss of function. Myelocele is often associated with an Arnold–Chiari malformation. With this the cranial nerves which are generally housed in the base of the brain (medulla) are present at the top of the neck (cervical vertebrae) rather than within the skull. This gives rise to hydrocephalus. If associated hydrocephalus is present in spina bifida an excess of fluid collects in the brain (due to a blockage in circulation), and under its pressure the child's head becomes progressively larger and the brain compressed and damaged. This added complication to spina bifida may occur at birth or in the first six months of life, but is unlikely to develop thereafter. Other abnormalities occurring may be club–foot (or talipes), or dislocation of the hips. Mental retardation is likely with severe hydrocephalus. Otherwise, the normal range of intelligence may be expected. Generally speaking, the higher up the spine the lesion, the greater the disability due to disruption of nervous tissue.

The treatment of spina bifida is a matter of some debate. Early surgery to remove the lump and cover the spinal cord is strongly argued by some medical experts, even though in spite of surgery, hydrocephalus, paralysis and incontinence in varying degrees may develop later. Psychologically, the mother is helped to feel that something is being done for her baby, whose initial appearance has been so distressing to her. Surgery also minimizes the risk of other infections, as there is less of the damaged area exposed, and facilitates treatment for the accompanying conditions. Arguments, however, have been put forward recommending no treatment for the most severely affected babies, in the hope that they will die.

Approximately 20% of babies with spina bifida survive (Hall, 1984) even without treatment, and deciding whether or not to operate immediately after birth is extremely diffcult for both doctor and parents concerned. Assuming that treatment is provided, the surgical removal of the lump is the first priority, and, thereafter, treatment for hydrocephalus described above and for paralysis and incontinence.

The degree of damage to the spinal cord in spina bifida will affect the amount of weakness and paralysis of the legs. If the defect is at the base of the spine, the muscles of the feet and ankles may be the only ones affected and the child may have to wear short leg braces to help with walking. If the defect is in the middle of the thorax, the child may require a wheelchair as there will be flaccid paralysis below the waist. Physiotherapy to aid walking and to ensure that the limbs are kept in a normal position are part of the treatment. As there is sensory loss in the limbs, checking for bruises and sores that cannot be felt prevents the occurrence of ulcers which may become difficult to treat, leading in extreme instances to the need for amputation.

The problem of incontinence of bladder and bowel is dealt with in a variety of ways. With girls in particular, surgery can be undertaken to divert urine from the bladder to an external bag by an ileal loop procedure. Penile bags solve the problem for many males. In some cases the problem can be dealt with by bowel 'washouts' or manual expression of the bladder. A common method nowadays is intermittent catheterization in which a catheter is inserted into the bladder for drainage. Urinary infection and damage to the kidneys may cause serious complications and care is taken to avoid them.

The management of the child with spina bifida, both at home in the early years and eventually at school, can be complicated by the wide range of handicaps accompanying the condition. Much of the first part of a child's life is spent in hospital, and normal cognitive development is consequently disrupted. The psychological problems of incontinence are also difficult for a child to overcome, particularly when venturing into normal social life. Incontinence is the biggest obstacle to a child's existence in a regular classroom. Even in special schools, a considerable amount of schooling is missed while a child is awaiting clean clothing, perhaps management and care.

Special education provision in some form is necessary to overcome possible visual, perceptual, intellectual and academic weaknesses for the majority of children with spina bifida. However, a large majority have no major physical or intellectual problems. A small proportion of children are severely intellectually disordered. For further reading see Hall (1984).

SPINAL DEFORMITIES

Spinal deformities are usually idiopathic or caused by congenital or neuromuscular disorders (such as spina bifida, cerebral palsy and muscular dystrophy). Other causes include tumours, infections and metabolic diseases. There are three types of spinal deformity: scoliosis, lordosis and kyphosis.

Scoliosis

This is a lateral curvature of the spine. One shoulder blade is more prominent than the other and one shoulder or hip higher than the other. Because of these changes, the alignment of the trunk may be distorted so that the pelvis, chest and head are not placed exactly over each other.

If scoliosis is untreated it usually progresses causing severe deformity. It can distort the rib cage leading to cardiac and pulmonary dysfunction. It can also distort the joints of the vertebrae of the lumbar region causing severe back pain, increasingly limiting movement.

Lordosis

This is a forward curvature of the spine when viewed from the side. It is an exaggeration of the normal anterior curve of the spine in the lumbar area. In neuromuscular disorders (particularly cerebral palsy, muscular dystrophy and myelomeningocele) it can be so exaggerated that sitting, lying and walking are difficult if not impossible (Rangaswamy, 1983).

Kyphosis

This is a posterior curvature of the spine when viewed from the side. It is an exaggeration of the normal backward curve of the spine in the thoracic area. In severe cases it can decrease lung capacity and also cause deformity with a shortening of stature.

Treatment of spinal deformities depends on the extent of the curvature, its location and the age of the child. It includes observation, orthotics and surgery. Early detection of spinal deformity is vital. The design and usage of braces and the timing and extent of surgery, particularly for a multiple-disabled child, is crucial and depends upon careful observation.

LIMB DEFICIENCIES

The cause of congenital limb deficiencies is little known. Only 3–5% of congenital limb deficiencies show an hereditary link. Most cases have been affected by some form of growth arrest between the fourth and sixth week of gestation when the limb bud is developing. A very few cases have been caused by amputation by constricting bands as the foetal limb grows. Since the banning worldwide of thalidomide, no drug has been found to have a similar disabling effect.

Acquired limb deficiencies (amputations) are caused by accident, disease or necessary surgery.

As the limbs are covered by over half of a normal body's skin surface, with its sweat glands, absence of limbs can affect the body's ability to control temperature and fluid balance. Sometimes high fevers will develop from minor infections. Limb-deficient children perspire freely and need to be dressed lightly.

The population of limb-deficient children has the normal spread of intelligence. Because they have had to strive harder to accomplish some tasks, they are often high achievers at school. If they have had the benefits of occupational therapy or physiotherapy from an early age they will have developed skills useful in school. Given the opportunity, they can work out for themselves ways to overcome problems arising from their disability. Sometimes prostheses are fitted. There is little danger that children will hurt themselves or others with these aids.

ASTHMA

'Asthma' means 'breathing hard'. The term was used originally by the Greeks to describe the panting and wheezing that was characteristic of a sufferer of the disease in an acute form. Here asthma is defined as 'clinical disorder characterized by intermittent bronchial spasm with symptom-free intervals. Its main symptoms are wheeze, shortness of breath, cough and sometimes tenacious sputum' (Simpson, 1973).

Asthma is the most common childhood pulmonary disease. It occurs in 3–10% of children and is more common among boys than girls. It frequently begins in early childhood but some children may not develop symptoms until late childhood or even early adolescence. Asthma can occur at any time of the year but is particularly common in the autumn.

Asthma is a complex disease which involves inflammation and spasm of the bronchi and the smaller airways of the lungs. The airways become constricted, thereby increasing the resistance of the flow of air in and out of the lungs, making it harder for a sufferer to breathe.

'Asthma can be provoked by a variety of stimuli, including allergies, viral infections, irritants, emotions and exercise' (Kraemer *et al.*, 1983).

Asthmatic patients often have a family history of allergic disorders, such as hay fever and a personal history of eczema. Other patients are more likely to be provoked by infection or emotional stimuli. The emotional factor can be seen in the personality of some children with asthma who are nervous, sensitive and sometimes disturbed. Often the cause of emotional stress is in the home and many asthmatic patients cease to have attacks on removal to boarding school.

Asthmatic attack

The attack comes on suddenly. In some children the onset of an attack is heralded by a running nose due to allergic rhinitis, which is often described as 'a cold'. This differs from the common cold in that the nasal discharge is persistenty clear. (A cough is another symptom preceding an attack.) In a severe attack the child becomes cyanosed (turns blue) and very frightened, thereby causing a vicious circle of increasing respiratory distress. Bronchospasm usually stops suddenly but the attack itself tails off rather than has a sudden end. One reason for this is that secretions become retained in the narrowed bronchi and must be coughed away before the lungs are clear. These accumulated secretions cause an alteration in the adventitious sounds from the chest which commence with an audible wheeze and change to a rattle.

Most children with asthma are of normal physical appearance but some have so-called 'adenoidal facies' (*sic*) with narrow maxilla, high palate and malocclusion. Children with chronic asthma tend to be slender and slightly below average in weight. Some develop barrel-shaped chests.

Treatment of an acute attack consists of physiotherapy and anti-spasmodic drugs.

Long-term treatment

Treatment may include environmental controls (i.e. removing sources of allergens in the child's environment), hyposensitization (attempting to build up resistance to allergens), physiotherapy and breathing exercises, use of drugs to relieve symptoms and measures to lessen emotional and psychological disturbances, possibly involving the help of a child psychiatrist. It is essential that the parents of an asthmatic patient are fully involved in the various aspects of long-term management and have all the measures properly explained to them.

Education

The greatest problem of educational progress for an asthmatic child is missed schooling. In addition, there may be anxiety at apparent failure at school. The emotional problems described above may be reflected in behaviour in the classroom. For teachers, a point worth noting is that in the period immediately before an asthmatic attack, when the child is showing preliminary symptoms, possibly unrecognized by the teacher, the child will probably not be 'taking in' what the teacher is saying. It is worthwhile, therefore, repeating that part of the lesson to the child later, when he has fully recovered from the attack.

There is also the effect of chronic illness on relations with a child's peers and loss of self-esteem. Physical activities may have to be restricted if exercise induces attacks. Side-effects of medication may include reduced attention span. In some cases drugs may have to be administered at school. It is important to know the correct dosage and possible side-effects. As emotional stress or over-excitement can cause an attack, the asthmatic child should be kept as calm and unstressed as is reasonably possible in the school environment.

With appropriate management and full co-operation between parents, medical staff and teaching staff, children with asthma should nowadays be able to enjoy a normal school life with minimal effect from the condition.

ARTHRITIS IN CHILDREN: JUVENILE RHEUMATOID ARTHRITIS: JUVENILE CHRONIC ARTHRITIS

The full cause of arthritis in children is unknown. It is, however, now generally accepted that the body's immune system is a major factor in sustaining rheumatoid inflammation. What triggers the auto-immune inflammation system is unknown. Children can be affected by as early as two or three years of age.

The disease is chronic and can have periods of remission with recurrent 'flare-ups'. Its prevalence is about 0.5 per 1000 children per year (Gewanter and Roghmann, 1983). Girls are affected more than boys.

Arthritis in children used, in Britain, to be called Still's disease, a term covering the disease generally. This was after Frederic Still, who first recognized certain special features of this childhood disease, which include a characteristic rash, high fever, enlargement of spleen and liver as well as joint involvement. Elsewhere the disease was called juvenile rheumatoid arthritis which is now the accepted term in the USA. In Europe it is now called juvenile chronic arthritis. Recent research has revealed numerous different patterns of arthritic disease in children. Nevertheless, in all patterns of the disease the joints are affected as in rheumatoid arthritis.

Between the bones of hinged joints (e.g. elbow and knee) and sliding joints (vertebrae) will be found cartilage covered by a greasy 'skin' called synovial membrane. In the ball and socket joint (e.g. shoulder and hips) the synovial membrane forms a bag or capsule between the bones which becomes filled with an oily fluid, given out by the membrane, called the synovial fluid. In arthritis, the synovial membrane becomes inflamed and secretes extra synovial fluid which begins to attack the cartilage. The joint becomes inflamed and swollen. Eventually the bones become demineralized at the ends (osteoporosis). This can be followed by periostitis (inflammation of the periosteum) in the region of the inflamed joint. In extreme cases, the bone ends fuse and become ankylosed (joined together) with the destruction of the cartilage. However, the process can stop at any time.

Some children have a systemic form of the diseaes. Others have the disease in numerous joints (polyarthritis) and some have it involving a few joints (pauciarticular). It is in the pauciarticular group that eye involvement is often found. It used to be the case that children occasionally lost their sight because of inflammation of the eye but nowadays, by early detection, drugs and surgery, this is less likely (Kanski, 1977). In about 5% of children with J.C.A. there is an associated bowel disorder. About 5% have an associated skin condition (psoriatic arthritis) (Craft *et al.*, 1985).

Treatment of arthritis in children consists of drug therapy, particularly aspirin, and physiotherapy, especially hydrotherapy. Surgery is sometimes used to correct a deformity or replace a joint. Measures to relieve pain and relax muscles and joints include wax treatment, 'hot packs' and use of the Faradic footbath (a footbath at the bottom of which are electric plates through which a current is passed). Orthoses, or splints, are widely used for both resting and working. Joint protection techniques are very important.

A few children, mostly girls, have a pattern of illness similar to that of adult rheumatoid arthritis. Although the age of onset can be as early as five years, usually it is at twelve years or later. This form often starts with involvement of small joints and spreads to other joints. The activity of the disease is persistent and can continue intermittently for years. Strong drugs, such as penicillamine are used as quickly as possible to halt the activity of the disease.

Another form of the disease, mostly affecting boys, is a form of spinal arthritis known as ankylosing spondylitis. The age of onset is usually nine to twelve years, although it can be much earlier. Thse children tend to carry HLA B27, an inherited antigen which can be identified by tissue typing. This helps in the early recognition of the disease (Ansell, 1976).

Effects of arthritis in children

Growth is affected by arthritis in children, causing them to be stunted and/or possibly causing anomalies of growth, e.g. one leg longer than the other. It can be a very painful disease, often necessitating strong dosage of drugs, with the consequent side-effects. The chronic nature of the disease with the intermittent 'flare-ups' frequently causes poor school attendance. Children also become fatigued, possibly necessitating rest periods or a shorter school day.

INHERITED DISEASES

A new understanding of the human structure springs from the work of James Watson and Francis Crick who, in 1953, revealed the organization of the DNA (deoxyribonucleic acid) molecule. Their discovery that DNA is the significant substance by which hereditary information is coded has given us a clearer idea of the way in which characteristics of one generation are handed down to another.

Watson and Crick indicated how each chromosome comprises two long strands of DNA which are wound around each other to form a double helix. Copying of the chromosomes occurs when one strand of the double helix unwinds. Each single old strand then forms into a new double helix by the sequential manufacture of its complementary partner down its entire length. Precise rules dictate the way 'bases' (organic substances adenine, cytosine, thymine and guanine) are paired. Bonding of the double helix is achieved by adherence to strict chemical sequencing and combination of each pair (adenine to thymine, and cytosine to guanine alone) to ensure genetic stability or continuity.

Biological information is stored in DNA. One of the functions of DNA is to replicate itself each time a cell divides. The other purpose is to ensure that living cells receive the necessary information for the manufacture of chemical compounds. In this latter process, genetic information is transferred from DNA to RNA (ribonucleic acid) and is then used to synthesise proteins from amino acids. Proteins are larger molecules which usually consist of many thousands of amino acids and undertake the biological functions of the cell. Each gene in the DNA provides the code for a specific protein.

It is now a possibility that scientists might intervene directly in the genetic process to correct hereditary anomalies, occasioned by sudden and persistent DNA changes, or when base or amino acid variations occur. Such mutations cause genetic disorders such as cystic fibrosis, muscular dystrophy, haemophilia, sickle cell anaemia, phenylketonuria (PKU), and Down's syndrome. The long-term hope is that it might be possible to correct DNA errors first, by prompt recognition of 'mistakes' in the foetus, and, second, by the *in utero* restoration of the orderly process of replication and genetic stability.

Under the direction of James Watson (see above), the ambitious Human Genome Project in the USA is progressing to identify every gene in the 'genome' – the name given to the entire cargo of the cell's genetic material. As each gene is identified, any disease for which it may be responsible can be diagnosed accurately. Then, having found out why it is so responsible, a cure may possibly be effected.

Gene therapy, as the replacement of genes is called, is already under way experimentally in a live patient in Bethesda Hospital, Washington DC, for the treatment of adenosine deaminase (ADA) deficiency. This rare disease causes the patient to be vulnerable to any sort of infection, similar to a person suffering from autoimmune deficiency syndrome (AIDS).

Many ethical questions have to be answered regarding gene therapy, and the use of the full knowledge of an individual's genes. At what point does man cease interfering with nature? Could knowledge of an individual's genes be misused? The genetic approach, however, promises to be the most exciting and hopeful area of research for cures of some of man's most persistent and distressing diseases.

MUSCULAR DYSTROPHY

This is a condition in which there is a progressive weakening of the various muscle groups. The muscle fibres swell, undergo what is known as 'hyaline degeneration' and become replaced by connective tissue and fat. These take up more space than the muscle they replace and the impression is given that the affected limbs have enlarged, hence the term 'pseudo-hypertrophy'.

There are different forms of muscular dystrophy which vary considerably in their age of onset, rate of progress and mode of inheritance. It is estimated that the incidence of Duchenne muscular dystrophy is approximately 1 per 3000 male births (Hall, 1984). Muscular dystrophy is caused by an absence of a protein, called dystrophin, in the muscles. The gene responsible for dystrophin was discovered in 1986 by Tony Monaco and Louis Kunkel at Harvard University. An absence or impairment of this gene results in the non-production of dystrophin and the muscles in the body begin to waste.

Recently, molecular geneticists at the Duke University Medical centre have implanted in animals with muscular dystrophy a mini-gene with enough of the missing protein to correct the disorder. The hope is that DNA therapy will work in human subjects.

In 90% of cases in its most severe and common form (Duchenne type) the transmission of the disease is sex-linked, mothers passing it in manifest form to sons and in carrier form to daughters. In the remaining 10% of cases, both parents must carry the recessive gene and either sex can be manifestly affected. Blood tests can identify children with the disease before symptoms develop and also 70–80% of carrier mothers.

A child with Duchenne type muscular dystrophy usually shows symptoms at two or three years. The condition begins in the muscles of the pelvic girdle, buttocks and thighs. The child shows a slowness in walking, an inability to run and difficulty in rising from a fall. When the disease is established, a characteristic way of rising from the floor is for the child to turn on to the face, put the hands and feet on the ground, and then climb the hands up the legs until the child is upright. The early presentation of the disease gives the child a waddling or clumsy gait, often attributed to the child being knock-kneed, lazy or flat footed. The shoulders usually slope and there is difficulty in raising objects or lifting the hands above the head. The muscles of the pelvic girdle, thighs, shoulder girdle and upper arm weaken. The pseudo-hypertrophy is most apparent in the thighs and calves. Eventually the child becomes severely crippled and is unable to move the muscles of his body except to be able to swallow and breathe. The child is often incapable of walking by about the age of eleven. Although nowadays some children survive for longer, death often follows between the ages of 14 and 20 years, either from pneumonia or cardiac arrest.

Limb girdle muscular dystrophy affects both sexes in equal numbers, beginning in the pelvic or shoulder girdle or both, where it may remain for several years before spreading to the other muscles. The condition may start in the second decade of life or even in some cases in middle or late life. Eventually a wheelchair life follows and the patient usually dies prematurely from some kind of respiratory infection. This form of the disease appears in the children of two unaffected carriers of the recessive gene.

Facioscapulohumeral muscular dystrophy also occurs in both sexes in equal numbers, usually in the second decade of life. The muscles of the face and the shoulder girdle are affected, the face assuming the expression of a mask. The patient has difficulty in closing the eyes or lips tightly and blowing out the cheeks or whistling. The disease, however, progresses very slowly and the disability is comparatively slight, so that most patients do not have a foreshortened life, as a result of it. The probability of the condition being inherited from an infected individual is one in two.

There is no drug yet available to cure muscular dystrophy. One approach for treating the disease is by a method known as myoblast transfer. This involves transplanting healthy muscle cells that normally produce dystrophin into the diseased muscle. So far the results of this treatment have not been very encouraging. The management of a child with this condition is usually directed at activity rather than passivity. Active exercise is desirable but over-exertion should be avoided as it may lead to falling or fatigue. Apart from sleep, more than one or two hours of continuous inactivity such as watching television, should be avoided. A prescribed diet should be followed to prevent obesity. Stretching the tendons, which are likely to shorten, helps to prevent contractures occurring. A general attitude of optimism surrounding the child can counteract the depression which often develops as the disease progresses. Most school activities are within a child's capability in the early stages of the disease. During the later stages modification of the pupil's timetable or even shortening the school day may be advisable to maximize the benefits of attendance at school. Fatigue and a lessening ability to take part in the full school curriculum tends to diminish academic progress. Death is usually caused by respiratory ailments, so evidence of respiratory problems should be reported. For further reading see Bourne and Golarz (1963) and Umbreit (1983).

CYSTIC FIBROSIS

Cystic fibrosis was first reported in 1936 by Dr Guido Fanconi of Switzerland. The earliest references to the disease in children dates to 1705. It is one of the more common inherited diseases in white children, the incidence being 1 in 2000 live births compared to 1 in 17 000 black babies. Orientals rarely contract the disease. Boys and girls are affected equally.

Cystic fibrosis is caused by a recessive gene mutation. A child inheriting the recessive gene from one parent will become a carrier; should both be inherited, the condition will develop.

The disease causes the exocrine (outward secreting) glands in the body to fail in their normal function. The exocrine glands produce thin, slippery secretions including sweat, mucus, tears, saliva and digestive juices. These secretions are carried through ducts (small tubes) to the external surface of the body, or into hollow organs like the intestine or airways. The exocrine glands and their secretions play an important part in maintaining the healthy working of the body.

In cystic fibrosis the mucus-producing glands often produce thick, sticky secretions. These secretions may block ducts and other passageways. These blockages occur most often in the lungs and intestines and can interfere with vital body functions, such as breathing and digestion.

Examination of the body fluids produced by endocrine glands from patients with cystic fibrosis reveals two basic abnormalities: abnormal electrolyte composition and abnormal mucus (Mangos, 1983).

The abnormality of the electrolyte composition is shown most clearly in the increased salinity of the sweat produced.

This has led to the development of the 'sweat' test which is now used as an accurate means of diagnosing cystic fibrosis. A sample of sweat is painlessly taken from a patient's skin and the level of salinity measured. Recordings over a certain level accurately indicate cystic fibrosis.

The symptoms of untreated cystic fibrosis appear in the first year of life. They consist of passing large, foul stools, increased appetite but little gain in weight, and an enlarging of the abdomen because of distension of the intestines. A persistent cough develops as thick mucus builds up. There is difficulty in breathing due to infections which gradually cause scarring and damage to the lungs, there is also clubbing of the fingers and toes. In time, because of the damage to the lungs, the exchange of oxygen and carbon dioxide is affected in the respiratory process and the heart becomes affected. Other complications may develop which may involve the liver, intestines, sinuses, growth and sexual development.

Once the condition is diagnosed, treatment consists of prevention and control of lung infection which, apart from drug therapy, includes breathing and coughing exercises, postural drainage and physiotherapy to keep air passages clear. Cystic fibrosis chidren need good nutrition for maintaining respiratory muscle strength, general growth and development to protect the body's defence against infection. Today, it is recognized that cystic fibrosis children can have a normal, well balanced diet with pancreatic enzyme supplements. It is now considered important and safe for the children to eat fats because they provide a valuable source of fuel for growth and development. Fat intake can be controlled by modifying the intake of pancreatic enzyme supplements. Children with cystic fibrosis also can be given water soluble forms of vitamins that do not rely on fat for absorption. Other treatments consist of surgery, particularly for heart complications, and the home use of oxygen.

Research into the genetic causes of cystic fibrosis is continuing in several leading medical centres in the world. American scientists claim that they have successfully corrected cystic fibrosis cells in the laboratory by introducing healthy forms of the gene into the diseased cystic fibrosis cells. They have also used genetically engineered viruses to introduce good copies of the gene into aberrant respiratory tract and pancreatic cells of affected patients. It is claimed that the affected cystic fibrosis cells gradually assume chemical normality (are able to absorb and secrete chloride molecules) as the sickly cells become more robust.

Other scientists, however, advocate caution in the claim that breakthroughs have occurred in the conquest of the disease. Professor Danks of the Medical Institute of Melbourne, Australia, argues that many more technological hurdles have to be surmounted before we are able to treat cystic fibrosis clinically outside the experimental laboratory test tube setting.

Nevertheless, there is an air of optimism even among the most conservative researchers with regard to gene therapy for cystic fibrosis sufferers. The use of viral carriers is not generally favoured. However, packaging the gene in a tiny fat-coated bubble which can penetrate cell membranes is recommended. Another possible method of delivery of the gene worth researching is by aerosol dispensers.

Problems at schools may include prolonged absences, persistent cough, interruptions because of medication and the demands of special diet. Emotional problems may arise with the uncertainty of prognosis and the lack of ability to compete physically with the child's peers. For further reading see Harvey (1982).

HAEMOPHILIA

This is a disease arising from a sex-linked recessive gene mutation, which is usually transmitted by females but apparent only in males. The defect is an absence or deficiency of Factor VIII, the substance which causes blood to clot. The blood of the haemophiliac may take several hours or days to clot, the result being bleeding, both internal and external, into the joints, muscles, soft tissues and internal organs. Haemorrhages are also a severe problem. The result of repeated haemorrhages into the joints, particularly the knees, is limitation of movement and permanent crippling.

The condition usually comes to light in early childhood when prolonged bleeding follows a minor operation. Subsequently, the condition tends to improve, possibly because of greater care taken to avoid any accident to the body. Periods of ill health and confinement to bed as a result of bleeding can result in arrested growth.

Treatment and management of the disease include every precaution to ensure the safety of the growing child. This may involve wearing protective clothing at all times, and special care during any dental and surgical treatment. The specific treatment to stop bleeding is the intravenous administration of Factor VIII, which is prepared from human or animal sources. This is in very short supply, but gene cloning (propagation from a single cell) seems certain to provide a more readily accessible source in the near future.

Haemophiliac children are of normal intelligence, and unless the condition is very severe, they can attend ordinary school, provided that staff know what to do in the case of injury, and that adequate precautions are taken in sport and casual play. There may be much absence from school due to injury, but facilities for home study can remedy this. Careful thought must be given to provide the right education for these chlidren, whose special medical needs and normal intellectual development present an awkward combination for any school to cope with satisfactorily

Many parents of such children feel dissatisfied with the current provision. The strain in terms of management of these children is great for both the child and the family.

In recent years, because of the worldwide spread of AIDS, haemophiliacs have suffered further problems. Their need for blood transfusions has resulted in some children having accidentally contracted the AIDS virus in their blood, with risk to their own health and social stigma in the community.

ACQUIRED IMMUNE DEFICIENCY SYNDROME (AIDS)

This disease is considered a scourge that has swept the world with alarming rapidity. It is caused by a virus that upsets the workings of the body's auto-immune system. A person with AIDS has antibodies that do not 'neutralize' or prevent the AIDS virus from entering a cell and then multiplying.

It has been discovered that the AIDS virus uses an enzyme called reverse transcriptase to make copies of itself. Only certain viruses have this enzyme which are not found in host cells.

Some scientists hope to develop a drug that targets the virus without damaging the host cells.

Genetic engineers have managed to stimulate the production of antibodies which act against the AIDS virus. However, it is not certain that these antibodies can offer protection to infected patients. The future cure lies in the field of molecular biology and biotechnology.

A growing number of children in western societies are being born with the AIDS virus. These children may share many of the symptoms of children with brain damage: slow development, learning difficulties, behaviour problems, clumsiness, etc. Societies which have a large number of AIDS victims, and they now include increasing numbers of women, will have to make provision for these children in the future or face increasing problems in schools.

SICKLE CELL ANAEMIA

This is an inherited condition affecting the red blood cells and is characterized by the production of an abnormal type of haemoglobin. It is an autosomal, recessive genetic disease. Sickle cell anaemia afflicts Mediterranean, Middle Eastern and African people. In the USA, one out of ten black people is affected.

In sickle cell anaemia, the cell becomes elongated, resembling a sickle, and loses the flexible property of normal red blood cells, which are round and flat. In this state the body attacks and destroys sickle cells at a rapid rate, causing anaemia, and jaundice. Furthermore, these rigid sickle cells block blood flow (vaso-occlusive crisis) causing cell death in organs, accompanied by extreme pain in parts of the body, akin to arthritis. Children with sickle cell anaemia may require transfusions of normal red blood cells during acute episodes of colds, fevers and infections.

There is no known cure for the disease, but survival to adulthood is not uncommon if vaso-occlusive crises are well managed.

Children with sickle cell anaemia need rest and exclusion from strenuous physical exercise. They will have short attention spans. If the central nervous system is affected then the psychological sequelae can mimic brain injury and affect intelligence and learning ability (Umbreit, 1983).

Part Two

Psychological issues

The aim of this section is to relate relevant medical, biochemical and psychological research to different areas of learning and to draw attention to the implications of this research to motor and neurological impairment in children.

3

The brain, learning and disorders of perception

The brain, together with the spinal cord, comprises the central nervous system (CNS). It is this phenomenal enlargement of the spinal cord at the head of the neural tube, together with a concentration of sense organs and an accumulation of nervous tissue, which carries out the specialized functions which characterize human behaviour. Thus, the brain efficiently collects information from the distant parts of the body, analyses the sensory data and, via a neural network, issues commands to the various muscles to carry out a range of tasks and activities.

The human brain represents the most sophisticated and elaborate response to environmental demands. It has taken millions of years to assume its present shape, structure and special organization from its primaeval beginnings. The human brain gives its owner a degree of behavioural flexibility enjoyed by no other organism. It is the human brain, in association with that unique manipulative tool, the hand, that has enabled man to adapt so readily to new environments, without having to undergo the laborious process of change through mutations and selection of specific genes, which normally make for successful adaptation to the environment and for survival in the animal world.

General appearance

The design of the human brain with its wrinkles, convolutions, relative small size and protective cranium reduces the risk of its exposure as a target to external trauma. The brain is roughly ovoid in shape. In colour, it is greyish with the consistency of soft cheese. The surface has convolutions which consist of ridges (gyri) and fissures (sulci). The more prominent of these provide landmarks for dividing the brain into anatomical lobes or areas (Figure 3.1). The surface area of the neo-cortex is greatly expanded by these features. The brain of an average adult male is about 1380 grams (approximately 3 lb), while that of the average female is somewhat smaller. This difference is partly offset by the differences in average body weight.

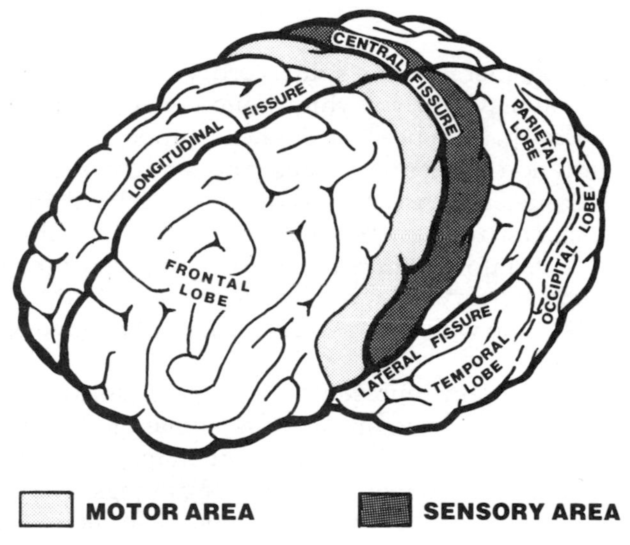

Figure 3.1 The lobes of the brain.

At birth the brain is approximately 25% of its adult weight and weighs on average about 350 grams. Over the next six months it doubles, and by the sixth year has attained 90% of its adult weight. Some racial differences in rate of brain growth have been reported, with Afro-Caribbean babies showing faster nervous system development than their Caucasian counterparts. However, individual differences within races are marked.

Divisions of the brain

There are two convenient ways of looking at the structure and architecture of the principal regions of the brain. The first method is by examining the bilateral arrangement of the left and right cerebral hemispheres. These are separated by a fissure running from back to front, and each hemisphere deals with the opposite side of the body. The second method is by reference to the brain's longitudinal arrangement. The principal structures of the brain are represented by the forebrain, midbrain and hindbrain (Figure 3.2).

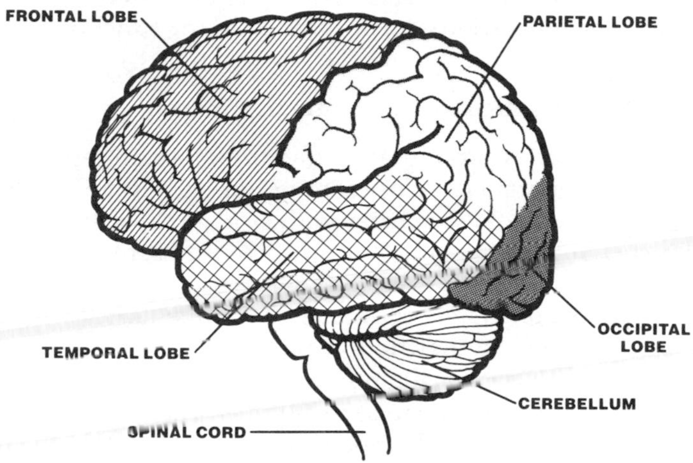

Figure 3.2 Side view of the brain seen from the left.

The forebrain in humans constitutes the largest part of the brain. The development of the forebrain permits the reception and registration of visual, auditory, exteroceptive and proprioceptive sensations, giving the human brain unparalleled reasoning powers.

The midbrain occupies a small area and forms an important link between the forebrain and hindbrain. This interconnecting system contains a rich network of ascending sensory and descending motor fibres.

The hindbrain contains the cerebellum (or little brain) and the pons and the medulla. The cerebellum also has a surface marked by sulci and gyri. The cerebellum is connected to the brainstem, vestibular nuclei and spinal cord. It sits astride both cerebral hemispheres. Among its many functions is the guidance and monitoring of movement, co-ordination of postural and locomotor activities through an information network from muscles, tendons, joints, skin and the semi-circular canal. The pons (bridge) is a unique structure with afferent and efferent fibres crossing over from one side of the brain to the other. It contains the cranial nerve nuclei and the reticular formation. The medulla connects the spinal cord to the higher centres of the brain. This is an important junction where most of the cranial nerves leave the brainstem to enter the head, serving various sensory and motor functions.

Plasticity of the human brain

The older subcortical structures in the human brain represent the full extent of brain development of our earliest ancestors. These phylogenetic old structures with storage capacity for the simplest behaviour are to be found in more highly evolved neural systems. However, even the lowly worm possessing only a reticular formation system is capable of rudimentary learning. Some workers believe that neural plasticity (modification of behavioural responses) facilitates information storage. Neural plasticity enables the organism to respond and adapt to internal and external stimuli. It is claimed that the functional value of each behavioural flexibility is the survival of the organism.

Evidence of functional plasticity of the brain has long been recognized, particularly from studies of aphasic patients. It has been shown that gradual damage to the left hemispheric speech mechanisms seldom resulted in aphasia, as was the case of sudden deterioration resulting from trauma or strokes. Broca, who carried out some of the earliest studies of this condition, reported that patients with unilateral damage to the left frontal region of the brain, regained normal speech following the transfer of motor speech to the right frontal part of their brain. The recruitment of atypical functioning of undamaged cortical structures is more effective in children than adults and better undertaken when the brain is immature. This suggests equipotentiality of some functions, especially language (Zangwill, 1975a).

Lenneberg (1967) has reviewed studies which indicated that up to puberty, the right hemisphere is able to compensate for damage to the language hemisphere, and that both hemispheres are actively engaged during the critical periods of language development.

Sex differences

Recent studies have revealed sex differences in the development of cerebral function. There is evidence that certain abilities and traits are unevenly distributed between males and females. (For a fuller discussion see Buffery and Gray, 1972; Cummins, 1988.) Consistent differences are shown in verbal and spatial skills. It is hypothesized that the female's greater facility in general in handling words and the male's superiority in general in performing tasks demanding perception, judgement and manipulation of spatial relationships are due to differences in the development and structure of male and female brains. It is known, for instance, that girls' brains develop more rapidly than boys'. This is particularly true of the cerebellum, which develops faster in females up to the age of three years. By six months the cerebellum weight in girls is twice as great as that in boys. It is suggested that it is this pattern of difference in growth and ability between the sexes (rather than psychosocial influences) that accounts for differential superiority in language, science and mathematics. There is some evidence to suggest that these differences persist until adulthood (Buffery, 1971).

A number of views have been advanced to account for observed sex differences in brain development and organization. Differential maturation is ascribed to hormonal differences. Buffery and Gray (1972) suggested that the superiority of left hemisphere functions in young girls accounts for their earlier linguistic skills development. Spatial skills are functionally distributed bilaterally and develop earlier in boys, which accounts for many boys' superiority in spatial tasks.

Buffery (1976) also observed that boys and girls between the ages of five and nine years tended to process easy-to-verbalize problems with their left hemisphere, and this preference was more marked as girls grew older. Buffery also noted that in difficult-to-verbalize tasks, both sexes preferred their right hemispheres. These findings suggest that girls are more competent than boys in processing verbal instructions and boys are better able to grasp spatial or pictorial material. Experienced teachers might consider matching the learning tasks to the child's cognitive strategy and learning style, utilizing the child's best hemispheric preference dominance to facilitate learning.

According to Beaumont (1983), the Buffery and Gray hypothesis has failed to receive widespread support among experimental neuropsychologists, because the results of experiments on sex differences are ambivalent, and the methodology of the studies unsatisfactory.

A substantial literature has grown up around the topic of sex differences in cerebral organization and a useful review of the subject is to be found in McGlone (1980) and Fairweather (1982).

Asymmetries of structures and functions

The human brain has developed specialized asymmetric cognitive functions for each hemisphere (see Figure 3.3). Both

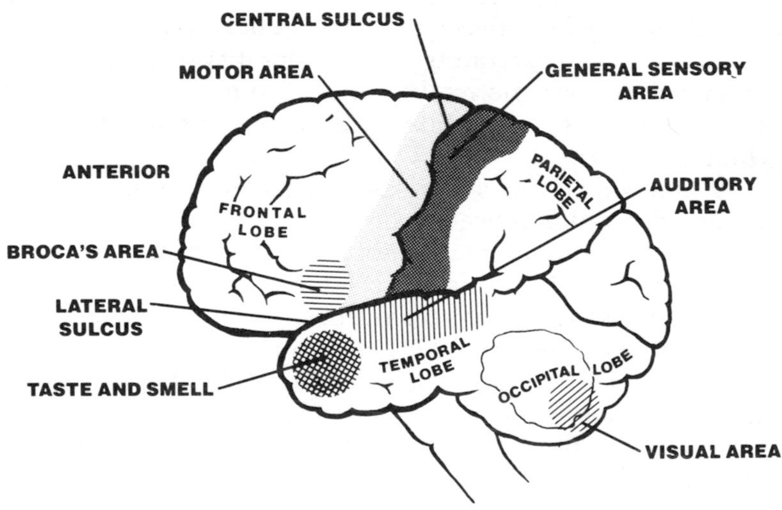

Figure 3.3 Side view of the brain illustrating the major localization of function.

hemispheres, however, are connected by fibres, which enable the two systems to interact with each other, and to integrate their functions. Visual and tactile information and activities of the left side, for example, are processed within the right hemisphere, while movement of the right limbs is organized by the left cerebral hemisphere. Hemispheric differences have been observed to occur in infancy and are developed *in utero*.

It is generally recognized that the left cerebral hemisphere is suitably designed and predisposed to recognize particular aspects of speech, especially phonological and syntactical information and the control of expressive language, reading, speaking and writing, and the performance of logical tasks in mathematical computations (Cole, 1977; Liberman, 1975; Pribram, 1976). The right hemisphere (non-verbal) exercises visual–spatial judgement and control, processing complex visual stimuli, musical activity, body schema and visual perception. However, language is not exclusively the domain of the left hemisphere (Rudel, 1978), as the right hemisphere has control of receptive language. The left hemisphere on the other hand is better able to perceive temporal patterns, make temporal order judgements and organize sequential motor tasks, without invoking linguistic processes.

The brain receives verbal and spatial information and these stimuli are delivered in the form of codes. Verbal information such as speech, seeking interpretation in the brain, is sequentially delivered – that is, it follows an order – whereas spatial information is rendered in simultaneous code – input and output overlaps. It is hypothesized that verbal information (sequential codes) is best served by neural structures of the brain which are adjacent and are localized and are predominantly lateralized to the left cerebral hemisphere. Such a topographic structure, it is argued, becomes 'specialized for the extraction of linguistic features in speech perception' and the development of verbal functions and language. It is further argued that localization has advantages because it can organize and handle information efficiently, and avoid messages being wasted by unnecessary involvement of mass neuronal activity. On the other hand, simultaneous coding is diffusely represented in the brain because general skills of crawling, walking, reaching and eye–hand co-ordination demand the co-ordination of input into the brain from eyes, ears and limbs and could not be handled efficiently by localized areas of the brain. What is well established is that language skills are organized in the left hemisphere but spatial skills are not absolutely biased, but well presented to the right.

Buffery (1970) suggests that there is some special structural attraction which invites the left cerebral hemisphere to serve the sequential coding – 'an innate, species specific neural mechanism which is usually lateralized to and localized within whichever cerebral hemisphere of the human brain is to develop dominance for language function'. Gazzaniga and Sperry (1967), however, have pointed out that even for right-handers (who normally have left-hemisphere dominance for language) language is not absolutely established in the left hemisphere. The right hemisphere does possess rudimentary verbal organizational facility.

Tests of vision and hearing have revealed differences in function between right and left hemispheres. The left hemisphere appears better organized to perceive alphabetical material, and familiar objects, while the right hemisphere has superior ability to recognize forms, the number and spatial arrangements of dots and the slope of lines.

The left visual field, controlled by the right hemisphere, has been found superior for face recognition. Geometric designs can be recognized with greater ease and skill with the left than with the right hemisphere. The reverse is true with handwriting (Cohen and Clark, 1979). In dichotic listening (simultaneous auditory stimulation of ears) the right ear has been found superior for discriminating digits, words and consonants. The left ear is better for non-verbal sounds such as melodies and simple pitch. In other words, there is right hemisphere specialization for discrimination of non-verbal sounds. Clinical support for this is to be found in cases of patients with right anterior temporal lobectomy (Milner, 1971).

There are other anatomical asymmetries in the cerebral structures, the left cerebral hemisphere being slightly heavier, occupying more space and having higher specific gravity than the right. Buffery and Gray proposed that the human neuronal or foetal female brain might reveal 'pre-language' structural asymmetry: this is supported by data (Wada, 1969; Witelson and Pallie, 1973) which confirmed functional precocity and greater myelination in female non-brain-injured babies that had been aborted or who had died peri-natally.

A number of theories have been advanced to account for the observed superiority of left hemispheric functioning in humans. One view offered is that the left hemisphere is committed to assume functional speciality by the earlier maturation of its neural structures. The relative immaturity, however, of the right brain enables it to assume functional control when the damaged structures are rendered inactive.

Figure 3.4 shows the cortical areas of visual, olfactory, motor and sensory localization in the brain.

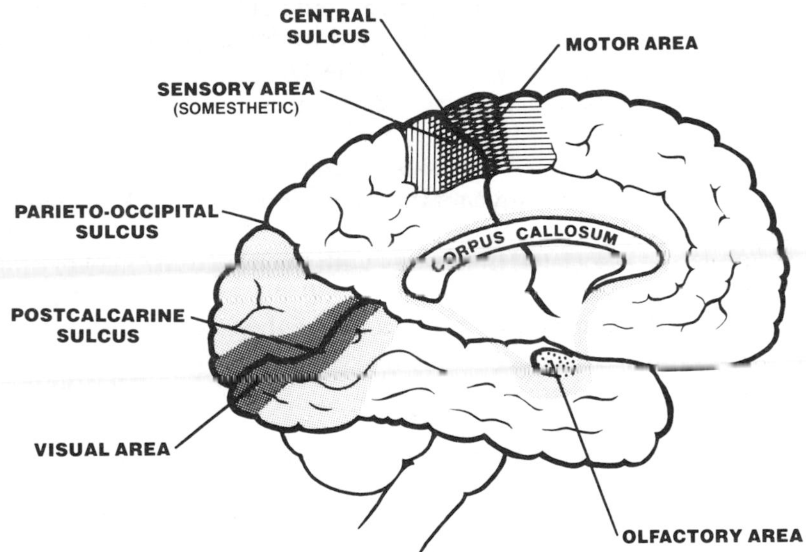

Figure 3.4 Cortical ares of visual, olfactory, motor and sensory localization in the brain.

The chemistry of learning and memory

In theory there may be a chemical base for learning and memory. A group of scientists at Oxford, who had been experimenting with tissue cultures, succeeded in implanting the nucleus of a cell from the intestine of a donor tadpole into an unfertilized egg cell of a tadpole of the same species; the nucleus of the recipient egg cell had been previously destroyed by ultra violet light. The frog's egg, equipped with its full complement of chromosomes, instead of only the half set, began to divide and behaved as if it had been fertilized conventionally. Finally, it grew into a tadpole. Whether bolder endeavours to control the effects of 'failures' in genetic mechanisms can be considered is a question of overcoming enormous technical problems and satisfying strongly held ethical objections. In the future it might be possible to remove damaged sections of the nucleus and replace them with healthy ones.

Watson and Crick were the direct inheritors of knowledge amassed by a distinguished and energetic line of molecular biologists, geneticists, biochemists and neuroscientists. In turn, the work of Watson and Crick led to developments in other fields. One hypothesis is that the DNA code is implicated directly or indirectly in learning, memory and other processes. The theory is that consolidation and maintenance of memory is dependent upon the production of particular proteins. Biochemists in recent years have contributed to our knowledge of mental processes by examining chemical substances which seem to be associated intimately with the transmission of neural impulses. Sir John Eccles and his colleagues at the Australian National University of Canberra, using the electron microscope and sophisticated micro-electrode techniques for probing single nerve cells, identified acetylcholine as one of these specialized compounds.

Learning and memory are two processes that are reported to be singularly susceptible to chemical agents in the brain. Sperry's (1963) work with goldfish, in which he cut the optic nerve fibres and observed their mode of regeneration (a feature of lowly vertebrates, amphibians and fish only) and the accuracy with which the nerve fibres of the right eye sought out the left side of the brain and *vice versa*, led him to speculate that an electrochemical basis for neural precision exists. Sperry holds that the rich exchange of signals, whereby cells recognize one another, is facilitated chemically.

The most exciting development, however, in this field was led by the brilliant Swedish neurobiologist Holger Hyden (1958), working at the University of Goteborg. Hyden, using sophisticated microknives and minute wire instruments to remove the smaller glial cells (glue-like structures or tissue) that surround the neuron, analysed each component for its protein synthesis, RNA production and content and other biochemical ingredients. He noted that rabbits and rats, for example, who 'learned' new tasks showed an increase in RNA synthesis and also that various stages of learning were related to levels of RNA activity. New stimuli result in small additional changes in the RNA synthesis and sensory impulses trigger off activities in neural DNA.

These and other experiments led to a number of 'cannibal' experiments which attempted to transfer RNA molecules from trained animals to naive subjects. Untutored worms were fed with portions of others which had acquired skills such as shock avoidance, and untrained rats were injected with brain extracts from trained rats. Attempts at replicating these memory transfer studies have been highly unsuccessful. Graver doubts may be expressed as to whether such a mode of transmission is possible in humans, as is claimed in the animal transfer experiments.

What is now known, however, is that the brain cortex of rats which 'learned' new skills weighed about 5% more than their untrained litter mates, and that marked differences were noted in the neural enzyme activity and an increase in glial cells in experimental stimulated litter mates. Furthermore, small amounts of an antibiotic (puromycin), a substance known to block RNA-mediated protein synthesis, inhibits the formation of long-term memory of newly learned tasks. Flexner *et al.* (1963) reported that mice taught to avoid electric shock forgot the habit when puromycin was injected into their brain. The period of memory loss was directly related to such factors as the interval between learned tasks (1–43 days) and the sites chosen (frontal, ventricular and temporal regions) for injecting puromycin. The findings strongly suggested that continued protein synthesis is necessary for the maintenance of memory.

If we are to survive we need protection from the overwhelming stream of energy impinging upon us. The function of the brain and nervous system is to filter the mass of information competing for our attention. How its complex system protects us remains unclear. What is known is that when selective or gross damage to various structures of the brain occurs through underdevelopment, disease or malformation, then brain working becomes disturbed and function impaired. The capacity of the individual to perceive, remember, plan actions, invent symbol systems and have access to other people's experience is markedly reduced. Neurophysiological psychologists have shown considerable interest in the effects of brain lesions upon function, and various explanations or descriptions have been offered as to the qualitative and quantitative effects of brain injury upon psychological operations. As has been shown, it is difficult to establish with certainty the precise relationship between anatomical structure and functioning. It would be unwise to relate weaknesses in function to the presence of lesions or to assume that specific learning difficulties in children can be attributed to neurological damage. The inadequacy of using cortical damage signs as predictors or explanations or disordered function has often been commented upon by other workers (Herbert, 1964). It would clearly be very useful in planning instructional strategies to have reliable knowledge of the extent to which healing and adaptation occurs, the manner in which intact areas take over from inactive regions, how spontaneous recovery of function takes place and the effects of loss of neural facilitation on unaffected cortical or subcortical areas.

Learning and disorders of perception

Intellectual abilities and their development are influenced by cerebral organization, which includes the central nervous system. A knowledge of the functioning of a healthy brain system is necessary, therefore, if one is to understand the process of learning and the way difficulties in learning arise if the brain is damaged. The unlocking of the secrets of the brain and an understanding of the working of the nervous system seem possible in the next few decades – advances made possible only as a result of work, begun many years ago, by scientists of various disciplines.

In the absence of techniques for measuring or observing brain function directly, early scientists and theorists conceived the notion of 'intelligence', the manifestation of brain performance. It has been recognized since the mid-nineteenth century that a healthy, well-formed brain is a necessary requirement for intelligence to be developed and sustained. Charles Darwin was one of the earliest scientists to recognize a progression from animal to human mental function. Later, the neurologist Lloyd Morgan (1894) offered a more technical view of this development. Herbert Spencer proposed that the more recent and complex mental mechanisms evolved from the older and simpler neural mechanisms. Darwin's writings clearly influenced Spencer's ideas which in turn influenced Spearman (1927), whose work on the nature of intelligence is best known for his theory that all intellectual performance is hierarchically organized and is influenced by general ability, or 'g'. Alfred Binet contributed much to our understanding of the nature of intelligence (Binet and Henri, 1896). He sought a direct measure of intelligence by observing an individual's performance in a range of activities such as attention, motor skill, comprehension, language ability and memorizing. There had been earlier attempts to give a systematic account of the relationship between the structure of the nervous system and specific functions – in 1824 Flourens had perceived the division of the nervous system into its six principal assemblies: the cerebral hemispheres, the cerebellum, the medulla oblongata, the corpora quadrigemina, the spinal cord and the peripheral nerves. His argument was that all these units acted in concert ('action commune') and he resisted attempts to relate specific mental functions – perception, memory, judgement – to areas within the cerebral hemisphere. Flourens held the view that 'one point excited in the nervous system excites all the others; one point enervated enervates them all; there is community of reaction, of alteration, of energy . . .' (Boring, 1957).

Huhglings Jackson (1874) developed Flourens' ideas and was more willing to link mental activities to hierarchical levels of nervous functioning, though Jackson too remained hesitant about identifying specific cerebral structures with higher functioning, such as judgement and memory. However, the arguments for localization of function within the cortex were becoming more convincing. As early as 1870 Fritsch and Hitzig showed that stimulation of certain areas of the cerebral cortex motor strip by a galvanic current evoked motor responses. Later, in 1876, Ferrier demonstrated that vision was localized in the occipital cortex. Other functions, such as hearing, speech and comprehension, had been traced to the temporal lobes by Broca, Wernicke and others (for a fuller account see Penfield and Roberts, 1959). Now began the era of the 'map markers' which led to some excessive zeal and optimism about the location of 'centres' for higher cognitive functioning within the cerebral hemispheres.

Lashley's meticulous work, started under Watson, spanned 40 years up to 1929. His search of the memory trace (engram) led him to propound the theory of cortical equipotentiality and mass action. Lashley believed that learning was dependent on the integrity and total mass action of the cerebral regions (equipotentiality) rather than on localized centres. He recognized, however, that specialized cerebral areas were responsible for certain sensory and motor functions. Lashley's views lent much support to the unitary character of intelligence 'g', but Lashley also believed the 'correlated development of different cerebral areas sustaining distinct functions was an equally tenable hypothesis'. In recent years there has been a return to the search for localization.

Intelligence

Interest now shifted to the development of intelligence in the individual. The British school of thought first propounded by Sir Cyril Burt (1940, 1955) was that intellectual development follows neurological maturation within the central nervous system and is organized hierarchically.

Since the 1940s, Hebb has exerted a powerful influence on ideas about the development of intelligence and cerebral organization. Hebb rejected Lashley's notion of mass action, demonstrating that the effects of massive cerebral lesions on intellectual function in adults was less severe than in children. A young child's language skills, for example, were more vulnerable to impairment than that of an adult who suffered a similar lesion provided it did not affect 'certain crucial areas'. This demonstrates that particular skills cannot develop if certain areas of the brain are damaged. An adult has already acquired the skill. If the whole brain were responsible for mental activity, child and adult would be affected equally (Figure 3.5).

Hebb's theory of two types of intelligence – intelligence A and intelligence B – is based on a neurological foundation. Intelligence A is commonly used to denote the 'capacity for development', a fully innate potential that amounts to the possession of a good brain and a good natural 'metabolism'.

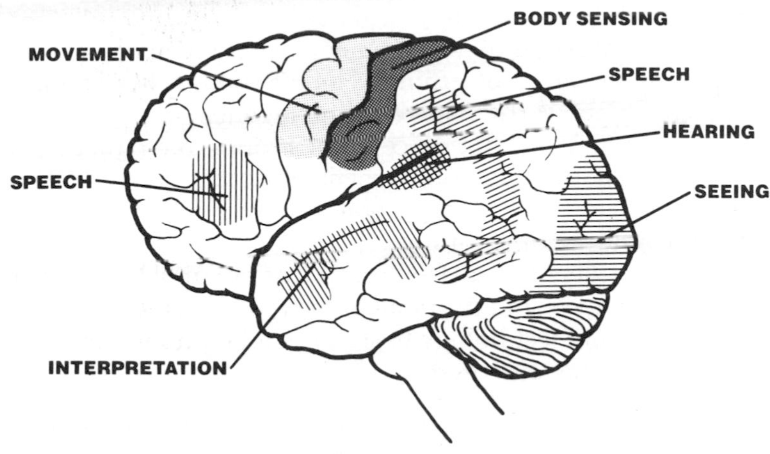

Figure 3.5 Brain structure showing areas in cerebral hemispheres associated with cognitive functioning.

However, Hebb maintains that the level of efficiency will depend upon the environmental influences; and this level can be measured directly – intelligence B. Hebb proposes that once intelligence B is established, it no longer needs the full powers of a good brain to be serviced and is affected only peripherally by brain injury or degeneration. Hebb stresses the dependence of the infant brain for intellectual performance on the hierarchical organization of intellectual skills. The theory is that learning results from activity in a complex closed loop called a 'cell assembly', which is developed through repeated stimulation, and that one or more cell assemblies simultaneously activated lead to elaborations called 'phase sequences'. Thus, the view that stimulating environments, particularly with animals, would lead to increased growth of brain structure and, conversely, sustained environmental deprivation retard cerebral growth, inspired much of the infant stimulation programmes in hospitals, pre-schools and socially disadvantaged groups.

Piaget's view of intelligence is also hierarchical. He regards intelligence as biological adaptation and its evolution as a result of human physical encounters with the environment. In a sense, it parallels Hebbs neurological descriptions of levels of nervous system organisation. Piaget's ontogenetic formulations about invariant stages of development increasing in complexity at each stage are not unlike Hebb's neurophysiological propositions about the nature of intelligence.

The important effects of cerebral lesions on intellectual development at particular ontogenetic stages become clear. The size, location and timing of cerebral insult would influence the level of cognitive functioning.

In Britain, Canada and elswhere, it was not until World War 2 that neurologists and psychologists came together to direct their interest and technology to study brain injury in humans. Two major issues emerged:

1. the need for more accurate descriptions of the major clinical conditions and of their aetiology;
2. the need for descriptions of the intellectual characteristics of brain-injured subjects and their relationship to cerebral dysfunction.

Among the more commonly studied psychological processes have been disorders of perception. These include:

1. visual;
2. auditory;
3. spatial;
4. motor.

DISORDERS OF PERCEPTION

Agnosia

Agnosia is a memory disorder in which an individual fails to recognize objects despite intact sensory systems, visual functions, or mental imagery. Agnosia occurs in the visual, auditory, and proprioceptive-sense modalities. **Visual agnosia** arises when the individual fails to recognize familiar pictures, colours, objects, faces etc., despite enjoying normal visual sensory function. Often they are able to recognize objects by touch. A subclinical feature of visual agnosia, prosopagnosia, is one in which familiar faces are not recognized. Some workers claim that difficulty in face recognition is commoner in individuals with right hemispheric lesions than those on the left

(Warrington and James, 1967; Hecaen & Albert, 1978; Gaddes, 1985).

Colour agnosia

Individuals suffering from colour agnosia are not colour blind but are unable to associate colours with objects.

Simultanagnosia

This condition, a specific disorder of form perception, is characterized by an inability on the part of an individual to absorb more than one element of a visual stimulus. Thus if more than one object is presented simultaneously (cup and a glass), the individual can only 'see' one of them. If sentences presented are long, only words generally in the right visual field are apprehended. Even single two-syllable words are misread. Thus the word 'bathroom' might be read as 'room'. Overlapping pictures are not recognized and single figures are picked out. Simultanagnosia should not be regarded as a form of stereoscopic rivalry which occurs in normal people, because there is significantly less fluctuation between perceptions, and a greater 'visual inattention' in this disorder. Kinsbourne and Warrington (1962a) suggested that the reason why four subjects who experienced difficulty with tasks involving visual recognition of pictures and extended scenes was that they had suffered damage in the anterior portion of the left occipital lobe. These subjects could readily recognize single forms; only after prolonged exposure to the stimuli could they recognize more than one form.

Milner (1958) demonstrated that removal of the right temporal lobe interfered with the ability to interpret pictorial material. Among other examples of visual perceptual defects provoked by specific neurological injury is that of size constancy judgements – consequent upon parietal lobe damage. People with unilateral cortical lesions reveal impairments in face recognition and discrimination of shape and position of lines. For further reading see Hecaen and Albert (1978).

Metamorphopsia

This is a disorder which is paroxysmal, associated with epilepsy and if of a persistent nature, traceable to ophthalmological problems or cerebral trauma. Two major types of metamorphopsia may be recognized, which results in single or complex visual illusions. In the former condition, perceptual qualities of an object are modified, while in the latter, alterations of three-dimensional visual space occur. For example, objects though recognized and named correctly are perceptually distorted, becoming larger (macropsia) or reduced (micropsia) tilted, fragmented, unstable, etc. Critchely (1965) reports cases of patients who described 'The furniture seemed to be turned away'; 'my husband seemed too big and yet a long way away' etc.

Auditory perception

There has been less research in auditory than in visual perception partly because of technical limitations. The effects of excision or disease to such areas as the auditory cortex in the left or right temporal lobes reveal differences in ability to discriminate pitch, volume, rhythm and ability to locate auditory stimuli (Milner, 1962).

The disorders have been studied more systematically in the areas of music and language, and relate to the ability to localise sounds. Disorders of auditory perception are different from those arising from auditory deafness. In the former, meanings of words are affected, whilst deafness leads to disorders of tone or pitch of the spoken words.

Route-finding difficulty

A less frequently mentioned disability is one in which a person has difficulty in finding his way about familiar surroundings. Such a person is unable to relate himself to a fixed point in space. Poor navigational performance and disordered judgement of motion have been reported by Goody, Benton, Brain and others (Benton, 1969). Some research workers ascribe this weakness to an inability to focus attention adequately, while others (Brain, 1941) attribute this disorder to 'confusion and complexity' occasioned in the individual when apparently random responses are demanded at decision points. They show a tendency to make right turns at these points on a route, become perplexed and make capricious responses at choice points. This is highlighted in hemianopic (blind in one half of the visual field) patients.

It is further suggested that children with movement disorders, who have proprioceptive and tactile weaknesses, experience difficulties in navigating in single, double or three directions (left to right or *vice versa*, up/down, forwards/backwards). Since spatial orientation has a neurological basis, this faculty becomes affected in people with specific neurological lesions (Goody, 1969).

DISORDERS OF MOTOR SKILL

Apraxia

This is a disorder involving poor control over limbs or muscular power (paresis) affecting motor skills in which the memory of a single motor act (waving goodbye) or an automatic complex sequence of motor acts (striking a match) is impaired. The person appears to have 'forgotten' how to perform familiar actions. However, such individuals are able to produce these behaviours spontaneously rather than on request. Debate surrounding the origin of this memory disturbance goes back to the 1900s (Liepmann, 1900). It has been represented variously; as a particular neuropsychological defect of gestural behaviour resulting from specific disturbances of movement or communication; or as a clinical feature of aphasia; or the results of intellectual deterioration.

The major forms of apraxia (Miller, 1987) are:

1. ideomotor;
2. ideational;
3. constructional;
4. dressing.

1. **Ideomotor apraxia** is a disorder in which simple often single gestures and pantomime (sign of the cross, wave goodbye etc.) or imitating gestures of examiner to verbal command, cannot be carried out. In all instances the

comprehension is unaffected and the gestures can be carried out spontaneously. There appears to be a severance between the 'idea' and 'motor' movement to carry out the task requested.

2. **Ideational apraxia**. In ideational apraxia, the individual's attempt to carry out a complex gesture is characterised by a disruption of the logical sequence and overall plan of the individual elements. Thus, the act of lighting a candle with a match cannot be carried out, because of defective planning of the discrete acts of the total action. Invariably, the individual attempts to strike the candle against the match box, or tries to light the candle with an unlit match.
3. **Constructional apraxia**. In this condition individuals have difficulty in exercising skills previously well established and practised, e.g. copying a design or building simple models with bricks, words incorrectly spaced, irregular direction of lines in writing. The defect apparently lies in the failure to transmit information from the visual perceptual mode to the appropriate motor action. Constructional apraxia is associated with a breakdown in different underlying neuropsychological mechanisms of the damaged hemisphere.
4. **Dressing apraxia**. This condition attracts more attention because of the social difficulties it poses for individuals. Again, though the individual's ability for dressing is not lost, organizing the sequence of acts for putting on clothes is disturbed. Thus the putting on of a coat or doing up buttons or trousers ends up with arms, sleeves, etc. back to front in total confusion. It is important to distinguish such a condition from that of dementia or severe psychiatric disorders.

Visuo–spatial disorders

These are characterised by marked difficulties in locating the relationship and position of objects in space. Thus children suffering from visuo–spatial disorders experience considerable problems in identifying which of two or more objects are above, below, to the left, right, nearer or further one from another.

Visuo-constructive weakness

The disorder may show up in such ways as an inability to build a tower of bricks, to construct a six-cube pyramid, or to copy a shape or pattern with sticks or plasticine. A child who is required to place one brick upon another must not only possess a degree of manual dexterity and eye–hand co-ordination, but be aware of the orientation of such objects in space and engage in an analysis of their interrelations – thus efficient muscular organisation and adequate spatial judgements are needed at the simplest level of visuo-constructive tasks. The essence of visuo-constructive weakness lies in being unable to translate adequate visual perception into appropriate visuo-motor actions.

Abercrombie (1964) has reviewed the literature concerning these disorders in brain-injured children including cerebral palsy subjects. Weddell (1973), in his account of learning and perceptuo-motor disabilities, warns against accepting general statements about the 'relationship between CNS defects and disabilities in sensory motor organization', since the findings of the studies are highly equivocal. For further reading see Calvin and Ojemann (1980) and Gaddes (1985).

Learning in children with neurological and physical disabilities

By virtue of their motor disorder, children with neurological and motor disabilities face a number of formidable difficulties over a whole range of learning tasks. The cerebral palsy child, for instance, is physically restricted in moving about freely in space and there are indications of the possible adverse effects of this on the child's ability to handle perceptuo-motor information. There is reason to suspect that in such children, judgements of space and orientation, crucial to the development of such personal social skills as dressing, feeding, toileting and playing are affected, especially if such children are raised in an impoverished social and physical environment. A number of studies have indicated that speech and language of such children develop more slowly than in normal children (Jones *et al.*, 1969). When such a child is faced with a dual handicap of motor and verbal limitation, the ability to relate language to practical experiences is reduced. The stream of discourse, such as 'eat your apple', 'give me the red pencil', and 'get into your bath', becomes a string of inconsequential sounds, if the task demands the carrying out of appropriate physical actions consequent upon verbal instructions.

Such limitations lead to further intellectual weaknesses, and a characteristic slowness to respond to complex environmental demands becomes evident. If one of the distinguishing aspects in humans is the speed and accuracy with which they process information, then a slowness to adapt in a learning situation, in the classroom or home, would disadvantage them in a range of living situations.

It can be argued that neurologically impaired children are slower ('less intelligent') because they do not employ appropriate strategies for extracting meaning from the ceaseless input of information from the environment. They are slow learners because they have not learnt to focus attention on the relevant aspects of the stimuli, or to exclude or filter excessive redundant information. These children differ from fast learners not only in their capacity to learn, but in their inefficient strategies of learning.

Implications for teachers

There are obvious implications for teachers and classroom practices in these matters. The early work of Cruickshank (1961) and Kinsbourne (1972) provides a notable attempt to relate difficulties and delays in the acquisition of academic skills to psychological theories. They attributed, for example, poor academic skills in brain-injured children (including those with CP) to disordered figure–ground perception, distractability, perseveration and other psychological characteristics described by the Gestalt psychologists. They tried to analyse the difficulties of these children in a systematic manner, looking at the visuo–motor, tactuo–motor and audio–motor skills and declared that impairment in these areas arose not only from corresponding sensory defects but could also be traced to disordered pathological conditions. It was pointed out that weaknesses in the perceptual integration and cognitive functioning in the child could lead to delayed or arrested development of academic skills.

Unfortunately, few psychologists or teachers have systematically followed up these leads in the classroom situation, which seems surprising in view of the significance attached by clinicians to the effects of brain damage on perceptual and other cognitive skills. Piaget (1950), on the other hand, offered a description of the developmental stages through which he suggested children progressed, and the kinds of knowledge they possessed at each of the stages. Piaget's use of systematic observational techniques to discover how normal children learn, the kinds of errors they make and how they overcome them, has been very little exploited for the benefit of children with neurological disorders. Teachers of such children do need sure knowledge of the normal and deviant patterns of child development and they require effective instructional skills to promote the appropriate level of learning in disabled children.

Skinner was one of the outstanding psychologists to have formulated a practical application of learning theory for classroom instruction. His methods setting out the range and availabilty of reinforcement techniques available to the teacher have been tested with normal children. Skinner demonstrated that children perform better when information presented is controlled and issued in manageable units (the optimum level for individual children should be determined by the class teacher). Teachers, he argued, should discourage guessing in children in order to reduce errors in learning. Repetition and practice to consolidate previously learned material is also incorporated in his approach.

Skinner also indicated that instructional technology is analysable, that 'negative information' is unhelpful and that a learner can best handle information that can be processed adequately. His suggestion that various features in the environment need structuring to maximize learning has been well received with normal children. Teachers need to apply similar techniques to enhance efficient learning in disabled children.

Teachers of disabled children have also been guided by notions which emphasize the use of incentives, the breakdown of the task, the spacing of learning, etc. The classical data presented by Hermelin and O'Connor (1970) pointed to 'deficits in acquisition rather than to poor perception, retention or transfer ability' as a major determinant of backwardness in speech and thought among the severely intellectually disabled.

It is suggested that a combination of the developmental approach of Piaget and a learning theory model of Skinner could be of considerable value to the teacher. An assessment of the developmental level reached by a child, including a systematic analysis of the particular areas in which the child's functioning is delayed or arrested would have to precede the formulation of any teaching programme in arithmetic, reading, writing, spelling or motor learning.

Here are some general guidelines for teaching children with learning difficulties a task or skill:

1. Assess the pupil's current level of achievement/level of development relative to the task to be taught.
2. Break down the task to be acquired into small steps.
3. Begin teaching at a slightly lower level than the child's level of achievement to ensure success from the outset.
4. Try to anticipate where difficulties and possible failure may occur and take steps to avoid them. This can be done by additional demonstration, explanation, etc. before attempting that stage of the task. This becomes easier with experience on the part of the teacher.
5. If a pupil begins to fail, break down the task into even smaller steps at the point of failure so that the child can succeed at each stage of the learning process.
6. Always give as much positive reinforcement as possible, i.e. encouragement, praise, pointing out where the pupil is succeeding.
7. Practise the task once it is learned in order to reinforce it.
8. Recapitulate on the task achieved before going onto the next stage.
9. Throughout, the teacher must observe the pupil closely to ascertain where and when he is going wrong, and to intervene at the crucial point.
10. Try using other sensory modalities, e.g. verbalizing during motor learning, moving to music; the use of colour, touch and movement in counting tasks; reading aloud with a child (or the child hearing the material on a cassette recorder) so that the written word is heard.
11. Always use the child's strengths (see 10. above).

4

Brain-damaged children

This chapter deals with the confusion surrounding the term 'brain-damaged child', a term which covers many different conditions.

Parents, neurologists, psychologists and educators are often confused about the meaning of the term 'brain-damaged child', which has become one of the diagnostic subcategories to which children with a diversity of learning and behavioural problems have been assigned. In the literature as many as 40 different terms are used to refer to these children but the most commonly accepted meaning is that of a child with a minimal disturbance of cerebral function rather than one suffering from cerebral palsy, epilepsy or mental subnormality.

Brain damage is not a unitary phenomenon. It emanates from a variety of conditions with differing effects. Earlier workers assumed that brain damage was due to a fundamental disturbance which arose from insult to specific cerebral regions. Thus, the administration of single tests to detect organic involvement were much in vogue and were claimed to distinguish psychiatric and normal subjects from brain-damaged individuals.

However, to ascribe the label of brain damage to an individual, there must be medical or clinical evidence of tissue damage, or other unequivocal signs of central nervous system damage, such as stroke, cerebral palsy, epilepsy, brain tumour or penetrating head injury, etc.,

To clarify the position for parents and professionals directly concerned with these children, the first part of this account will attempt to trace the ways in which the confused terminology arose and examine the intellectual and behavioural patterns it has come to imply. Ways in which the term may most usefully be redefined will then be suggested. The second part of the account will deal specifically with the learning disorders associated with actual damage, particularly cerebral palsy.

In the 1920s a German neurologist, Dr Strauss, examined the children in a school for mental defectives in Michigan in the USA and found that a large proportion had some kind of neurological impairment. From these findings, Strauss postulated that mental defectives could not be considered as a homogeneous group, but rather that they consisted of an 'endogenous' and an 'exogenous' group. The endogenous group showed no history of peri-natal or later childhood damage to the nervous system and their backwardness could be ascribed to an inherited low intelligence. The exogenous group showed actual damage to the central nervous system, or the brain. Collaborating with a psychologist, Dr Laura Lehtinen, Strauss drew attention to the fact that there were differences in both cognitive and emotional behaviour between the two groups and that the exogenous group showed specific learning difficulties and abnormal patterns of behaviour. For example, small demands or changes in the children's routine could result in an unpredictable show of temper. The term 'brain-damaged' subsequently came to be applied to the exogenous group.

The criteria Strauss used for the recognition of cases of brain injury were:

1. Injury to the brain by trauma or inflammatory processes before, during, or after birth.
2. Slight neurological signs indicating a lesion.
3. Severe psychological disturbance together with intellectual retardation, despite normal family stock.
4. No mental retardation but the presence of psychological disturbance discovered by means of qualitative tests of perception and conceptualization.

Unfortunately, both exogenous and endogenous groups of children were found to conform to some of Strauss' criteria, although it is true that a child who shows these signs is more likely to be brain-damaged than one who does not. Difficulties still arise from the rather loose application of the term 'brain-damaged', since children have been found depicting one or more Strauss criteria but showing no clinical signs of brain damage. Others who are definitely known to be brain-damaged have been found to display none of these criteria. For example, contrary to the prevailing neuropsychological convictions of the time that loss of the prefrontal lobe would lead to immediate and severe intellectual retardation, Hebb (1942) reported the case of a young man who obtained 'a perfect score' on the Standford–Binet test after total removal of his left prefrontal lobe.

The other notable case was that of Dr Penfield's patient, who had both his prefrontal lobes ablated (15% by weight of the total mass of the cerebellum) because of fits, psychotic behaviour and severe intellectual impairment, and who obtained an IQ of about 95 following the operation.

It has also been shown that right- and left-sided lesions do not produce similar effects and that left and right temporal lobe patients reveal a quantitatively different pattern in their IQ scores (McFie *et al.*, 1950; Milner, 1954). Again, it has been argued that 'a large brain injury need not reduce intelligence in proportion to its size, because of the conceptual development that has occurred before the injury' (Buchtel, 1984).

Today, there is greater recognition among neuropsychologists that the behavioural characteristics of individuals with brain damage vary according to the type, site, and onset of the condition, as well as their age, sex and their psychological background. Furthermore, different individuals with similar lesions could display widely differing behaviour disorders.

Attempts to overcome the difficulty by using terms such as 'soft neurological signs', 'minimal cerebral dysfunction' (mcd), 'diffuse' or 'non-focal', 'minimal brain dysfunction' (mbd), are again begging the question, since 'brain damage' is being implied. It has been pointed out (Birch, 1964) that a distinction should be made between the fact of brain damage and the concept of brain damage.

The fact of brain damage is the presence of any anatomical or physiological change of a pathological nature in the nerve tissues of the brain. Thus, a child with cerebral palsy is, in fact, brain damaged.

Birch (1956) argues that:

1. There are individuals with brain damage.
2. We have instruments for examining the behaviour of these individuals.
3. These instruments are often inadequate for the detection of changes in behaviour produced by this damage.
4. We have to produce better methods of approaching analysis of behaviour.

The extent of the functional disturbance resulting from brain damage will depend on a number of factors. These include:

1. Size of the lesion.
2. Site of the lesion.
3. Whether the lesion is progressive or static.
4. Whether it is diffuse or focal.
5. Whether the damage occurred during the pre-natal or neonatal period. If there is an early primary lesion, there may be secondary consequences, since interrelated areas, dependent on the damaged area for stimulation towards maturation, may fail to develop.

The concept of brain damage is a term used to designate a certain pattern or set of patterns of behavioural disturbance (Birch, 1964). Brain damage is generally inferred because the individual displays abnormal patterns of behaviour, with disturbed interpersonal and social features. For example, in family relationships, a child's disturbances may affect parental attitudes and the child, who cannot control or understand its own behaviour, may be rejected. Such rejection could lead to further behavioural disturbance. Clearly, such dysfunction may lead indirectly to impaired development of self-image, since this is derived from the way others view the child (with possible hostility or impatience) and from the way the child sees itself (bad, stupid or doomed to failure). Unfortunately, these beliefs lead to unrealistic expectations to succeed or attempts to gain attention by clowning or aggressiveness. The concept usually refers to a certain pattern of behavioural disturbance, and this stereotyping has meant the neglect of consideration of other behaviour disorders in such children.

Disturbances in spatial perception

Right hemispheric damage is likely to cause disturbances of spatial orientation. The outcome could be influenced by the extent and site of the lesion, as well as the sensory modality being examined and the choice of tests used (see Figure 4.1, which shows how damage to a particular section of the motor cortex results in physical impairment to the equivalent function). Carmon (1970) found that patients with right hemisphere lesions used kinaesthetic feedback rather poorly to improve their performance on a posture maintenance test.

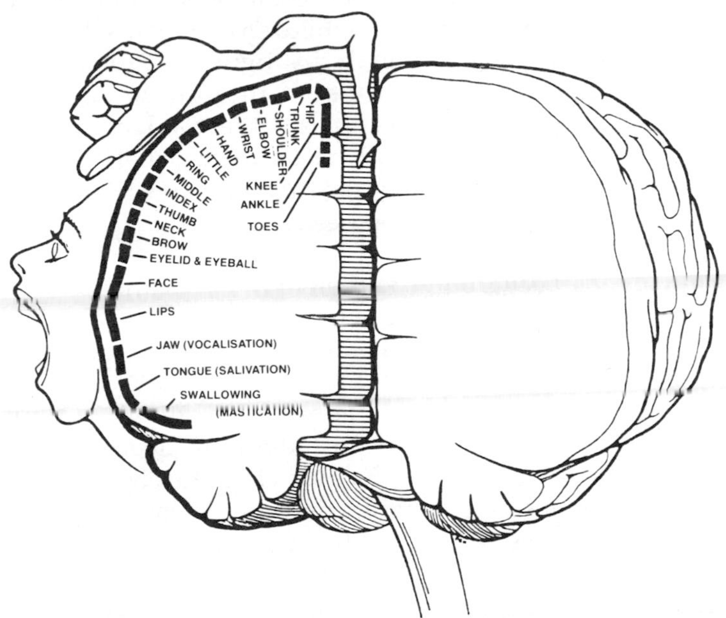

Figure 4.1 The motor cortex of the brain. Damage to a particular section of the motor cortex results in physical impairment to the equivalent function.

Strauss and Lehtinen believed that the behaviour of the children they studied indicated perceptual disturbances which were in many ways similar to those of brain-injured adults. For example, the children would examine intently certain interesting details of the teacher's clothing, such as belts or buckles and seemed oblivious of anything else; or they might be attracted to the minute details of pictures but disregard the conceptual contents of the picture as a whole. The children experienced particular difficulty in writing and arithmetic and performed erratically and incorrectly on puzzles and performance tests. In order to objectify these clinical impressions, various perceptual and motor tests, such as the marble-board test, were administered in which brain-injured children showed a qualitatively different performance from the familial mentally deficient child or younger normal child. The results of the marble-board and other perceptual tests suggested that brain-injured children had particular figure–background difficulties and this hypothesis was supported by results of a test in which children had to perceive embedded figures; the children experienced greater difficulty than normal children in distinguishing foreground from background. It was considered that the foreground–background disturbance might apply to other modalities (i.e. to the tactual and auditory fields as well as to the visual field) and results of a variety of tests suggested that this was so. It appears that brain-damaged children experience constant instability between foreground and background so that there is a fluid and fluctuating background to the child's adjustment to the normal world. This is obviously a handicap in all learning processes; in reading, for example, children may be unable to attend to the essential word (the 'figure') long enough to make an appropriate response. Since the hundreds of other stimuli (pattern, spaces and angles) may distract his attention, clearly there is a relationship between such difficulties and the cognitive disorders which Strauss and Lehtinen drew particular attention to, that is, the difficulties of these children in concept formation and in forming abstractions. Obviously a child will have difficulties in abstracting the class characteristics of a stimulus pattern (and in reducing it to a standardized de-particularized problem) if its detailed particularities cannot be cut out (e.g. size and colour). The foreground–background confusion and the inability to see things as wholes may also be closely related to some of the behavioural disorders noted in brain-damaged children (see Fig. 4.2)

Behavioural disorders

General characteristics

Strauss and Lehtinen found behavioural disorders to be the most conspicuous manifestations of abnormality in brain-injured children. Most of these disorders should be regarded as manifestations of exaggerated responsiveness to stimuli. It appears that the inhibiting responses which are normally built into the nervous system may be interfered with. The young brain-injured child reacts in a manner which is beyond the reach of effective cortical control.

A general picture of such behavioural disorders was given by Strauss and Lehtinen who found that the brain-injured group as opposed to the normal were erratic, uncoordinated, uncontrolled, uninhibited and socially unacceptable. Another characteristic behaviour manifestaton is the 'catastrophic reaction' similar to one described by Goldstein in adults – when confronted with a task beyond his ability such a person may experience a strong sensation of rage, despair, anxiety or extreme depression, with all the accompanying bodily reactions. Birch (1964) refers to the same thing when he says that the conduct of the brain-damaged person may be 'dramatically unpredictable'.

Among the specific characteristics described most frequently are those of distractability or abnormalities in attention span, perseveration and what is variously known as hyperactivity or the hyperkinetic syndrome.

Distractability

Teachers and other observers have commented on the short attention span of brain-damaged children, here labelled as 'distractable'. It is assumed that such children lack cortical control which prevents them from being able to attend to a given stimulus or group of stimuli for a sufficient period to make an appropriate intellectual response. Instead, these children appear to be reacting constantly to inessential stimuli, whether these are visual, auditory or tactile. This results in an abnormally interrupted cognitive development, since the child has difficulty in focusing and maintaining attention.

Perseveration

On the other hand, these children may also be characterized by a disturbance known as 'perseveration', that is the attention

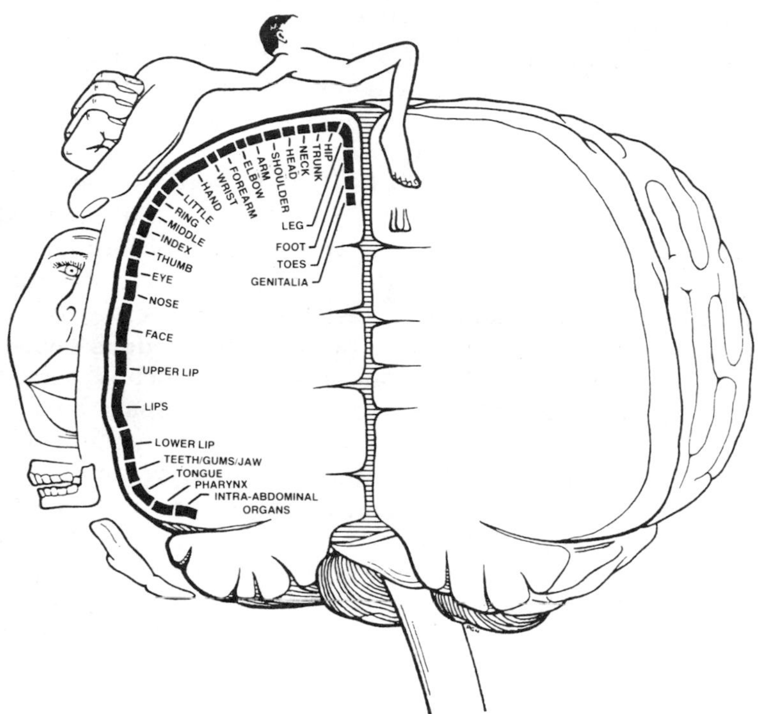

Figure 4.2 The sensory cortex of the brain. The localization of each function corresponds with a particular section of the sensory cortex.

to a simple stimulus for long periods of time. Examples of such behaviour would include the child in the classroom who in writing seems unable to initiate a new sequence of acts and repeats the letter he has just completed.

While a child may appear to have a short attention span, perseveration may have some of the opposite characteristics, and it is probably better to describe the child's attention as 'capricious'.

Hyperactivity

Not all children who are called 'brain damaged' are hyperactive. Some hyperactive children are grossly brain damaged, while others are not. Nevertheless, hyperactive children pose one of the major problems to the teacher. One aspect of hyperactivity is sensory hyperactivity. The majority of those who use the term, however, are thinking largely of its second aspect, that is, of motor hyperactivity, possibly more correctly called 'motor disinhibition', which is the inability of the child to react to a stimulus which produces a motor response.

The hyperkinetic syndrome is characterized by severe and disorganized overactivity. While such a child may not be more active than the ordinary child, its activity is irrelevant and without clear direction. Also such children may be impulsive and meddlesome; they must move, touch and handle objects and are often destructive. This uninhibited behaviour may affect several aspects of their social functioning so that while they may appear cheerful and over-friendly they generally do not get on well with other children, are often aggressive and may display outbursts of rage. This behaviour is most striking in the first year or so of school when it is seen in 1 or 2% of children, who are often found to have fits (Rutter, 1966; Rutter *et al.*, 1970a). In middle or later childhood this overactive pattern of behaviour is often gradually replaced by an inert under-activity.

Rethinking the concept of the brain damaged child

The above account covers some of the most striking features generally accepted as characteristic of the 'brain-damaged child', but does not solve the problem of confused terminology. We suggest rethinking the term 'brain-damaged child' along the lines put forward by Rutter (1966). Rutter suggests that the term can be used in a general way to cover a number of different syndromes or patterns of difficulty which are the result of some impaired functioning of the brain. This use of the term would include two broad groups:

1. those 'involving definite abnormalities of function' (such as cerebral palsy and epilepsy); and
2. those in which there are 'limits or delays in the development of normal functions'.

In the latter cases it may be very difficult to determine whether the disorders are due to brain damage or just to maturational delay. More boys are affected than girls in both cases. Rutter suggested four main syndromes of developmental disorders.

1. *Retardation of speech development (developmental dysphasia)*
   This may result in lack of speech or understanding of sounds or a delay in the acquisition of speech. Difficulties in reading may occur together with a lack of concentration and a delay in the development of logical and abstract thought. This is much commoner in boys than girls.
2. *Severe clumsiness (developmental dyspraxia)*
   Here the child is backward, ungainly and maladroit in fine and gross motor skills (doing up buttons and laces, catching and kicking a ball or gymnastic games), may have difficulties of perception of shapes and delays in speech and reading. However, these are not usually permanent disorders.
3. *Reading retardation (developmental dyslexia)*
   Here many of the above-mentioned difficulties occur, more often in boys than girls. Difficulties of distinguishing right and left, motor impersistence - the inability to sustain a voluntarily initiated motor act such as keeping the eye closed, and problems of concentration.
4. *The hyperkinetic syndrome*
   This has been outlined above.

Defined in this way, therefore, brain damage can be seen as a very varied and common problem affecting up to 5% of all children. It is more acceptable as a definition than earlier restricted and misleading ones because, although broadly based, it is clear.

The specific learning disorders of such children, and those with cerebral palsy in particular will now be discussed and suggestions made for their remedy.

Incidence of visuo-perceptual and visuo-motor disorders in the different types of cerebral palsy

The three main types of cerebral palsy, divided according to the motor disorder involved, are spasticity, which forms 60% of the cerebral palsy population, athetosis, which forms approximately 25%, and ataxia 5–10%, the rest being a mixed type.

Two distinct types of disorder may be involved in cerebral palsy; visuo-perceptual disorders (the impaired ability to perceive spatial relationships) and visuo-motor or constructional disorders.

A review of the findings by Abercrombie (1964) shows that where there is a spastic disorder of movement there is also a greater than average difficulty with visuo-motor tasks, in some cases slight and imperceptible, in others severe and permanent. Visuo-motor disorders are less frequent and less severe in children with athetosis.

Visuo-perceptual disorders

Studies of the perceptual ability of cerebral palsied subjects - Strauss and Lehtinen (1947); Dunsdon (1952); Cruickshank *et al.* (1957); Cruickshank (1976); Hecaen and Albert, (1978); Gaddes (1985) - indicate that children with cerebral palsy, and spastic children in particular, have a poorer perceptual ability than the normal child. Most studies relate this, not to cerebral palsy, but to levels of intelligence in the child. The main deficits found are the inability to distinguish figure from ground and the inability to organize individual stimuli into a whole (Figure 4.3). The tasks which these children find difficult in practical learning terms, therefore, are the matching of objects and processes of abstraction. In reading there is difficulty in the recognition of familiar words (the tendency being to confuse words with similar configurations of letters), and there is a tendency to omit letters. Among the most widely known tests which claim to examine these difficulties is the Frostig Developmental Test of Visual Perception (DTVP) which deals with problems of position in space, spatial relationship, perceptual constancy and the relation of figure to background. Factor analytic studies, however, have refuted the claim that five separate areas of visual perception and visuo-motor skills are identified by the DTVP.

Visuo-motor disorders

Visuo-motor skills may be defined as those skills requiring movement under visual control. The difficulties that the cerebral palsied child may show in copying a pattern or a

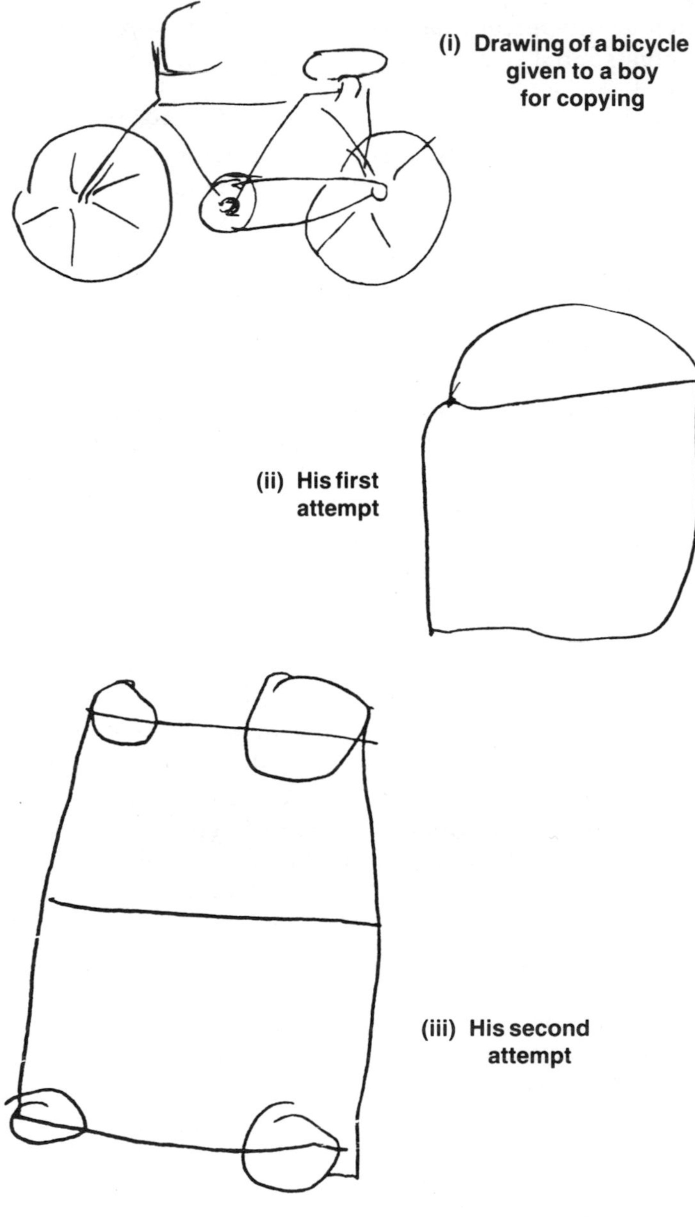
(i) Drawing of a bicycle given to a boy for copying
(ii) His first attempt
(iii) His second attempt

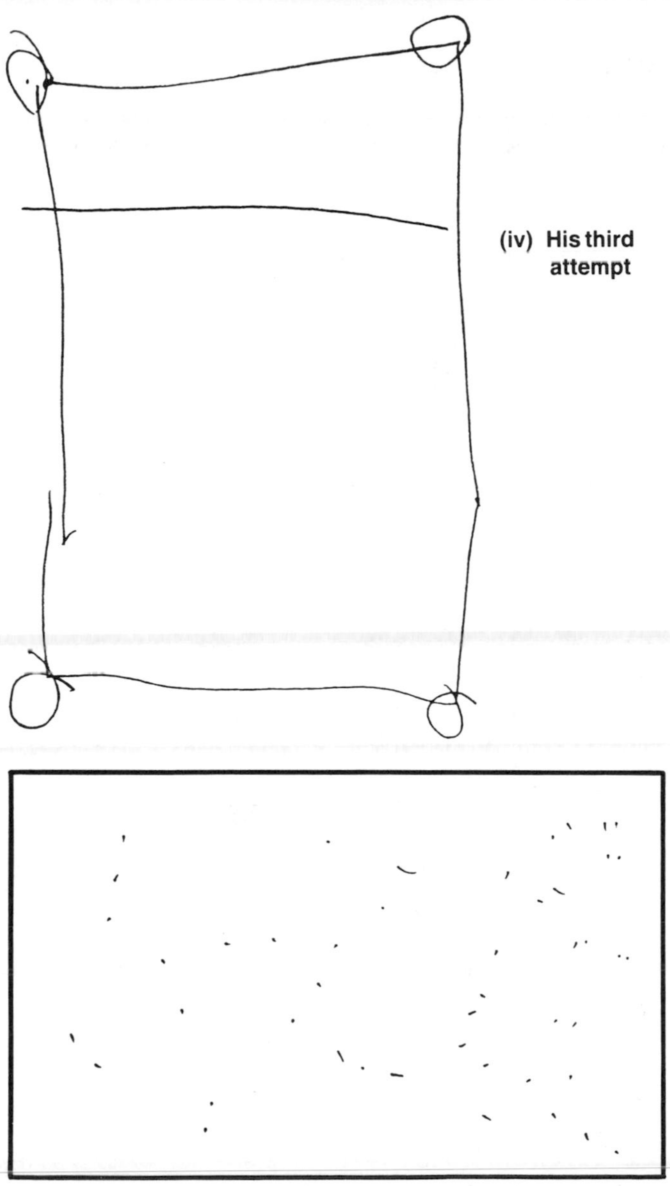

The same boy's attempt to reproduce a straight dotted line thus: . . . .

Figure 4.3 The practical effect of a visuo-perceptual disorder. A 13-year-old boy's attempts at drawing a bicycle.

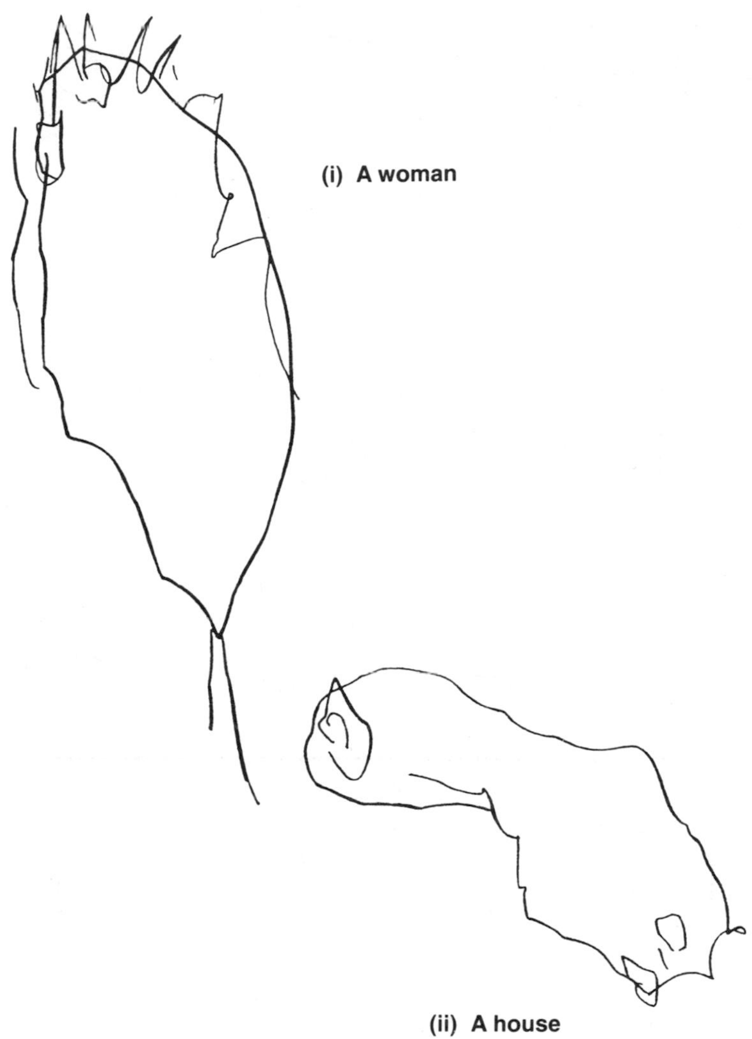

Figure 4.4 The effects of visuo-motor disorders on a 10-year-old, below-average ability spastic girl's drawing.

shape include the failure to get the size and position of the angles correctly and a change of direction at the angles (Figure 4.4). The tendency to reproduce a mirror image of a model is also common. An inability to synthesize the information as a whole is evident. Tests for disorders of visual–motor–spatial-constructional impairments include Wechsler Performance Subtests, Benton Visual Retention Test, Benton Finger Localization Test, Finger Praxis, Beery Test of Visual Motor Integration, etc. There is doubt as to whether a visuo-motor disorder represents a developmental lag or a permanent disturbance. What effect other sensory and motor handicaps have upon it is not clear.

Relationship of disorders to other disabilities

Visual defects, especially occulo-motor weaknesses, occur in over 50% of the cerebral palsy population and these include errors or refraction, visual field defects, various developmental anomalies and disorders of the movement of the eyeball (disorders of vergence and version) and difficulties of fixation – Smith (1963), Abercrombie (1963), Haskell and Hughes (1965), Haskell (1972). Hebb has pointed out that 'eye movements contribute essentially to perceptual integration' and it has been shown that cerebral palsied children are less efficient than normal children in following horizontal moving targets, so that the relationship of eye movements to cerebral palsied disorders needs to be further examined.

Motor handicaps may have two possible effects on perceptual learning in cerebral palsied children. Although by themselves they do not produce perceptual impairment, they may cause a poverty of sensory experience, due to the restriction of contact with the physical world. They may also cause a distortion of sensory input due to weak, restricted or disordered bodily movements. Further research is necessary here.

Educational problems and their remediation

The practical effects of the disorders outlined above as regards learning are many. Caldwell (1956) listed the effects of lack of spatial ability in cerebral palsied school children which hindered their normal development as the following: difficulties in realization of position and direction with regard to self; dressing difficulties; difficulties with apparatus involving comparisons of colour, shape and size; difficulties in drawing, tracing, copying and writing; the reading difficulties outlined earlier and difficulties in number work of counting and grouping.

Remedial programs

Strauss and Lehtinen (1947) suggested that visual–motor perception in the brain-damaged child could be strengthened in the pre-writing phase by tasks which accentuated the differences of figure and background. They used colour to help the integration of perceptual patterns and beads to facilitate the abstract process of counting. They included the motor activity of the child wherever possible.

Cruickshank (1976) has concentrated in particular on the behaviour disturbances of the brain-damaged child. He first assesses the level of ability of the child, then he provides a remedial program which reflects the child's disorders. The program is highly structured and allows conditioning to take place. The classrooms are designed to reduce distracting stimuli and have monotone rooms with typewriter, walls, furniture, woodwork and floor coverings all the same colour. Windows may have opaque glass to reduce stimuli from outside, and the room may be sound-proofed and have wall-to-wall carpeting. Tasks for hyperactive children are approached in order of increasing difficulty with a strictness of regime that reduces the possibilities of behaviour problems. Generally, the children are treated in an authoritarian manner and there is a strict frame of discipline. Kephart (1960) concentrates on the large motor components of visuo–motor tasks and provides a series of exercises to develop gross muscle movements. He also has a program to develop skills of direction and orientation by means of aids or prompts which are gradually reduced. In Britain, Morgenstern *et al*. (1966) have produced a series of developmental toys for disabled children.

In Britain and some European countries the programs widely used are 'Training in Basic Cognitive Skills' and 'Training in Motor Skills – Haskell and Paull (1973a, b). These programs consist of a series of booklets for children involving carefully graded exercises to help develop skills of visual perception and discrimination, concept formation, abstract reasoning and visual motor ability.

The training program for motor skills consists of a series of systematic and graded visuo–motor exercises for young children. These exercises are designed specifically to provide children with an opportunity to practise eye–hand co-ordination and control in the form of pre-writing skills. For example, starting with a straight line along a wide road, the exercises progress through curves and angles to following dotted line patterns, which finally lead to the formation of single letters of the alphabet.

The approach is varied in form, so that interest is maintained in developing motor skills in a number of different situations. Apart from learning to control a pencil, children receive training in using a pencil in a left-to-right direction on a paper.

The goal of writing the letters of the alphabet is achieved by leading young children through an organized sequence of the simpler components of writing activity until mastery of writing proper is achieved. This technique is based partly upon the recognized educational method known as programmed instruction.

Remedial and training programs should be designed to help teachers plan systematic but flexible exercises for young children. It should not be based on extreme theoretical views about the invariant stages of cognitive development, but rather in the belief that teachers can best facilitate learning when optimal conditions for training basic skills necessary for higher cognitive learning present themselves.

These include individual training exercises to develop competence in perceptual discrimination, concept formation, sequential reasoning, eye–hand co-ordination, etc. Much practice and drill in these exercises is necessary for the acquisition of these skills.

Recent advances in micro-computer technology have led to the development of programs suitable for children with learning difficulties. Learning tasks are presented in an eye-catching manner, incorporating colour and sound. The stages of learning are small. The programs can be used repeatedly.

The touch-screen, whereby a subject can touch the screen elucidating patterns, colour and lines provides an immediate reward. Programs are available for counting, drawing and attention fixing, as well as hand–eye co-ordination.

In Britain, the inclusion of Information Technology into the recently introduced National Curriculum ensures the continued development of such programs.

5

Motor learning and development

There are a number of reasons why the study of motor learning and development is important for those interested in the habilitation and rehabilitation of people with physical disabilities. With babies and young infants motor responses provide evidence of the normal functioning of the nervous system. Motor responses such as reflexes are therefore useful tools in the early identification of motor, perceptual or intellectual abnormalities. The second major issue is that in the years prior to adolescence motor activity, such as exploring the physical properties of objects, is vital for learning fundamental concepts such as weight, shape, size, speed and spatial relationships. The third important area is that of self-help skills. Adequate motor abilities are required for acquiring skills such as feeding, dressing and cleanliness. Finally, a degree of motor skill is needed in leisure, recreation and physical education activities, which are considered to be important for a person's physical and social development.

Each of these areas of interest has its own body of literature and procedures for instruction and evaluation. In this chapter we will undertake a broad discussion of motor learning and development and examine a number of fundamental principles and concepts common to all the above areas of specialisation. Our first undertaking is to discuss the concept of motor learning and also to describe some of the principles underlying the learning of motor skills.

This chapter is an attempt to provide some straightforward principles based on an extensive body of relevant research for teaching motor skills to those with physical disabilities.

MOTOR LEARNING

Motor learning is a branch of psychology dealing with how people learn motor skills. It has been defined as follows:

> Motor learning is a set of processes associated with practice or experience leading to relatively permanent changes in skilled behaviour (Schmidt, 1982).

Change in motor behaviour is registered using measures such as the time taken to perform the skill, the degree of accuracy or the number of errors made while performing the skill. The permanence of the performance is determined from observations over the period of time during which the individual is involved in practice at the skill in question. For any motor skill we can draw a learning curve to measure the success of our training or remediation program.

Figure 5.1 shows the type of curve or graph that we could produce from observing any skill over a period of practice. The ordinate is our measure of performance on the task, for example, the time taken or the number of errors made. The abscissa is the number of practice trials or, if you like, the number of

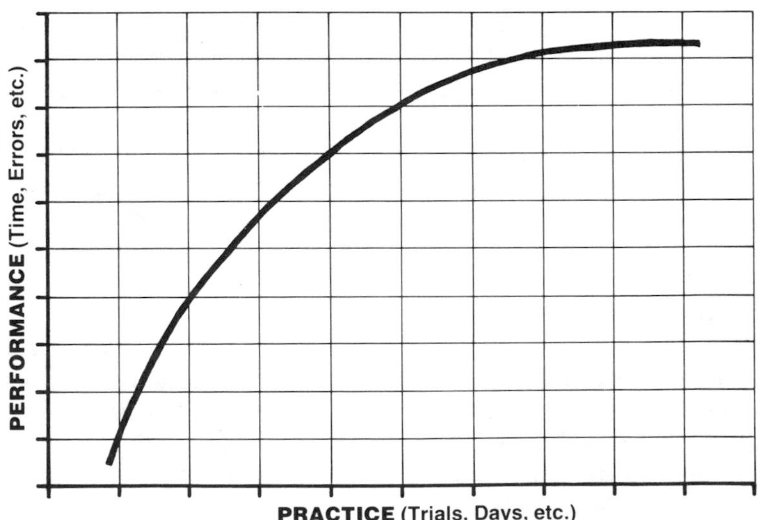

Figure 5.1 Idealized learning curve showing changes in performance with practice.

attempts at producing the required movement. As can be seen, there is great improvement at first but after a time the achievement of the performance levels out.

In the opening paragraph we discussed various categories of motor skills that are of interest to those concerned with physically handicapped individuals. What do we mean by 'motor skills' and the related concept 'motor abilities'?

Motor skills and motor abilities

Motor skills can be thought of as the real-life everyday motor activities that are our major concern when undertaking a motor skill training program. Independent living skills, recreational activities of the functional motor skills of young children, such as walking, reaching and grasping, are motor skills.

Motor abilities are the components of motor skills. They are the basic underlying physical attributes that contribute to the performance of motor skills. Some of these abilities are related to physical growth. Such abilities are directly related to physical attributes such as strength, speed, flexibility or physical fitness. For convenience, we can call these 'physical abilities'.

Another class of abilities are those related to attributes such as balance, co-ordination, dexterity, timing and speed of reaction to various stimuli. These types of abilities may also be thought of as 'motor abilities'. In general, these abilities are the less easily measured and verifiable components of motor skills. The ability to perform motor skills effectively depends on a combination of these two types of abilities.

Key principles of motor learning

The literature on motor skill learning offers those dealing with physically disabled people a number of key principles that may guide the evaluation and design of motor training programs. The first of these is practice.

Practice

By far the most important consideration when conducting a motor training program is practice. The greater the number of practice trials or repetitions of the activity, the greater the amount of learning. The rule, therefore, is to maximize the number of times that the individual is required to repeat the skill.

One question that is often raised in relation to practice is, 'How much practice should be given relative to the period of rest?' Surprisingly perhaps, laboratory studies have shown that although continuous practice with no rest, so-called 'massed practice', may depress performance due to boredom or fatigue, such prolonged practice periods have no effect on learning. For practical purposes, however, it is often recommended that practice should be alternated with a reasonable amount of rest. This is called 'distributed practice'. Distributed practice might be more effective because the subject does not lose the motivation to continue practising the skill due to the inhibiting influence of boredom and fatigue. The ratio of practice to rest that is adopted will depend on both the nature of the task and the motor abilities and physical abilities of the learner.

Knowledge of results and knowledge of performance

It has been emphasized that practice is essential for skill learning. Practice alone, however, is useless without some information from the instructor about the success of the performance. Information about how well the task was performed can be of two kinds. The first type of information given to the learner is 'knowledge of results'.

Knowledge of results

This is information about the **outcome** or end-product of the movement. In most cases this information is given verbally as an instruction, such as, 'You moved too far that time', or 'Try to move your right hand faster'. Quite simply, knowledge of results (KR) is information about how the subject's attempt at the desired movement fell short of the prescribed goal. KR also serves an important purpose in reinforcing the student's behaviour and helping provide the necessary motivation to continue practising.

Knowledge of performance

A second type of information that can assist the disabled

person who is trying to learn or re-learn a motor skill is called 'knowledge of performance'.

Knowledge of performance (KP) also fulfils the reinforcing and motivating functions of KR but is information about the movement **pattern**. Instructors provide information of this kind using verbal instructions but also demonstrations and physically guiding the limb in the desired manner convey an understanding of the required movement pattern. Commands such as 'Lift your arm higher' and 'Keep your head up' convey movement pattern information. A demonstration by the instructor with some physical assistance during movement execution are also useful ways to provide KP. Another way of understanding the role of KP is to consider how it helps in improving co-ordination. What do we mean by the often ill-defined concept of 'co-ordination'?

Co-ordination

Co-ordination is used to refer to two aspects of the movement. The first of these is that concerned with the **relationship** between the movements of different parts or segments of the same limb. We call this 'intra-limb' co-ordination. In walking, for example, it is important that the lower leg and the thigh maintain the proper relationship to each other throughout the stride cycle. This is necessary to produce what we would call a 'well co-ordinated' movement. Here we are describing the **relative** motion of the segments of a single limb.

The second type of co-ordination is called 'inter-limb' co-ordination. This defines the extent to which **different** limbs are moved with the correct spatial and temporal relationship to each other. Taking the example of walking once more, it would be said that the disabled person showed good inter-limb co-ordination if the right leg and the left leg moved in the appropriate manner in relation to each other. A physical disability producing a limp, for example, would lead to poor inter-limb co-ordination. Similarly, it is possible that the same individual's unaffected limb might show quite satisfactory intra-limb co-ordination. The concept of co-ordination is therefore very useful in describing the habilitation or rehabilitation of disabled people in providing a description of the relative motions of the limbs or parts of a limb affected by their disability.

MOTOR DEVELOPMENT

So far, our discussion has centred on the meaning of skill learning and the main principles by which the motor skills of physically disabled people may be taught and assessed. Assessments can be made of the quality of inter-limb and intra-limb co-ordination. Motor skills can also be assessed by recording the success of the movement outcome in relation to the task goal. The guidelines to teaching are that the subject should receive as much practice as possible with information given about the movement pattern (KP) and/or the movement outcome (KR).

Motor development also involves learning but there are two other considerations when evaluating the motor performance of infants, children and adolescents. The first of these is maturation.

Maturation

Maturation can be thought of as synonymous with ageing. As the organism ages there are some processes at work that cause changes which proceed in an orderly fashion. These changes are caused by the interaction of the organism and its environment. The kind of changes that we observe as a result of maturation we refer to as growth.

Growth

While maturation may be considered as the 'invisible' processes that are part of the natural ageing process, growth is the measurable physical and biological changes that accompany maturation. Increases in height, weight, strength and changes in bodily proportion are characteristic growth variables in the study of motor development. Motor development is therefore due to an interaction of growth, maturation and learning. The child's performance at a given chronological age will be determined by age (maturation), growth and learning.

In non-disabled children maturation and growth proceed in a fairly orderly and predictable fashion. In physically disabled children we expect this sequence to be disrupted.

Disruption of the normal course of neurological changes has two main consequences:

1. Direct and specific deficiency in perceptual–motor function as a consequence of neurological damage.
2. Indirect and non-specific disruptions due to lack of perceptual–motor experience, e.g. that produced by lack of mobility.

As a result of these two influences, the motor development of physically disabled people is likely to be highly specific, depending on the nature of the impairment and quality of motor experience.

Approaches to study of motor development

Despite the difficulty in cataloguing the characteristics of motor development in the physically disabled, it is possible to refer to a number of different approaches to the study of motor development. These four approaches have been described previously by Wade and Davis (1982) and are as follows:

Descriptive approach

The descriptive approach considers only the **outcome** of the child's performance at a given chronological age. It is not concerned with the nature of the movement pattern, that is, the degree of co-ordination which we discussed earlier. The child's motor development is charted by examining the chronological age at which certain 'milestones' or clearly identifiable levels of achievement are reached. From normative data obtained from large samples of non-handicapped children, it is possible to compare the attainment of the physically disabled child at a particular chronological age. For example, the milestone of being able to walk independently has an average or normative age of achievement with which we can assess the motor development of the physically disabled child.

Process-oriented or diagnostic approach

By 'process' we mean the neurological mechanisms underlying the control of movement. The aim of the process-oriented or diagnostic approach, however, is to develop tests of motor abilities and physical abilities. The tests would then be used to examine certain central nervous system (CNS) and peripheral nervous system (PNS) processes, with the aim of diagnosing the problem associated with the motor dysfunction. Many tests of this kind have been developed based on the pioneering work of the Soviet investigator Oseretsky in the 1930s.

Process/descriptive approach

Here the child's performance is judged on an **individual** basis against a 'criterion' or 'mature' movement pattern obtained from the established literature on the biomechanical characteristics of motor performance. By criterion or mature movement pattern is meant the optimal or most efficient pattern of co-ordination. In addition to describing the movement pattern an attempt is also made to determine the nature of the CNS and PNS **processes** that are responsible for producing the observable limb movements. This serves the same purpose as that of the process/diagnostic approach, in trying to ascertain the nature of the PNS and CNS mechanisms, that are responsible for the disabled person's atypical movement pattern.

Reflex testing

The motor development of infants is characterized by various reflexes. They provide some adaptive function for the infant at a given stage of development. Such reflexes permit responses such as feeding, defensive reactions, grasping and postural control. The persistence of reflexes beyond a given developmental level, however, is **dysfunctional**, inhibiting the production of voluntary controlled movements. There are well documented accounts of various reflexes and the consequences of their persistence in various physically disabling conditions (e.g. Fiorentino, 1981). Here is a summary of the characteristics of reflexes and their importance in the developmental assessment of the physically disabled.

1. Initiated by a simple proprioceptive stimulus (moving a limb) or tactile stimulus (touching a limb).

2. The response is largely involuntary, it cannot be inhibited.
3. The response is rapid and stereotyped.
4. Reflexes seem to fulfil some adaptive function that is appropriate to the child's stage of development.
5. A reflex may provide the foundation for later complex and less involuntary movements.

Reflexive responses can be examined with the purpose of diagnosing sensori–motor defects and also with a view to devising therapeutic measures. For example, the training techniques devised by the Bobaths (e.g. Bobath 1966, 1971) are designed to adapt reflexive responses to more flexible, purposive activity.

Active and passive movements

Normal vision involves an active motor system, which also involves the extraction of key spatial and temporal features of objects or scenes. Active movements give stability of perception, but passive movements make for instability of perception (Hecaen and Albert, 1978).

Held (Held and Hein (1963) and Held and Bauer 1967) and his co-workers demonstrated that plasticity in sensori–motor systems is dependent upon information provided by movement, to provide perceptual constancy. Also that in the earliest stages of development, normal sensori–motor co-ordination and visuo–motor adaptation require voluntary movement, and sensori–motor feedback. The failure of visuo–motor co-ordination to emerge is linked to a 'dyscorrelation' between movements of the subject and changes in visual stimulation. For a fuller discussion of the topic see Hecaen and Albert, (1978).

Active movements refer to self-induced movements, passive movements to externally produced movements. Held and Hein (1963) in their studies with animals and humans demonstrated that certain types of contact with the environment are necessary for the development of sensori–motor co-ordination. Kittens, severely restricted in their movements, but not visual experience, failed to develop normal movement discrimination skills, such as guiding their forelimbs towards an object. Held and Hein devised an apparatus in which kittens, reared in darkness, were harnessed in pairs to a bar device rotating

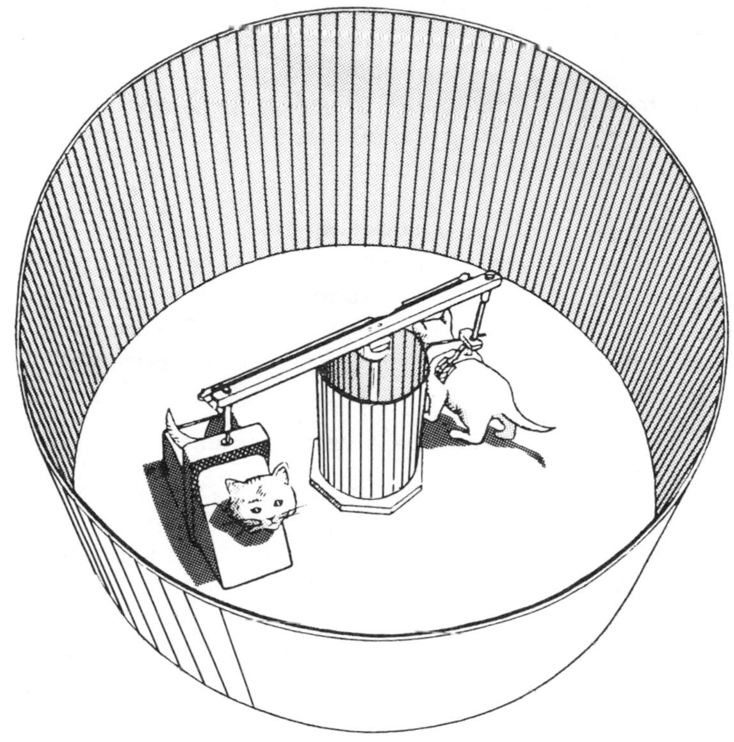

Figure 5.2 Active and passive movements in Held and Hein's kitten experiment.

on a pivot (Figure 5.2). One arm carried a 'gondola', in which a kitten was restrained. The passive kitten received the same visual stimulation as the active one moving about freely. The free kitten transmitted its gross movements to the passive animal by the chain and bar arrangement. At the end of the 30-hour experimental period, the passive kittens, unlike their active partners, failed on such tasks as avoiding the steep side of a visual cliff and blinking at the approach of an object. They were grossly inaccurate in their visual placing movements (such as the extension of forelimbs to avoid collision). The last response was elicited by holding the animal by its body and hindlimbs and allowing its forelegs to move feeely down towards objects with interrupted surfaces. Refinements of this technique were used with kittens in experiments in which the animals were allowed to move about freely but without sight of limbs which were obscured by a large collar. The control kitten made 75% accurate placing responses, while the experimental animals were only able to guide their paws accurately to the solid parts of the interrupted surface in fewer than 50% of the trials.

Infant monkeys showed similar deficiencies in grasping visible objects if reared in circumstances which denied them sight of their limbs and bodies (Held and Bauer, 1967). Interest in the sensori–motor development of human infants severely restricted in motor experience such as cerebral palsied children, is a highly relevant issue. White and Held (1966) in a series of benign experiments using the technique of enhancement instead of deprivation, examined the effects of handling, i.e. cuddling and playing with normal babies between the age of 6 to 36 days, for an extra 20 minutes each day. Infants handled for such extra limited periods showed a significant increase in visual attentiveness.

As in the animal experiments, experimenters considered the importance of self-induced movements in accelerating perceptuo–motor development. They chose as their subjects young babies in hospital. White and Held devised a set of 'enriched crib environments'. They suspended toys, multi-coloured sheets and other apparatus to encourage babies to pay greater heed to their immediate environment (crib) and wider environment (ward activities). By lowering the sides of cribs and flattening the mattresses, the infant's head, arm and trunk mobility was increased when the infant was placed in a prone position for 15 minutes after each of three feeds. The babies were able to swipe at objects and take in more of the ward scene.

White and Held reported that this regimen led to a significant advance of babies in sustained hand regard (increased viewing of their hands) and swiping (the tendency to strike at nearby visible objects). Children were able to do on the 60th day what, according to the Gesell scale, a normal child can do on the 84th. This experiment clearly indicates that the notion of a gradual unfolding of sensory motor skills in human infants is inadequate and pays insufficient regard to the differential consequences of early contacts in modifying rates of development.

Concept of noise

An individual's ability to execute skilled movements is dependent upon feedback from his own movements – mediated by internal 'signals'. The process whereby this is effected is by rapid selection of the relevant information from the neuromuscular activity. It is held that children with cerebral palsy have extreme difficulty in filtering the relevant from irrelevant cues. When information is detrimental to the system it is termed 'noise'. If the noise is too disturbing or intense – be it internal or external – it can mask the 'signal', i.e. the essential message. Too much information or too little information can disrupt performance. Children with cerebral palsy may suffer from both problems (Connolly, 1970).

On the one hand, these children appear to have difficulty in handling an abundance of information; they may find it difficult to focus attention selectively and to take in relevant information from irrelevant stimuli in the environment. On the other hand, children with cerebral palsy tend to lack kinesthetic feedback.

> The problem then is one of augmenting feedback – such that the child can discriminate signal from noise. If motor responses can be brought under control by increasing feedback in another modality (visual) then it might be possible to shift control to kinesthetic/proprioceptive systems by suitable training procedures (Harrison and Connolly, 1971).

Harrison and Connolly (1971) investigated the ability to learn to recognize and achieve a fine degree of neuromuscular control of the forearm flexor muscles on specific command of four normal and four spastic diplegic adults between the ages of 18 and 25 years. The subjects were provided with simultaneous visual feedback from an oscilloscope. The training procedure consisted of a graded set of activities in which the subjects were made to relax, then maintain light activity to command. Next, they were trained to recognize muscle activity ('spike activity') and achieve adequate control to avoid hand, finger and upper arm movement under augmented visual feedback. Finally, subjects were requested to produce spike activity at the command 'now'. No significant differences were noted between spastics and normal subjects, though the former group took longer to achieve discrete motor control. The results indicated that spastics were as able to achieve fine motor control as normal subjects. It was hypothesized that a spastic 'can learn to control the hyperactivity inherent in his neuromuscular system given additional information concerning ongoing activity' (Harrison and Connolly, 1971).

Instructional methods

Having considered some principles of motor skill learning and development, we now turn our attention to methods of instruction. This concerns how we should teach motor skills. Before deciding this, however, we must consider what skills to teach. Let us tackle this question first.

A major controversy surrounding the choice of motor activities concerns the issue of whether we should teach skills or, alternatively, teach basic movement patterns that are assumed to assist in the performance of a wide range of skills. This practice of general motor training rests on the assumption that whatever is learned will transfer positively to skills. This assumption is highly speculative and unless the skill and the practised movement pattern are very similar it is unlikely that performance of the skill will be improved. The best solution seems to be that, just as with non-disabled individuals, we should provide the opportunity for active recreation and physical education, while also teaching essential self-help activities.

Teaching any motor skill usually begins with a decision about how to break down the skill into more easily learned parts. This process is sometimes called **task analysis**. How the task is broken down will depend on the nature and degree of the client's disability and the nature of the task. There should be no hard and fast rules for doing this, and the breakdown into parts will depend on the instructor's experience, intelligent observation and trial and error. Some programs of motor skill training involve teaching a progressive sequence of parts resembling those observed in the typical developmental sequence. For example, crawling, creeping, and standing with support, might be suggested as progressive parts for teaching independent walking. In teaching physically disabled individuals, however, there does **not** appear to be any theoretical rationale for utilising the progressive, stage-like sequence of movement patterns observed in the normal course of motor skill development. The specifics of the child's disability in combination with growth, maturation and learning should dictate the choice of progressive stages.

Below are a number of instructional methods which can be utilized in conjunction with our earlier principles of practice, KR and KP.

1. **Whole method**
   The whole skill is taught, the subject(s) then attempts the whole skill.
2. **Part method**
   Successive parts are taught, the subject performs them all, e.g. teach Part 1, subject practises, teach Part 2, subject practises, teach Part 3, subject practises. Finally, subject performs all the parts, completing the skill.
3. **Progressive part method**
   Teach Part 1, subject practises, teach Part 2, subject practises Part 1 **and** Part 2, teach Part 3, subject practises Part 1, Part 2 and Part 3, completing the skill.
4. **Whole-part-whole method**
   Teach the whole skill, Part 1, whole skill. Then whole skill, Part 2, whole skill, etc. such that each new part is immediately practised within the whole skill.
5. **Reverse chaining**
   Subject executes the final part of the skill **first**. Subject performs Part 4, Part 3, Part 2 and, finally, Part 1, i.e. it is the 'part method' in reverse.
6. **Conceptualizing techniques**
   The three types of conceptualizing techniques – imagery (thinking about the movements necessary for performance), directed mental practice (directing the thinking of the performer through specific instruction) and verbalization techniques (the performer describes movements or associated feelings through the spoken or written word) – are used in 'conductive education'. As we have seen, these three techniques have proven value in improving motor skills.

Physical disabilities manifest themselves in a bewildering variety of motor responses. The methods recommended for teaching physically disabled people motor skills, the rationale for these methods and their purported benefits are equally varied.

Doman–Delacato

This approach, based on the work of Glen Doman and Carl Delacato in Philadelphia is attracting considerable attention at present and so we have included a brief description and discussion of their theories' reference. Delacato maintains that 'if the problem lies in the nervous system, we must treat the nervous system', and that ontogenetic development reflects phylogenetic development. Basically, their theory is that to some extent normal human development parallels the evolution of the human race. They consider that this evolution goes from fish to amphibians, to 'land-animals', to primates, all with their developing types of movements, to end in man, who is capable of rational thought. In a way man's neural development parallels this evolutionary development from the beginning, when the baby is in the period of gestation, to the time a child reaches about eight years of age.

According to Delacato, neurological organization takes place with the increase of myelinization, starting at the spinal cord and working towards the cortex. The development is systematic and dependent upon each level being organized at the correct stage. The process ends with the organization of the cortex with one hemisphere being dominant. According to this theory, abstract thinking, present only in humans, is dependent upon hemispheric dominance.

At birth the spinal cord and medulla are the most highly organized structures. At about four months (crawling stage), when the child is becoming mobile, he leaves the level of organization paralleling that of the fish and enters that which parallels the amphibians. At six months neural organization has reached the mid-brain – this brings the infant to the level paralleling 'land-animal'. The infant can now crawl, and has binaural hearing and binocular vision. Neural fibres associated with sight, sound, balance, posture and movement are linked. At this stage the child can move the opposite hand and leg simultaneously. At 12 months, organization parallels that of the primates and the child can walk. The cortex is now organized. Finally, at about eight years, cerebral dominance is well established and the child is capable of abstract thought.

Doman and Delacato insist that children who do not go through these stages because of damage to their central nervous system have to be taken through them before they can progress normally. Such a child going for assessment is clinically examined and the point at which neural organization has broken down is determined. Treatment is aimed at re-organizing subsequent disorganized levels. For example, according to Delacato, if a child's neural organization has reached the level of the medulla only and yet has problems of movement although several months or years old, such a child should be programmed for organization at the next level. This would mean making the child use any reflex movements it has managed to develop, and any of which the child is, at the time, incapable are passively imposed on it by several adults in a 'patterning' program. At the level of cortical organization, in an effort to evolve dominance of one of the cerebral hemispheres, there is retraining of sleep patterns (considered important by Doman and Delacato). Then dominance, right or left, of foot, hand and eye is trained (Doman 1974).

The neurological and theoretical views of Doman and Delacato have been severely criticized over the years. A comprehensive review of this literature (Cummins, 1988) has concluded that there is neither a proper scientific basis to the Doman–Delacato theory nor reliable evidence that these techniques have any special efficacy. Although a number of children undergoing the Doman–Delacato program have shown spectacular improvements, these could well be due to the high levels of motivation and attention of parents and therapists. Moreover, since the parents who become involved in these programs are induced to expend much money and energy, they should be offered help and advice before committing themselves to this particular form of 'therapy'.

Part Three

Pedagogical issues

This section is an attempt to relate the subject matter of the preceding chapters to the education of motor and neurologically impaired children. As it is impractical to include the whole curriculum in this book, four basic subjects have been chosen for discussion: reading, arithmetic, spelling and handwriting. Arithmetic, spelling and handwriting are subjects which have attracted comparatively little attention in research until recently, and still less thought has been given to these subjects with regard to physically disabled children.

Each chapter gives a brief historical background where relevant, followed by an analysis of factors and subskills required for a child's success in that subject. ('Spelling' follows a slightly different pattern in this respect.) Attention is drawn to areas of possible difficulty encountered by a motor or neurologically impaired child and, where possible, lines of approach for their remedy are suggested. In the chapter on reading, no specific remedies are put forward as there is a large amount of literature on the subject already and because opinions on methods of teaching reading vary so widely.

6

Reading

Up to the early part of the nineteenth century, the accepted method of teaching reading was alphabetic, where a child was taught the names of the letters which spelled a word. Then, in an attempt to overcome the problems of letter names not corresponding to their sounds in words, the phonic was evolved, whereby the syllabified sounds of the letters were substituted for the letter names. The next development came early in the twentieth century, when phonics were supplanted by the look-and-say method, by which a child is required to respond to whole word units. Subsequently, fashion has swung back and forth between these two methods. More recently, i.t.a., the Initial Teaching Alphabet, has been devised. (See Chapter 9 and note.) One may summarize research on teaching reading as having confirmed that the look-and-say method is advantageous for vocabulary acquisition but that the phonic approach is superior in a number of other respects. For a fuller discussion see Jorm and Share (1983).

Ninety per cent of all children learn to read by whichever method they are taught, irrespective of the environment in which they are taught, that is, despite impoverished or unstimulating backgrounds, over-crowded classrooms and teachers inadequately trained in the teaching of reading. An understanding of the way in which reading is normally acquired is important for a study of the 10% of children who have reading difficulties of various kinds. It is our opinion that learning to read is, like learning to speak, potentially present in all human beings, and that, theoretically, every child is capable of developing the skills needed in order to be able to read. Any degree of impairment of the body or the brain will interfere with this capability and will reduce the number of necessary skills, relevant to reading, which he can acquire. As a result there will be slow, inadequate and apparent non-readers, depending on our definition of these terms. There will, however, be no child without some ability to read, and, therefore, no environment in which some form of reading cannot take place.

Reading difficulties

There are certain children who, in spite of normal intelligence, maturation and appropriate instruction, are unduly slow in learning to read and write. While emotional and environmental factors account for a proportion of cases, others appear to represent failures in some relevant aspects of cerebral maturation. These children seem to lack certain abilities for the acquisition of reading skills. This difficulty may be associated with an extensive and varied pattern of neurological deficits (Critchley, 1964), as well as impaired cognitive function (Lovell and Woolsey, 1964). Kinsbourne and Warrington (1963a) suggested that two main categories of reading disorders in young children existed. The first group were those deficient in language development and the second in the development of spatial skills relating to the recall and recognition of sequences.

It is useful to describe reading difficulties in children in terms of reading backwardness and reading retardation. These definitions have been refined by Rutter and Yule (1973). Reading backwardness, according to them, is a 28 months or more lag in reading accuracy and comprehension on the Neale Reading Test (Neale, 1966) in relation to the chronological age. Boys are twice as backward as girls in this respect. Reading retardation is defined as a 28 months or more lower reading attainment than could be predicted on the WISC IQ scale. Three times as many boys as girls are reading retarded. The distinction between reading backwardness and retardation has educational and psychological significance and is a helpful notion to teachers and remedial workers because the outlook for retarded readers is significantly worse than that for those who are backward readers.

Viewpoints on reading

The quantity of literature on the teaching of reading and on how children learn to read is enormous. It is appropriate, therefore, to discuss some major viewpoints on the assumption that they most significantly enhance our knowledge of what reading is. These are: Piaget's biological/developmental approach, which defines the cognitive stages through which all children pass; Kinsbourne's contribution, which involves an analysis of human skills, in particular, those appropriate to the ability to read; an attempt to explain the act of reading as described by Smith (1978a); the phonological encoding model and the interactive schematic model.

Piaget's approach

Piaget's assumption that there is a definite sequence in which physical and intellectual abilities develop in the child provides us with a set of expectations and a criterion of assessment for every child, disabled or otherwise. The notion of a fixed order is reassuring, as is the notion of movement forwards. Terms like 'developmental delay' or 'early attainment' of 'milestones' encompass all kinds of children, the brain-injured and the gifted, each taking his position on the line of forward movement.

At the stage of development which Piaget calls sensori-motor, before the development of language in the infant, exploration of the environment through the physical senses takes place. The gradual awareness that events are repeated builds up expectations in the child, and familiar sounds begin to be associated with objects. The introduction of books, which can be handled and played with, encourages the perception of familiar household objects in two-dimensional form, and the sounding of words which correspond to the picture establishes certain ideas for the child. The child begins to perceive that pictures and letters are both means of saying the same thing in different ways, that certain words or groups of letters represent particular objects and that the words for these objects may be distinguished from one another and recalled by their different lengths, shapes and configurations. At this stage, reading is a process of interpreting and gaining meaning from pictures.

The implications for motor- or brain-injured children, who may possess sensory deficits that impede their natural urge to explore and understand their surroundings, are that parents, or those to whose care the children may be entrusted, need to encourage as active a response as possible to situations in the child's life. Stimulation and informed encouragement, the provision of simple tasks and objectives and the familiarizing of what may be a strange and incomprehensible environment (as the Peto method of conductive education – see Chapter 14 – attempts with children who have cerebral palsy) should begin early and be maintained. Difficulties with feeding and dressing and generally moving from place to place need not take up the whole time either of child or parent, if the priorities of intellectual activities are recognized.

At the pre-operational stage, according to Piaget, the child begins to make generalizations on the strength of his growing experience, probably seeing only one or two factors rather than all, and therefore making errors in the selection of what he believes to be relevant. With frequent exposure to print, however, certain patterns emerge in the printed word. The child begins to anticipate certain combinations of letters, sees smaller words within larger ones, sees words as having spaces on either side of them and takes particular note of beginning and ending letters. At this stage the word is mainly a visual image. The continued development of the child's own spoken language throughout this time provides opportunities of memorizing and symbolizing experiences, particularly through the activities of creative play, and these acts of crude representationalism contribute to an understanding of the symbolism of the written word. The gradual awareness of the relationship of sound to visual shape follows and the child realizes that words can be split into sound groups as well as letter groups.

By the next stage, that of 'concrete operations', the principles of 'reversibility' and 'conservation' operate. The child classifies objects and experiences in terms of differences and similarities, realizing, for example, that a letter may alter its sound according to its position in a word, and that small and capital letters represent the same sound. He also learns to recall the sequence and position of letters and realizes that the same groups of letters in a different order mean a different word. Reading aloud helps to answer problems of pronounciation. Finally, at the 'formal stage', as Piaget calls it, sufficient skill for phrasing and expression is attained. The child adjusts the reading rate to the difficulty of the material, organizing the reading of the text to comprehend its meaning.

Piaget's developmental model of reading acquisition assumes the presence of certain human skills, without which delays or halts may occur. An analysis of these follows, as an accompaniment to the picture of the normally developing reader, assuming that a detailed understanding of each of these skills enables the parent or teacher of the child with reading difficulty to prescribe remedial treatment.

Kinsbourne's approach

The skills that many psychologists, and Kinsbourne in particular, have defined as determining the acquisition of reading are mainly perceptual. We shall also refer to other factors which are thought to affect reading progress. Kinsbourne describes 'beginning reading' as acquiring certain mental operations, each marking a stage in one of a set of parallel developmental sequences.

> The child who is insufficiently advanced along any one of the relevant developmental sequences is not ready to read. If he has reached the requisite stage, then the better he is at the relevant operation, the faster will he acquire information (translating his competence into performance), and the sooner will he be ready for the next level of reading instruction. This level will call for new operations, possibly related to new developmental sequences. Whether progress continues depends on the degree of development of these new operations. But further progress along the previously useful developmental sequences is irrelevant. For reading, many processes must function at a given level of efficiency. Greater efficiency than this is redundant, because once an operation ceases to limit further development of the overall reading skill, it will remain idle while waiting for what has now become the performance limiting operation to be concluded (Kinsbourne and Warrington 1962b, 1963a; Kinsbourne, 1966, 1967).

Reading: subskills

This approach emphasizes the attainment of a given level of competence of the skills relevant to a particular stage of reading, without which a child may be unable to read. These skills are thought to be:

1. General motor skills.
2. Visuo-perceptual skills.
3. Auditory-perceptual skills.
4. Speech and language.
5. Concept formation.
6. Intersensory integration.

General motor skills

Through its first movements a child begins to find out about itself and the world around. These experiences form the foundation upon which the child's knowledge is based and they play a major role in intellectual development. The ability to orientate its body and achieve a correct posture whether lying, sitting or standing and eventually walking, will affect the degree to which a child can handle objects with ease and therefore learn about their properties. Early development of flexible, balanced and co-ordinated movements provides a child with an accurate picture of its body and its relationship to different parts of the self and to other objects.

Delays in crawling, sitting and walking, together with unco-ordinated and clumsy movements and confusions between the right and left sides of the body have been shown to be related to reading retardation (Rutter, *et al.*, 1970a). Children with a specific motor and neurological disorder such as cerebral palsy, and those with minimal disorders of the brain can be expected to show either severe or mild reading retardation.

Visuo-perceptual skills

A child's ability to steer and control the movement of its hands by the use of the eyes is usually referred to as 'eye-hand co-ordination'. Before this a child must first be able to distinguish the left side from the right side and also be able to control the two sides of its body separately or simultaneously. Initially, a child's movements are bilaterally symmetrical.

Accuracy of eye–hand co-ordination is necessary for the child's inspection of the printed page and the various directional movements involved in seeing letters and words in sequence. Confusion between right and left may mean that a child fails to scan a page of print from the correct starting point and sees no difference between a 'b' and a 'd'. Crossed laterality is sometimes found with a child who has reading difficulties, though precisely why this occurs has not been established.

The ability to discriminate between letters, to note the relevant differences and similarities in terms of orientation and spatial position, to be able to retain a series of shapes in its memory and the ability to distinguish figure from background also play a part in reading. Some brain-injured children are known to have difficulties in distinguishing figure from background, due to over-attentiveness to the background.

The presence of any defect in vision such as short or long sight, squint, tunnel vision or astigmatism may affect the process of reading for a child. Partially sighted children, however, can be taught to read well provided that they have sufficient skilled help from a teacher and sufficiently clear print from which to read. A teacher can do much to enable a child to use sight effectively by concentration on essential features of a display. Blind children, by substituting touch for sight, can learn braille. Tactile perception then replaces visuo-perception. Lack of sensitivity in the fingers, or lack of control in finger or hand muscles will impede progress in learning to read braille, just as deficiencies in sight or learning will impede progress in reading by the normal method.

Disabilities in constructional tasks, such as copying basic shapes using matchsticks, defective perception of shapes and poor motor co-ordination were found among the retarded readers in the survey of the Isle of Wight (*op.cit.*)

For many workers, the issue of whether visuo–spatial difficulties precede reading problems or co-occur is not resolved satisfactorily and hence the prescription of visuo–spatial activities in reading instruction is still debated.

Kinsbourne (personal communication) has shown deficiencies in a child's perception when overloaded with data and he makes some suggestions for their remedy. Kinsbourne's tests on beginning reading (personal communication) confirm that children most readily learn letters or letter groups if these are presented singly for successive comparison with displays which differ from them by single cues. In this way attention is focused without distraction on the crucial aspects of the array, one at a time. He suggests that failure in beginning reading is due to failure to attend to all points on a given dimension, and to all dimensions when more than one is represented, and to all items of a multiple display. Simplifying presentation to highlight a particular cue might indicate how children are overloaded with data, which they fail to interpret correctly.

Auditory–perceptual skills

The ear receives and transmits sounds to the central nervous system where they are registered initially as noises with no meaning. The child first responds to the middle, then the lower and finally upper frequencies of tone, and the central nervous system then extracts meaning from the pattern of sounds transmitted to it.

Auditory comprehension increases gradually in the developmental phase which precedes the acquisition of speech. The young child uses gestures and other visual clues to increase the understanding of sounds. At the first stage, high-information words, such as nouns and verbs, are selected by the child and stored in the brain. As sounds are occurring in great frequency, the child must quickly learn to discriminate between them and retain them in its memory system.

Poor performance in auditory discrimination at five years has been found to correlate with subsequent failures in reading. Delays in the acquisition of speech as a consequence of poor auditory perception will also affect reading progress.

Speech and language

Linguists believe that normal speech development is essential for the acquisition of reading, and that this is made possible by good auditory perception and memory. Learning to read must normally be preceded by a background of meaningful, articulate and clear use of language, at home and in school. Deaf children, however, taught from an early age by special techniques from highly skilled and dedicated teachers, can achieve high standards of reading and written work.

The normal development of spoken language occurs from the time of the first cry, the first production of sound. If there is brain injury, muscles of the mouth may be affected. Consequently, swallowing and general tongue movements preparatory to normal speech will be impaired. At the stage of development when sounds are recognized and discriminated, sounds are associated with objects and the use of consonants is being gradually developed, so any hearing loss will result in distorted hearing and reproduction of speech. Defects of articulation will produce inaccurate and incorrect sequences of sounds, omissions, substitutions and transposition of vowels. At the next stage, when the sounds that others make have meaning and when the child's own thoughts and expression of needs are accompanied with meaningful sounds, deafness will produce limited understanding of speech. The comprehension of verbal communication and development of receptive language is vital. Retarded motor development will also affect the use of speech in accompanying actions. Emotional conditions may cause speech defects – for example, hesitation or stammering. Skilled help at an early age is, therefore essential for children affected in the ways described if later progress in reading is to be achieved.

Concept formation

The development of language facilitates organization of abstract thought. When a child names an object, it is associated with sounds. Gradually the child acquires a store of labels for everything in its environment. A child will have difficulties in forming concepts if there is difficulty:

1. in organizing perceptual information, e.g. distinguishing near from far or left-facing objects from right-facing objects;
2. in recognizing relationships between objects in the environment, e.g. hammer/nails, cup/saucer;
3. in noticing common elements in sets of objects, e.g. that different types of knives (carving, pen, tea) are still

knives and distinguishing sets or groups within larger numbers of objects, e.g. teaspoons within spoons.

The ability to transfer learning from one situation to another is also involved in concept formation. Reading is an abstract concept. Many children fail to understand that the spoken word is represented by the one written on the page. They have to discover that the written word has spatially organized groups of letters which correspond systematically to temporally ordered sounds. The acquisition of such a concept is related to normal cognitive growth. The brain-injured child has difficulty in developing concepts, not necessarily because of a lack of experience but because the experiences are not well integrated and cannot be manipulated freely. If the child cannot make any sense from the environment in the ways described, it will be unable to cope with reading.

Intersensory integration

Related to concept formation is the ability to integrate information arriving in the central nervous system from different sense modalities. In the process of reading, for example, information arriving via the visual field must be related to that arriving from the auditory field. As the child matures, proficiency in integrating information increases. This ability is related to the child's intellectual and maturational level, and most rapidly improves between the ages of five and seven, when most children are learning to read. A disturbance in motor ability, touch, sight or hearing will affect a child's ability to integrate the sensory information received from stimuli in the environment.

Other relevant factors

For reading competence and progress other relevant factors are:

1. intellectual;
2. biological;
3. emotional;
4. social;
5. educational.

Intellectual factors

In a section describing readiness the Bullock Report (1975) states that 'very high intelligence on the one hand and very low intelligence on the other certainly have a significant bearing on readiness. But apart from these extremes early reading success is not closely associated with intelligence test measures.' It is also pointed out here that, later, a teacher's expectations of a pupil's ability may be significantly affected by the knowledge of that child's IQ. These expectations in turn will affect that child's performance in reading and in other subjects.

In the Isle of Wight survey, it was found that children with specific reading retardation were in fact of average intelligence, but their verbal skills tended to be inferior to their performance skills as measured by sub-tests of the WISC. Those groups of children which the survey defined as suffering from physical disorders (asthma, eczema, epilepsy, cerebral palsy, orthopaedic disorders, heart disease, deafness, diabetes and other miscellaneous disorders) contained a high proportion of children, whose reading was below the level expected on the basis of their age and intelligence, than in the normal population. Apart from the asthmatic group, whose scores on tests of verbal intelligence were found to be significantly above the mean, the verbal IQ and to a lesser extent the performance IQ of the children with other types of physical disorder (except eczema) were slightly below the mean of the normal population. The authors of the survey felt that poor attendance at school may have had a slightly retarding effect on intellectual development and academic progress.

Biological factors

It has been pointed out frequently (Rutter and Yule, 1973) that more boys than girls have reading difficulties. The physical maturation of boys is much slower than that of girls, and therefore a similar biological process may be responsible for specific reading retardation in boys, through the slow development of certain parts of the brain. Goodacre (1971) also maintains that there are more very good and very poor readers among boys than girls, whereas among the girls there is a narrower range of difference. Although a biological explanation in terms of maturation may partly explain these differences, Goodacre suggests that as boys and girls have different attitudes to learning there are also different teacher/pupil relationships. Because girls usually begin to talk earlier than boys, they bring a more sophisticated level of speech development to the reading readiness stage (see Buffery and Gray, 1972).

Emotional factors

A correlation between specific reading retardation and certain patterns of behaviour was revealed by the Isle of Wight Survey. Children who were retarded in reading showed poor concentration and were over-active and fidgety. In addition, reading retardation was associated with anti social disorders such as truancy, destructiveness, fighting, disobedience, lying, stealing and bullying. The explanation for this was hypothesized:

> The reading retardation handicaps the child in all his school work. Educational failure then leads to the child's reacting against the values associated with school. With status and satisfaction denied him through school work he rebels and seeks satisfaction in activities that run counter to everything for which the school stands. By this means he becomes involved in antisocial activities.

Social factors

The Isle of Wight survey established as affecting reading ability certain social features of the lives of the children it studied. These included the presence of a family history of reading difficulties or of speech delays in the parents or siblings of a child; family and household size which affected the degree and quality of verbal interaction between parents and child (i.e. the larger the family the less the interaction); overcrowded accommodation; the prolonged absence of the mother, either at work or for other reasons and the general attitude towards reading shown by the parents. Evidence from the Bullock Report confirms the importance of the attitude of the home towards reading in terms of regular reading aloud by parents and such things as visits to the library.

Educational factors

A child who has pre-school education and early encouragement to read at home will not necessarily be successful in learning to read as a complex network of factors and skills is involved in the process of reading and some of these may be lacking at any one time in a child's progress. However, this early stimulation towards reading should at least be reflected in a child's speech, conceptualization and general perceptual skills, all of which are necesary preliminaries to reading.

Once a child starts going to school, regular attendance becomes important. Some children whose physical disorders require frequent and sometimes lengthy absences due to treatment or the condition itself become discouraged in all their work, lose confidence and morale and so fail to make progress. The provision of remedial classes does not always have the success that well-intentioned planners hope for. The extra attention to the reading problem may benefit one child but highlight for another its own deficiency and prove counter-productive. Frequently, such classes are run by staff untrained in remedial teaching and selection of pupils for the classes is made arbitrarily.

Other educational factors relevant to a child's progress in reading are: teacher turnover, which is high in urban or educational priority areas, co-operation between the home and the school in the reading program, and the presence of skilled additional help for the teacher of reading such as a speech therapist or an educational psychologist who can diagnose and advise on the treatment of specific difficulties. We suggest that comprehensive records be maintained on the educational progress, and the behaviour and health, where relevant, of every child with reading retardation; these should be made available to all those by whom the child is taught. Social circumstances should also be made known where appropriate. When prescribing treatment, the relevant history of the child should be referred to as well as the diagnostic tests applied before remediation.

If a child is learning at school to read in a language which is not normally spoken in the home enormous difficulties will be encountered, especially if the cultural background is not reflected in the reading material. A large proportion of such children in a class will affect the progress of the indigenous pupils. Special provision must be made to cope with these problems.

Knowledge of a child's cognitive development and of the skills involved in learning to read, as well as factors which may influence reading progress, have been outlined. The third viewpoint for an understanding of the act of reading is the feature-analytic approach described by Smith (1973, 1978a, b).

The feature-analytic approach

This is a psycholinguistic analysis of reading, which assumes that a child's innate cognitive capacity for language is an important part of an ability to read. The ability to abstract rules from all the language made available to the child cannot, according to Smith, be taught. A child must be able to construe meaning, not so much by being presented with certain rules, but rather by being exposed to the regularities in which the unknown rules appear to be exemplified. A child's perceptual and cognitive skills then come into play and the appropriate rule discovered and how it works in a particular context. The child must, however, be allowed to test hypotheses on the basis of the information given, and risk errors and receive appropriate feedback as to progress. A certain degree of inaccuracy is tolerated temporarily, although always corrected, in the young infant learning to express itself orally, which is not accorded to the beginning reader. According to Smith, children are frequently prevented from formulating a potential rule in reading by being expected to be accurate the first time and not positively reinforced for correct interpretation.

Smith considers that the basis of reading is what he calls 'distinctive features', that is elements in the visual configuration of words and letters. Although he does not say exactly what a 'distinctive feature' is, we are meant to assume that it is related to the obvious aspects of letters such as the ascenders of 'b', 'd' and 'h' and the curved strokes of 'c', 'o' and 'a', Smith's own examples. Any one distinctive feature conveys some information about the letter or word to which it belongs, though perhaps not enough information to permit its precise identification. The greater the number of distinctive features that are discriminated the greater the number of of alternatives that are eliminated. Smith suggests that any five distinctive features are sufficient to distinguish all the letters of the alphabet. Discrimination of barely a dozen or so features may permit identification of a word among scores or thousands of alternatives, provided the reader has acquired some knowledge about which sets of features are critical for particular words.

The way in which a word is identified is through categorization. A category is a 'unique cognitive grouping to which particular visual configurations can be allocated together with a name'. Each category is specified in the brain by descriptions which Smith calls 'feature lists' that determine which configurations may be allocated to that category. A word is thus immediately identified by the discrimination of distinctive features which are then assigned to a particular word feature list which in turn signifies a category of word and leads to the word name. The way in which reading is slowed down, according to Smith, frequently by the wrong teaching method, is by the 'mediated word identification process', as he calls it. Distinctive features are discriminated, assigned to letter 'feature lists' identified in terms of letters, instead of word 'feature lists' directly, which then leads to a word name which in turn arrives at a word category. This method is slow because it is a matter of going from words to meaning, whereas in fact, reading is a matter of going from meaning to words, that is, with a hypothesis of what might be meant which the words then confirm. This last point is confirmed by Smith's study of what the eye tells the brain and what the brain tells the eye. From this he proposes that:

1. reading has to be fast since information is delivered by the eye in packages, four times a second, to a sensory store, the visual image, where it stays for not much more than half a second;
2. the reader must be selective, since only four or five items pass into the short-term memory, and these must be the ones that suit information needs; and
3. the reader must use prior knowledge in order to process the information in larger and larger units of meaning (i.e. not letter by letter).

Although this is only a brief outline of a large and exemplary piece of work it must suffice and the implications for the child and the teacher can be defined.

Smith's hypothetical feature-analytic model of how we learn to read suggests that a child will extract the information required provided that the appropriate informational environment is presented and that the child's visual system is sound. The appropriate environment is one in which opportunities are given to make comparisons and to discover what the significant differences are between letters and between words so that a child sees what a letter or word is not like as well as what it is like. Reading instruction can provide motivation and feedback, but the formation of rules is left to the child to deduce. The teacher of a remedial reading class, therefore, has to draw attention to those rules which a child has failed to perceive. Thus, according to Smith, the child has to discover itself, the distinctive features of print, in order to be able to distinguish letters or words.

Phonological recoding

The phonic approach (or word-analysis, phonological encoding approach) would probably rank now as a fourth approach. Several investigators are arguing now (for example, Jorm, 1983; Bradley and Bryant, 1985) that reading problems are associated with difficulty using particular phonological analysis and encoding strategies. This approach argues that the encoding of the visual information precedes the identification of words, and the construction of the meaning of the print. This approach contrasts with Smith and Miller (1966) and Smith (1969) and Goodman's (1968, 1969) approach, which proposes that the use of visual information and phonological strategies are secondary to language-based strategies.

Jorm and Share (1983) claim that children use a phonological code ('an internal representation of speech to access the lexicon') when learning to read. Beginning readers who have difficulty identifying printed words visually, employ phonological recoding to identify individual words. It is further claimed by Jorm and Share that when the visual mode is unavailable to young children, they use phonological recoding as a self-teaching mechanism, not only to identify but to comprehend words. The process itself is said to be carried out among beginning readers by employing grapheme/phoneme correspondence rules, and that it plays a critical role in reading acquisition.

Poor readers, it is argued, are poorer at word recognition using phonological recoding. A test of this process is the ability to read ordinary nonsense words, which poor readers are especially weak at. When the letters in the nonsense words were increased, then poor readers were slower than good readers at reading the words. Therefore, according to Jorm and Share, teachers who emphasize phonics in beginning to read programs promote more efficient reading strategies in young children.

Other workers (Bradley and Bryant, 1978; Fox and Routh, 1980) have pointed to the close relationship between phonological processing skills and reading ability. Poor readers, they claim, are weaker at analysing the phonetic structure of words and have difficulty associating print to sound (decoding) accurately.

Bradley and Bryant offer the view that learning to read in young children depends on 'breaking words into phonological segments' as is carried out in rhyming. They argue that for children to detect rhyme, they must analyse the word and identify the common unit shared by the words. For example, 'hat' and 'cat' must be recognizable because the words share the identical phonemes and because these units are represented by a conventional writing system. The authors claim that phonemic skills contribute to reading success and that a significant relationship existed between sound categorization and reading and spelling achievement in 368 four- and five-year-olds, which persisted over three years. While a causal relationship was difficult to establish, Bradley and Bryant sought to explore this aspect further in a study which included 65 children divided into four gorups and identical for age, sex, IQ and initial sound categorization. The first group was trained to categorize by sounds. The second group was also trained to categorize by sound and reinforced to represent sounds with plastic letters. The third group was trained to categorize words using conceptual categories instead of sound, and the fourth group served as a control group and was given no training.

The training for the first group consisted of rhyming and alliteration of tasks, in which the children were taught that the same word will be arranged in different ways in different groups, e.g. 'hen' and 'hat' and 'hand' all shared the initial first phoneme, but that 'hen', 'men' and 'sun' also shared the end phoneme, and a further category could be used with the middle sound being shared by 'hen', 'bed' and 'leg'.

The second group received similar training and in addition were assisted in their tasks with plastic letters. The third group were encouraged to clarify by concepts, thus 'hen', 'fox' and 'dog' belonged together because they were animals.

The results of the Bradley and Bryant study showed that beginning readers taught to categorize by sounds achieved higher scores on standardized tests of reading and spelling than those not trained in this strategy, while those who also received phoneme sequalization and alphabet letter training achieved the highest success in reading and spelling.

Liberman and Shankweiler (1985) declare that the Bradley and Bryant experiments 'offer the strongest evidence to date of a possible causal link between phonological awareness and reading and writing abilities.' Their approach strongly indicated that beginning readers, taught to categorize by sounds, obtained higher scores on standardized tests of reading as well as spelling. Moreover, children who received such instruction, plus training with alphabet letters, were superior in reading and spelling to other children taught by other methods.

Interactive or schematic model

Over the past eight years a fifth model of reading has been developed – the 'interactive' or 'schematic' model of reading. This model tends to integrate or synthesize the meaning-based (or feature-analytic) approach and the phonic based approach. It suggests that the reader uses a variety of reading strategies selectively, and samples the print according to the perceived purposes for reading and properties of the print.

Studies investigating the psychophysiological correlates of reading, using measures of physiological activity to establish levels of attention and arousal in reading tasks and language processes have been reported by Rentel *et al.* (1985). They indicate that the physical characteristics of the stimulus material influence the reading task itself. Also, that workers have sought to identify the factors which promote reading and the accompanying psychophysiological changes (cardiovascular, electroencephalic, blood flow, etc.) which occur during the reading process.

Metalinguistic aspects of reading

Some studies found that young children beginning reading have very limited understanding of the reading task or understanding of the metalinguistic term **word**. Bowey *et al.* (1984) and others (Gough, 1972; Mattingly, 1972; Downing, 1978) claim that reading for the young child is essentially a discovery of the correspondence between speech and print, or learning that the 'speech he or she has been producing and comprehending for years is, in fact, made up of sequences of word units' (Bowey *et al.*, 1984). Bowey argues that the child, while having a mastery of word concepts, may be unaware that these units are called **words**. She carried out a number of experiments to examine children's understanding of the metalinguistic term **word**, and its relation to spoken language was examined. Her findings indicated that children's reading improved as a result of brief training sessions, in which they were 'taught to attach the metalinguistic label **word** to their developing concept of the word as a unit of spoken language'.

Neurological aspects of reading

At the later stages of learning to read the proficient reader appears to depend on efficient left hemispheric verbal perceptual processes. Other evidence is offered that reading in the early stages is dependent on right hemispheric dominance. Also that not all children employ identical strategies in learning to read, since some children adopt left hemispheric approaches and others right hemispheric strategies. The latter are more alert to the perceptual properties of stimuli, exploring the visual features more systematically, resulting in slower but more accurate reading. The left hemisphere strategists are faster readers, guess more readily and also examine the perceptual elements of the visual configuration more carefully.

Older children who persist in using the slow but accurate study become inefficient readers and the dependence on right hemispheric processing for reading is evidence of developmental lags in hemispheric lateralizations. When both hemispheres compete to serve reading function it is a further cause of reading difficulty. After the silent reading of a passage by 18 right-handed children (mean age 8.09 years), whose brain-wave activity was monitored with EEG recording, the children showed greater right hemispheric involvement when answering comprehension questions on the passage (Rentel *et al.*, 1985). Children who missed the comprehension questions showed greater left hemispheric activity, than did the superior readers. One explanation for the shift from right to left hemispheric processing is that these children were focusing on the perceptual features of the stimuli, and the receptive, rather than expressive language elements invoking the right hemisphere.

The findings that poor readers showed more left hemispheric activity than the better readers in comprehension tasks suggests that there is a close link between reading comprehension and bilateral functioning. Or that the right hemisphere's role in attending to the perceptual configurations and receptive linguistic information was paramount during the silent reading phase, whereas the retrieval of information (comprehension) demands a shift in operation invoking processing in both hemispheres. Clearly, these results point to difficulties for children with recognized brain damage whose bilateral functioning is impaired.

Our picture of the beginning reader is of one who has the potential to learn, but who has many restrictions on the effectiveness of that learning. A teacher undertaking the task of easing the process of learning to read has to take account of a child's cognitive stage of development and physical deficits where relevant, take social, emotional and intellectual aspects of the child into account, make a breakdown of the skills and weaknesses in terms of reading which that child reveals and provide the appropriate total environment in which successful reading can begin.

7

Arithmetic

The development of arithmetical skills has attracted far less attention than the development of reading skills in both normal and handicapped children. Up to two decades ago, over 12 000 research reports on various aspects of reading had appeared. During the same period, studies of disorders of calculation in both normal and disabled children had been meagre by comparison (Haskell, 1973). The reason for this disparity is not clear since calculation, like reading, is essential for survival in both simple and complex technological societies. It is puzzling to understand why there has been so little research in this area when methods of examining and assessing the conditions leading to disorders in number operations are so readily available.

In normal children there are many and varied causes of backwardness in arithmetic. A number of research workers have considered the differential and developmental factors associated with the development of skill in arithmetic (Dutton, 1964). These have focused on, for instance, arithmetic readiness, pupils' attitudes to the subject, level of conceptualizing, learning strategies and cognitive styles. Teacher competency and structured apparatus have been studied and instructional material has been evaluated. Sex differences in arithmetical attainment have been examined as well.

However, before we can understand disabled children's difficulties we need to know what the process of calculation entails in normal children. In arithmetic, a number of discrete operations must be carried out in their correct sequence. For instance, addition involves the organization of digits in strictly conventional order. Symbols are employed to indicate the nature of operations to be carried out, for example, the sign + is an order to add. In all these operations unambiguous rules govern the spatial arrangements of the notation system. Sets of units, tens and hundreds are placed in vertical columns and, in our denary scale, increases in power always take place to the left of each column of digits. Mistakes in vertical and horizontal operations or confusion of the visuo–spatial or left/right orientation disturb the most rudimentary calculation system. Examples of remedial exercises to develop accurate left/right, up/down judgements are given in the Training in Basic Cognitive Skills series by Haskell and Paull (1973a).

Teachers could devise additional individual programs which require the copying of columns of figures on squared paper. Children with intellectual, motor and neurological disabilities may encounter even more difficulties. However, it should not be assumed that a disabled child will necessarily encounter difficulties in learning arithmetic or be permanently weak in calculating skills. We describe here the more important factors influencing arithmetical attainment.

It is not always recognized that home influences affect the arithmetical readiness of children when they attend primary school for the first time. Those fortunate enough to find school an extension and enrichment of home experiences tend to maintain the initial advantage they had over those less well prepared. A number of research studies (Douglas, 1964; Deutsch, 1966; and Smilansky, 1967; Chazan, 1973) have indicated also that depriving conditions at home (and indeed at school), in the form of lack of suitable play materials and appropriate language experience as well as poor motivation towards school learning can retard educational achievement in general, and specifically the attainment of number concepts in young children. It should be emphasized, though, that consistent parental support at home rather than social class or income level is a determining factor in children's arithmetical success and enjoyment. Negative attitudes towards school at home inevitably lead to poor motivation and lowered aspirations in children, for wealthy and poor alike.

Children with intellectual, physical and neurological disabilities make additional and unusual demands on parents; this factor may reduce their opportunities for learning. Early opportunities for successful training in arithmetic such as counting stairs, sharing sweets and judging distances, weights and heights are, therefore, frequently missed (Haskell, 1973). A combination of factors (restricted mobility, poor eye–hand co-ordination, restricted play experiences and fewer opportunities to learn appropriate arithmetic language) reduce the prospects of an orderly emergence of skills.

The introduction by teachers of such concepts as number, conservation of quantity, weight and so on, without first finding out what developmental level the child has reached is unwise and could hamper his educational development. There is evidence that carefully planned programs based on a wide range of experience (Weikart and Lambie, 1970) aimed at stimulating and training cognitive and motor skills such as perceptual discrimination, spatial judgement and motor co-ordination can accelerate arithmetic abilities in young children (Brownell, 1941; Dutton, 1964). Uzgiris and Hunt (1971) have devised developmental scales based on Piagetian concepts, offering guidance to teachers in identifying these cognitive skills and the framework for training these abilities utilizing sensori–motor activities. 'Rote learning' is inadequate preparation for a child to master the four rules of arithmetic; instead active exploration of the immediate environment, through play and other physical experience, is a necessary prelude to formal instruction in the classroom.

Piaget's contribution to this discussion is universally acknowledged and enjoys a firm place in the literature (Piaget, 1952, 1953). He postulates that all children reach invariant developmental 'milestones', which are organized hierarchically before mathematical concepts are mastered. In the early stages of 'sensori-motor' development the infant is dependent on perceptual information derived mainly by physical activities. Later, with the availability of verbal skills, the infant is able to progress through a 'pre-conceptual stage' to more abstract 'formal operations'.

Initially, at the pre-conceptual stage, only the simplest perceptual judgements are attempted. When the infant arranges and manipulates objects, rudimentary number relationships are established as a result of what is seen and touched. It is only after the infant has 'mastered the concrete operations stage' that he is ready to engage in 'formal operations', and a true knowledge and understanding of number relationships emerges. Piaget recognizes that, although these stages are reached by all children, the age at which they reach them is influenced by maturation and experience.

Piaget proposed that the integration of information obtained from different aspects of sense experiences (sense modalities) serve to establish firm 'schemata' in young children. Schemata are regarded as conceptual frameworks containing the salient characteristics of an experience. These, therefore, provide basic organizational structures for the incorporation ('assimilation' and 'accommodation') of new information. Schemata are built up during successive environmental encounters, enabling children to interpret new experiences.

It is through the conscious exploitation of, and the experimentation with, the various play equipment commonly available in nursery classes, such as beads, cubes and rods, that children eventually discover concepts of 'more' and 'less', 'higher' and 'lower', 'longer' and 'shorter'. For a concept to become fixed permanently the performance of the same tasks over and over again is essential, especially if it involves cross-modality skills. Bortner and Birch (1971), however, argue cogently that a distinction should be made between cognitive capacity and cognitive performance. Children might possess a concept but remain unable to make use of it because competing stimuli prevent abstraction occurring. For instance, in a simple matching task, when required to match a model object from among alternatives, unlike older children, young children are strongly influenced in their choice by the stimulus properties instead of the functional relationship of the alternative objects. In the Birch and Bortner study younger children were asked to match a red button (model) with a red lipstick case or a blue, round poker chip or a spool of thread. They relied heavily on the striking sensory information, selecting either the red lipstick case for colour or the round poker chip for shape. Older children chose by using the functional relationship represented by the spool of thread (Birch and Bortner, 1966). Birch and Bortner (1967) maintain that if the test conditions for matching tasks are altered, both for normal and brain-damaged children, and the range of choice is based on sensory properties, then the same children would find matching according to functional relationship easier.

Support for this notion comes from the conservation of number study by Mehler and Bever (1967). Two rows of pellets were set out with the shorter row containing more pellets than the longer one. As expected, children pointed to the longer row as containing more pellets. However, when Smarties (M & M) were substituted and the children allowed to 'eat the row of their choice, the children more frequently took the shorter row'. Bortner and Birch (1971) suggest that the capacity for correct judgement, though present, becomes affected by the nature of the object, the task demands, and motivation. In one case (clay pellets) 'more' meant the visual extent whereas in the other, 'more' (Smarties) meant more things to eat. The teacher should be aware of the child's level of development so that appropriate experience can be supplied for the child at that stage.

Another aspect of the nature of learning should be considered, namely that one experience, no matter how valuable, is in itself insufficient to establish a concept. As Harlow (1949) demonstrated a single encounter offers a subject only the most limited opportunities of learning the rules or adopting effective strategies. Harlow discovered that, when required to solve simple discrimination problems, monkeys and children learn in two stages – a trial and error, and later an insight stage – provided that several learning occasions are offered to the subject. This observation is particularly important when considering the learning needs of disabled children. It does not develop spontaneously but by laborious and systematic training. The success of this operation depends upon a brisk interchange between sensory input and motor output. According to Harlow, concepts, the raw materials for 'human thinking', require this rich interchange between the organism and its environment in order to become firmly established. The number of uncontrived and contrived experiences, both in the home and at school, and the skilful engineering of the 'arithmetical environment' of the young child by the teacher, will determine when and how concepts of number, quantity and space will be acquired. Activities such as setting the table at home and at school for the correct number of people and the arrangement of knives, forks, spoons, place mats, glasses, etc., which stress right/left, up/down discrimination provide natural (and regular) training opportunities for these children.

Physically disabled children are often restricted in their physical interaction with the environment and unless opportunities are specially created for them, they miss these important stages and experiences.

Consequences of sensori–motor deprivation

At the simplest level, disorders of the sensory organs which affect vision, hearing, proprioception, kinaesthesia, tactile and other modalities give rise to disturbed psychological processes of perception, attention, conceptualization and regulation of movement. In the more severe cases involving lesions above the brainstem, the effects on arithmetical abilities are hypothesized by Strauss and Lehtinen (1947) thus:

> the brain-injured organism lacks the ability possessed by the normal child to discover spontaneously the significant relationships of the number system. Accepting the thesis that a perceptual scheme of visual–spatial organization is the basis of calculation, it is reasonable to anticipate that the organism whose ability to construct such a perceptual scheme has been disturbed will be hindered in any activities which require its use.

Cerebral palsied children, with disorders of movement and posture due to cerebral lesions, experience special difficulties in performing with proficiency and ease such functions as locomotion, feeding, dressing and sitting. Children who are severely physically disabled also tend to be restricted in their range of purposeful motor activities and consequently their general arithmetical development is delayed. As mentioned earlier, Held and Hein (1963) demonstrated that in both animals and man, physical mobility, together with appropriate perceptual experience, is a necessary pre-requisite for normal perceptual development.

It would be useful to refer to the work of White and Held (1966), which showed that infants raised in enriched environments (visually attractive cribs and surrounds, suspended toys, mobiles and pacifiers with interesting patterned backgrounds) exhibited marked perceptuo–motor precocity with respect to examining and manipulating their hands, prehension and visual attention.

Both in movements and variety of visual, auditory and tactile experiences, motor-handicapped children appear severely underprivileged. We would expect, therefore, that motor-handicapped children's intellectual and arithmetical development would be affected if the physical constraints of movement are so gross as to disrupt such basic cognitive functions as sorting, classifying and matching (Haskell, 1973). The consequences of reduced contact with the environment are serious and the resulting arrested development of sensori-motor skills increases the risk of educational failure. Parents and teachers could provide children with toys which offer a variety of sensations, sounds, colour, textures and temperatures. Toys designed by Morgenstern *et al.* (1966) encourage exploration, compatible with the physically disabled child's mental and physical development. For further reading see Riddick (1982).

Interruptions in school attendance

Absence from school of both normal and disabled children affects attainment in arithmetic more than in reading or most other school subjects. Schonell and Schonell (1957) maintain that because arithmetic involves understanding sequential steps and children progress by mastering each step in succession, irregular attenders who miss critical stages find it hard to keep up with their peers as they have nothing on which to base their next work. Teachers should be aware of the feelings of anxiety which repeated absence from arithmetic lessons may create in certain children.

Haskell (1973) found that the use of Programmed Instruction (PI) for children with cerebral palsy had certain obvious advantages when continuity of attendance during the term was interrupted by illness or accident. This method was also helpful for children in classes with excessively wide ranges of intellectual ability. Individual children benefited from PI because the pace of learning was directly maintained by the child and not by arbitrary standards imposed by the class situation. Nowadays with computerized learning in the classroom, commercially or privately produced software comprising arithmetic programs can fulfil a similar function.

Emotional and temperamental factors

Failure often leads to anxiety and negative attitudes to the subject, which in themselves may contribute towards arithmetical failure. There are even cases reported of repeated failure in arithmetic leading to maladjusted behaviour (Gregory, 1965). Some studies by Lynn (1957) and Biggs (1959) indicate that children who are anxious or temperamentally unstable tend to display negative attitudes to arithmetic. It is not uncommon for some children to identify with the unfavourable attitudes of parents and teachers to the subject (Biggs, 1959). In addition, where teachers are unsympathetic to a pupil's poor performance in arithmetic, the fear and anxiety of the child increases. There are indications that a child's temperament may contribute to success or failure. Some children, however, like arithmetic because of its orderly pattern and structure.

Active and passive movements

Disabled children, especially those with motor disorders arising out of central nervous system dysfunctioning, require greater opportunities for physical experimentation in order to learn how to solve simple problems than do normal children. To appreciate abstract concepts, such as conservation, a child needs to practise activities such as rearranging a collection of wooden bricks in space, inspecting and verifying its properties and studying the altered pattern produced by rearranging a similar number of objects.

At a certain stage of a child's sensori–motor development a normal child enjoys experimenting with toys itself instead of having an adult's helping hand directing movements (see Figures 7.1, 7.2 and 7.3). This is regarded as a significant developmental milestone, according to Piaget, because the child is 'trying out' all the schemata available for discovery learning. A child with severe motor disabilities, on the other hand, has greatly reduced opportunities to learn by experimentation and the framework on which to build schemata is weak, because the child cannot 'discover' for itself by playing and experimenting. For instance a young child, given ample play opportunities to rearrange a collection of objects by

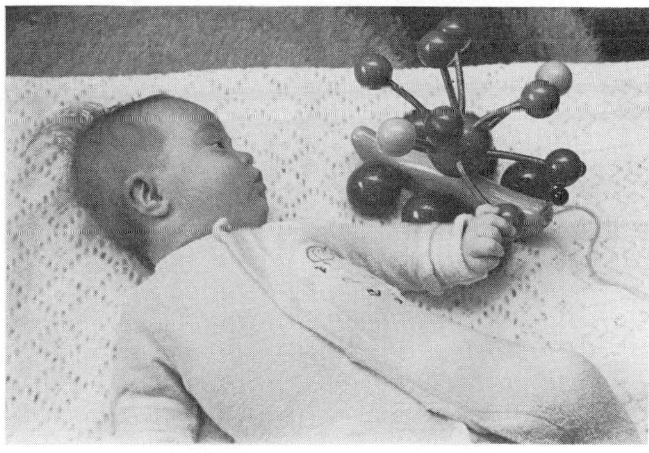

Figure 7.1 Kouvalis toys designed for cerebral palsied infants with poor hand control.

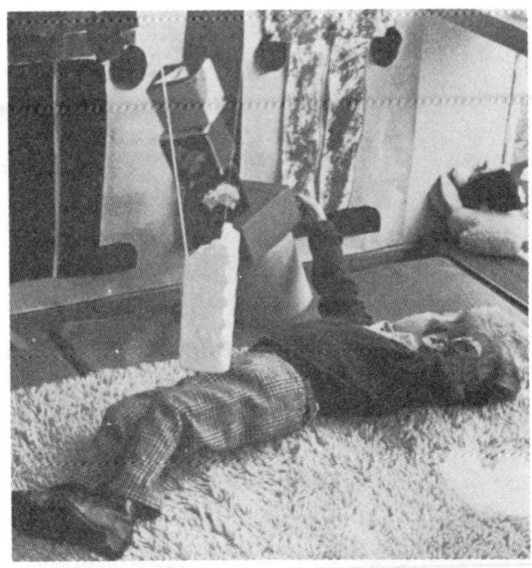

Figure 7.2 Older motor disabled child knocking down a stack of light foam bricks.

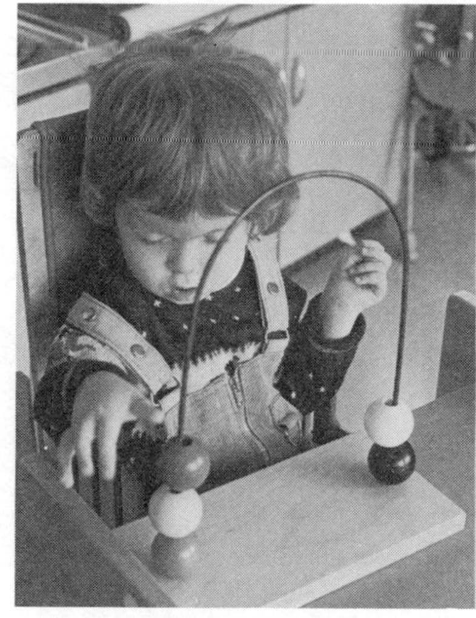

Figure 7.3 Morgenstern Arched Abacus: teaching a child to grasp and move a ball in a specific direction.
Source: From Riddick, B. (1982) *Toys and Play for the Handicapped Child*. London: Croom Helm, with permission.

reversing its pattern and then returning the objects to their original position, will develop concepts of reversibility more easily than if denied this practice.

Brain-injured children encounter special problems in transferring from three dimensions of an object to the two-dimensional representation of it. To overcome these difficulties such children require skilled help and systematic training, and active participation by the child is essential. Learning by proxy or passive movements, is far less effective, e.g. when the physiotherapist manipulates the child's limbs as happens so frequently with severely handicapped children. Children with physical disabilities need to carry out 'volume conservation' experiments with containers of varying sizes to discover for themselves by direct observation that volume retains its capacity and is 'conserved' in whichever shape of container it is poured into. It is through successive actions reinforced with approriate language that true understanding grows, concepts and schemata develop and serve as a basis for mathematical reasoning.

In a similar way, brain-injured children encounter problems learning the four basic arithmetical operations. Proficiency in arithmetic requires a grasp of the underlying concepts, which indicate which operation should be used. In shopping, for example, various operations are required, in the correct order. Many brain-injured children have difficulty in learning these procedures. Munro (1986) showed that when such children learn the mental actions as corresponding to physical actions, and then gradually internalize these, their arithmetic performance can be improved significantly. In an ongoing study, Munro taught motor-disabled children to add by incrementing along a number ladder, and to subtract by decrementing, for example '32 − 3 = ' was computed by beginning at 32 on the path and counting down 3 steps. The children were then taught to use their knowledge of counting to picture mentally part of the number path and to take the corresponding actions. For the subtraction problem above, the children recalled the numbers around 32, pictured them in descending order, and imagined going down three steps. The children learn to multiply and divide in similar ways, using bead chains. The physical action of using these chains made the mental process underlying each table more salient, showing the students that the three times table, for example, could be generated by counting in steps of three at once. This emphasis on physical actions leading to the corresponding mental actions assists motor-disabled children to integrate or unify their mathematics knowledge, and to manipulate the more formal aspects of arithmetic, capacities that had previously been believed to be beyond many of them. Practice is clearly essential for consolidating a newly learned skill, especially calculation or learning tables. For arithmetical responses to be organised with precision and speed, children need considerable rehearsal in each of the four rules of arithmetic. The ultimate aim should be to free the child from conscious planning and long hours of tedious procedures such as recalling multiplication tables (Schonell and Schonell, 1957).

Ocular–motor disorders and calculating difficulties

A high percentage of ocular–motor defects are present in brain-injured children (Smith, 1963). The frequent occurrence of refractive errors, strabismus (squint), visual field defects and various developmental anomalies hold in abeyance the normal attainment of arithmetical competency in young children. As Hebb (1949) pointed out, much early learning is dependent upon the integrity of visual functioning. Cerebral palsied children with visual disorders seem highly vulnerable (Abercrombie, 1960, 1963, 1964) to arithmetical failure. It is important to remember that an ocular defect does not necessarily mean that the child will have difficulties in visual perception. Nevertheless, alternating squints, severe nystagmus, tunnel vision, defective visual scanning of a set of numbers and disordered eye movements could affect simple calculation functions and other skills requiring movement under visual control.

Memory for visual and spatial sequencing

Another function related to calculating skills is memory for visual and spatial sequencing. The ability to retain and recall the correct order of digits or composite numbers is demanded at the simplest level in a computational task. Brain-injured children have been known to experience selective impairment of this function (Kinsbourne and Warrington, 1963b). The association between calculation and sequential difficulties suggests an underlying disorder of arranging a collection of objects in their correct spatio–temporal sequence (Lefford, 1970).

Distractability

These children are sometimes described as 'hyperactive, hyperkinetic or stimulus bound', being unable to ignore the variety of stimuli which they receive. When carrying out arithmetical operations, these children have the greatest difficulty in inhibiting their response to the competing stimuli of extraneous digits and symbols and selectively focusing on and attending to a limited field. On the other hand, these children may become unnaturally attached to a single stimulus for long periods of time or 'perseverate'. (For fuller discussion see Chapter 4 on brain damage).

Perseveration

According to Grewel (1969) perseveration is a

> general disorder which is found in all varieties of sensori-motor disorganization (apraxias, agnosias, aphasias) and may hamper calculating ability. After an operation is carried out, the child may persist in continuing with the same operation, for example, after being asked to add 4 + 4, the child will with the next problem, 3 − 1, answer 4 (repeating the operation of addition) or given 4 × 4 answer 8. The child may get unnaturally fixated to a single number or numbers and ignore the requirement to perform the arithmetic operation; for 3 + 3 the child answers 33, or when asked 20 + 15, he answers 25. There may be persistence in rote counting. For example when directed to perform an operation such as 11 + 5 the child ignores the + 5 and answers 12.

Arithmetical ability in cerebral palsied children

Phillips and White (1964) noted that motor-disabled children with brain injury fared poorly on arithmetic compared with motor-disabled control groups without congenital brain injury. On the Revised Southend Arithmetic Test in Mechanical Arithmetic, the mean arithmetic achievement of the 23 cerebral palsied children was significantly poorer, after controlling for age and IQ differences, than that of 32 physically disabled children without neurological involvements. Another study which revealed severe weaknesses in arithmetic as measured on the Burt Four Rules and Ballard One Minute Test in Oral Addition and Subtraction was the East Scotland Survey carried out by Henderson (1961). Of the 153 cerebral palsied children 93.5% were backward, compared with normal children.

Dunsdon (1952) concluded that 'weak gestalt' (poor appreciation of form or configuration) as measured on the Bender Gestalt test was commoner in athetoids than spastics, and contributed to their lowered arithmetic attainment. Dunsdon studied a highly selected group of 35 cerebral palsied children, drawn from her own large sample of 916 pupils, and based her scoring on the mental age norms provided in the manual. In her sample, 60% of the cerebral palsied children showed a closer relationship between their Bender and Arithmetic scores, compared with 46% which showed similar relationships between verbal reasoning and visual memory factors (based on various items of the Stanford Binet Intelligence Scale (Terman and Merrill, 1937).

Haskell (1973) carried out a study in which a program of instruction which covered the four basic rules of arithmetic was used and applied over a period of 13 weeks to a group of 21 cerebral palsied children between the ages of 9 and 16 years. A matched group of similarly disabled children was taught by conventional methods. Both groups showed gains in arithmetic and both methods had merit. However, restless and withdrawn children taught by conventional methods benefited less than their counterparts instructed by programmed instruction. Progress in the four rules of arithmetic showed direct correlation with spatial and non-verbal items of the test.

Neurological factors

From a psychological point of view, it is of absorbing interest to trace any link between cerebral insult and deficiency in number operations. However, attempts to establish causal relationships between localization of lesion and specific deranged functions have proved inconclusive. Grewel's (1969) scholarly review of the acalculias (impaired ability to perform simple calculations) is recommended, and should convey some notion of the difference in views expressed over the last half-century. His survey of the clinical evidence for the localisation of lesion in the occipital, temporal, frontal and parietal lobes and disturbances in calculation, mainly in adults, is still a classic study.

Lesions in the occipital region tend to impair visuo-perceptual and visuo-spatial functions and are reflected in confusions due to misreading numbers. Multiple digits are mistaken for discrete units, e.g. 89 read as 8.9. Tasks involving analysis and synthesis cause difficulties and since visual imagery is implicated, patients with occipital lesions develop fewer useful calculating skills.

Some patients apparently experience uncommon difficulties in arithmetical calculations if the material is presented auditorily. Some of the features of parietal lobe lesions, it is claimed, are difficulties in auditory discrimination, recall of digits and cross-model transfer from auditory stimulus to the written expression of the same. This view has not won general acceptance, partly because of insensitivity of tests used in studies and partly because efforts to ascribe auditory digit recognition to highly specific cortical regions are quite unconvincing.

It is claimed that one result of frontal lobe damage is weak abstract reasoning in mathematics, and that multiplication and division are more likely to be affected by lesions in this region than are addition and subtraction. The assumption that the former two operations involve more abstract reasoning skills than do addition and subtraction has little, if any, support. Clinicians have given much attention and speculation to the effects of damage to the parietal lobe. Among the functions affected, it is claimed are calculating skills. Acalculia is reported to result from lesions of the angular gyrus. Fifty years ago the German neurologist Gerstmann (1924) described a complex of four systems in which right–left disorientation, finger agnosia and deficiencies in writing and counting resulted from left parietal lesions. Evidence for this claim has been disputed by Benton *et al.* (1951), who criticized the so-called supportive data offered by Strauss and Werner (1938) and Werner and Carrison (1942).

Kinsbourne and Warrington (1962c, 1963a), on the other hand, claim that impairments in serial orderings (items arranged in definite sequence) were implicated in spelling, finger recognition, calculation and right–left orientation, and that constructional disorders were signs of development delays. In the absence of motor paralysis, a failure to carry out motor operations, such as block-building or copying a pattern, under visual guidance and monitoring, might be due to an inability to put elements together as a whole. In other words, a constructional disorder might not be a single dysfunction but a disturbance of several related functions, including spatial manipulative ability.

Lesions in the right hemisphere, including the thalamic, medial and posterios cortical areas, affect spatial perception and visuo–spatial memory, which in turn impairs calculation skills (Ojemann, 1974).

Luria (1966) noted that adults with damage to the parietal–occipital areas of the brain demonstrated disturbances of spatial imagery, resulting in loss of ability to perform arithmetical calculations.

Bilateral electrical stimulation of the thalamus produced differential disturbances in arithmetical ability. Left thalamic stimulation increased calculation errors and accelerated the rate of counting backwards, while right thalamic stimulation increased errors in calculation and slowed down counting (Ojemann, 1974). Since the right thalamus controls number reading, spatial functions requiring the setting out of digits horizontally, left to right in an evenly spaced manner, become deranged.

Luria (1970) devised a test which examined systematically the nature and degree of calculation disorders in adults. Luria claimed that damage to the language dominant areas of the brain led to inability, reduced ability to read numbers and the confusion of one number with another. Hecaen (1972), on the other hand, found that right hemisphere lesions led to spatial dyscalculia, while bilateral disturbances led to acalculia ('a' suggests massive loss and 'dys' partial loss).

Critchley (1953) reported that left parietal lobe symptoms often gave rise to arithmetical computation weaknesses, such as those found in individuals with Gerstmann syndrome. It should be pointed out that the use of these prefixes is used rather imprecisely by workers and that some caution should be exercised in translating the findings of number disorders in adults to that of children with development number retardation.

Dyscalculia in adults has been extensively studied by neuropsychologists (Levin, 1979), but the focus of interest has been on the nature of the disorder, rather than on its treatment. An analysis of errors made of acalculic individuals revealed that failure to use spatial representations, set out digits in their correct sequences, and copy out subtraction operations, were caused by parietal lesions.

Rourke and Strang (1983) compared the mechanical arithmetical skills of two groups of children between the ages of 9 to 14 years referred for neuropsychological assessment. There were 15 children in each group matched for age and WISC IQs, but which differed in their neuropsychological and neurodevelopmental status. They noted that children in the first group with deficient language skills were delayed in the acquisition of age-appropriate arithmetic abilities. There was confirmation that the 'neuropsychological strengths and weaknesses of the children were consistent with problems that may underlie their arithmetic calculation difficulties'. Children in the second group showed better arithmetical than reading and spelling scores. These children also performed well on visual–spatial/visuo–perceptual tasks. In a follow-up study, these children also performed well on complex psycho–motor and tactile–perceptual tasks. Rourke and Strang suggest that the arithmetic impairments of such children arise from disorders in central processing and neurological make-up.

Conclusion

Arithmetic is a highly sophisticated skill and is based on hierarchically organized subskills rather than a single underlying ability. Calculation depends upon the efficient functioning of several processes including sensory, perceptual, motor, intellectual and social factors. The lack of any relevant skill, or delay in its development in both normal and disabled children will set limits to arithmetical attainment. The role, therefore, of the teacher is to identify the development stage reached by a particular child, to specify the nature of the learning task and to set the educational scene, in order to exploit a child's existing skills and to generate new competencies.

The general guidelines on teaching children with learning difficulties as suggested above (Chapter 3) are directly relevant to teaching arithmetic. In addition, much direct practical experience of every preliminary stage of computation is essential, i.e. sharing, sorting, matching, counting, handling money, reacting with the environment such as counting going up and down stairs, counting movements backwards and forwards. When the stage is reached of representing concrete objects by mathematical symbols, the symbols should be clearly and boldly depicted. Time must be spent on recognizing them and what they represent (e.g. 2,3, etc.). The position of placement values must be stressed. Each new operation should be demonstrated in concrete form, worked through with the child, left with the child for him/her to work on his/her own successfully before moving to the symbolic written form. The use of as many different forms of counters as possible should be employed so that children obtain the concept of number, rather than relating number to a particular set of objects, e.g. plastic discs, or buttons. Each stage of operation must be understood thoroughly and practised correctly by the child before moving on to the next. In teaching arithmetic to children who are finding it hard, breaking down operations into smaller and smaller steps is crucial.

8

Handwriting

Humanity's desire to create a permanent record of its way of life was first reflected in drawings on the walls of caves. This urge and the need to communicate with others has led, down the centuries, to sophisticated writing forms. These record not only messages but great literature, advanced conceptual thought and symbols of technology. In early writing systems, simple pictorial representations wee made of objects and ideas. The step of greatest importance was the invention of phonetic writing in which sounds were given symbols, thus linking speech with writing. Phonetic writing became simplified into sets of two or three dozen symbols or alphabets.

It is estimated that the number of languages spoken today is approximately 2800 – excluding minor dialects. There are three main types of character or symbol used in writing:

1. word–concept characters – as in the Chinese language;
2. syllable–sound characters – as in 'Tulisan' in the Malay language;
3. letter–sound characters – as in the English language.

The eye movements required for reading these characters vary from culture to culture. They may be from left to right (as in our own), up and down (as in Chinese) or from right to left (as in some systems in the Middle East). Reading and writing are closely linked. The ability to read precedes meaningful writing. In a modern technological society, anyone who canot read and write is seriously disabled.

In this age of typewriters and word-processors it is sometimes suggested that children do not need to be taught handwriting at all. We disagree. An important reason for teaching handwriting is that the writing process is an integral part of the development of reading skills; the reproduction of the written form by perceptual–motor processes is a valuable part of this development. It is also important to be as independent of machines as possible and to be able to cope by one's own effort when the occasion so demands. Undoubtedly, children now at school will probably not, as was once the case, need handwriting as a commercial asset. Nevertheless, there are many occasions when a typewriter or word-processor is not available. A further argument for the teaching of handwriting is that as an art form it can be a source of great pride and satisfaction to all children, including those with disabilities. In any case, it is advisable to encourage severely disabled children to use a writing tool as much as possible, even if it is only to write their name – a social necessity. It must be recognized, nevertheless, that some physically disabled children are so poorly co-ordinated that typing or keyboarding is the only sensible course for them.

Certain subskills are needed to enable a child to put thoughts into the conventional writing system of their culture. The following are suggested for English writing:

1. the ability to see and perceive the shape, form and orientation of letters;
2. sufficient motor control to be able to pick up, hold and guide a writing tool across the page, with the necessary rhythm and fine variation of pressure to make handwriting legible;
3. sufficient hand–eye co-ordination to be able to direct a writing tool to form the letters;
4. adequate memory to learn and recall the motor pattern for each letter and, subsequently, word;
5. the ability to plan the necessary motor movement (praxis) for writing.

Inadequacy in any one of these subskills will produce difficulties in writing. It is essential to find out at which stage a child is failing before one can plan remedial help for that child who, though physically capable of producing legible handwriting, finds difficulty in so doing. Speed is another factor to be considered when teaching handwriting; for all except artistic purposes, a child or adult needs to use writing to record information or communicate as quickly and efficiently as possible without sacrificing legibility.

National curriculum

In Britain handwriting has been included as a subject in the National Curriculum (1989). Statements of Attainment have been set down for four levels:

Level 1 Pupils should be able to begin to form letters with some control over the size, shape and orientation of letters or lines of writing.

Level 2 (a) Produce legible upper and lower case letters in one style and use them consistently (i.e. not randomly mixed within words).

(b) Produce letters that are recognizably formed and properly oriented and that have clear ascenders and descenders where necessary.'

Level 3 Begin to produce clear and legible joined-up writing.

Level 4 Produce more fluent joined-up writing in independent work.

Levels 5, 6, 7 Handwriting joins with spelling as presentation.

The aim is 'to develop a comfortable, flowing and legible joined-up style of handwriting'.

The criteria for assessing the final product are not precise and leave room for subjective judgement. The inclusion of handwriting in the National Curriculum (1989) reflects a growing concern over the standard of handwriting in school leavers nationally.

Guidelines have been set for teachers establishing programs of study for children to achieve the attainment targets. These guidelines include beginning by building on children's early interest in letters (particularly in their own name); teaching the alphabet; teaching letter formation; close observation of the child as letters are formed; linking sounds to writing; purposeful handwriting practice and use of text-handling programs on computers. Handwriting and presentation of work are linked.

British children now have the legal right to be taught handwriting properly, a subject which some schools have been neglected in recent years.

In Australia and New Zealand formal guidelines have been laid down by education authorities for the teaching of handwriting (Alston and Taylor, 1987).

Subskill 1: perception of letters

Poor spatial perception may result in mirror writing, reversals (especially of b and d, p and q) and horizontal/vertical confusion (p and d). Difficulties in spacing letters and words, poor sense of direction and confusion in relative sizes of letters are also attributable to visuo–spatial difficulties. In the early stages of writing, normal children often present many of these problems but with practice and maturity these usually disappear. Children with neurological or sensory impairments may continue to show these faults at a much later age than do able-bodied children.

Interesting work has been done on incorrect orientation of letters. Schonell (1948) found that letter reversals usually disappear from children's handwriting at about eight years of age, slightly earlier than in reading. Boys were making reversals at a later age than girls. Chapman *et al.* (1970), in a study of 328 children between the ages of 7½ and 8½, found a similar difference between boys and girls. The children were required to write ten 'reversible' lower case letters and seven 'reversible' numbers to dictation. Some children were still making orientation errors. Wedell (1973) observes:

> An analysis of the types of error showed that most were reversals. The most frequently rotated letters and digits were those which represented another letter or digit in the alternative position (d or 9). This indicates that a child is more certain of a letter or digit when it is meaningful in only one orientation.

Following from this study, Chapman *et al.* (1972) investigated some of the factors which had been put forward as contributing to uncertainty of letter formation. A battery of tests was selected covering areas postulated as being associated with reversal errors, namely left/right discrimination, visual perception, lateral hand or eye preference, and knowledge of left and right sides of the body. From the original 328 children, two groups were chosen, matched for age, sex, school class and scores on a verbal ability test; one group (R group) made rotation or other errors in at least three out of five letter and digit writing tasks and the other group (NF group) made none of these errors on any of the tasks. Mean scores were significantly different on measures of only two of the tests. One was the Frostig Position in Space sub-test, in which a subject matches similar shapes in the same orientation among those in different orientations. The other was Kephart's 'Crossing the Midline' task which shows knowledge of left and right sides of the body. (In this the child is required to stand in front of a blackboard and draw a line joining two points, one to his right and one to his left. The points are arranged horizontally and then diagonally. The task was scored by a standard stencil fitted over the line drawn.) One is led to ask why measures on only these two tests were significant, especially as the two groups of children were not significantly different in their knowledge of the distinction between left and right sides of their body nor in their lateral hand and eye preference and other aspects of visual perception. Body image and spatial perception seem to be important, but further research is needed. The R group's reading and spelling scores were significantly lower than those of the NR group. Wedell observes that the R group's poorer spelling, but not their poorer reading, can be seen as contributory to their difficulty in writing. When the letter and digit-writing task in the original study was altered to copying rather than writing from dictation, fewer mistakes were made.

It seems that letter orientation errors are reduced when the letters occur in words rather than in isolation, as is shown in the Chapman *et al*. study, by the results from the Daniels and Diack (1964) reversible words sub-test. In their experiment, Marchbanks and Levin (1965) found that children pay most attention to initial letters in reading words. If this is a general truth, children would be more likely to remember the orientation of initial letters. This is tentatively supported by the Chapman *et al*. study, and the authors suggest that this may be one way in which experience in reading helps to reduce children's uncertainty about letter orientation. Wedell suggest that the R group's poorer orientation contributed to their poor reading, which in turn led to their continuing uncertainty about orientation of letters.

The link between reading and writing is emphasized by the studies described; the two must be taught together, especially for remedial purposes. There are perceptual programs available for children who have basic perceptual difficulties. These, however, serve only as a preliminary to letter discrimination; the teacher must devise ways of enabling a child to differentiate between reversible letters and numbers. Illustrated alphabets in which the letters are incorporated into a picture of a word beginning with that letter, for example, W is made to look like a worm, can help because the letter has a meaningful association for the child (see above). The Letterland Series with its colourful characters with alliterative names for each letter is enjoyed by children. Series of words beginning with the letters which a child confuses (for example b or d), chosen and illustrated by the child and set on opposite sides of the page, can be helpful. Hooton (1975) suggests methods of teaching basic letters. Many of these methods can be used for children with physical disabilities.

Together with these approaches, a careful observation of how a child in difficulty actually makes each letter is essential, followed if necessary with a demonstration at close quarters of the correct writing movement by the teacher. If a child is having difficulty in forming a letter correctly, an adaptation of a sand tray is sometimes helpful. A shallow box with a black bottom, covered with rice or uncooked porridge oats, is placed in front of the child. The required form is drawn with the forefinger in the box leaving the letter shape in black. A quick shake of the tray makes the letter disappear. The contrasting colours of white and black make the letters easy to see, a useful factor for children with poor sight. Children also enjoy writing in chalk on small blackboards. Both these aids have the advantage of producing letters which are easily erasable. Often children are reluctant to produce a permanent letter when they lack confidence in writing and feel that their efforts may be poorly formed. Other helpful aids include felt letters, indented plastic letter forms which can be traced with fingers or ball-bearings or pen, raised letters, letter jigsaws.

Another aid for children with partial or poor sight is a pencil with a soft lead, making the writing blacker on the page. They may do even better with a black fibre-tipped or roller ball pen. Lines may have to be drawn, possibly in green at the top and red at the bottom, indicating that one starts where it is green and ends where it is red. This is a gimmick that can be used for any child unsure of direction of writing movement. We believe that, in spite of current theory and practice, lines are needed to guide children who are experiencing writing difficulty, if only so that they can get the proportion of sizes of letters correct. In a normal exercise book, heavy ruling of every other line may help a child in this respect while letters with ascenders, such as h, l and capitals can take up two spacings. Copy books, now being printed once more, can be used (Paull and Haskell 1977a, b).

Books with wide-line spacing are also available and are useful for children with sight problems. An argument against using lines is that it cramps a child's natural style and size of writing. An enterprising teacher, though, can observe a child's natural size of writing and rule lines accordingly. If necessary, in order to guide the child, the teacher can adjust the spacing of lines to increase or decrease the size of the child's writing. For those children whose writing is uncertain and cramped and who need to gain confidence, writing patterns in the Marion Richardson tradition are useful. An adaptation of normal infant methods involving some gross motor exercises and large-scale writing and drawing may also help in this respect (Cambridge and Wedell, 1974). Using a paintbrush on an easel to produce letter patterns and firm brush strokes in interesting colours is an example. These techniques have been used with success by the authors.

Subskill 2: motor control

To help a child with poor motor control, close consultation and co-operation with the occupational therapist or physiotherapist is essential. Exercises to develop the fine motor movements required for writing, for example, clenching and unclenching a fist, must be devised and a program worked out and understood by both teacher and therapist. Crafts such as weaving, modelling (plasticine is still very useful for developing muscle strength and co-ordination), leather work, basketry and mosaic work all play their part. Also useful are balsa wood modelling, lino cutting, printing, constructional toys and clay modelling. Children with poor hand grip because of deforming or painful illnesses such as juvenile rheumatoid arthritis find biros with round stems and with a ridge above the point preferable as writing tools to angular biros, which these children may find hard to grasp; they may even prefer the round-stemmed biros to pens, which have no ridge and require the fuss of refilling. Triangular rubber or specially shaped plastic pencil grips which are now on the market can also be useful. The teacher could experiment with all kinds of unusual tools as writing implements for variety and for testing different aspects of hand/eye control and hand/elbow arm muscle control. Examples are: writing with large, thick or fine paint brushes, with fat chalks, with charcoal, writing with the length rather than the tip of chalk, writing with fingers dipped in paint.

Research, such as there is, supports the common-sense observation that, at speed, both pressure and rhythm vary, and increasing illegibility results (Harris and Rarick, 1959). A child must therefore know how to form letters correctly so that when writing fast, and being certain of the basic formation, there is less likelihood of distortion. A suggestion for an activity which would develop skills in rhythm and pressure, and is fun as well, is the use of an object such as a sponge or half-potato dipped in paint, tapped on to a large surface to a rhythm given by the teacher.

Subskill 3: hand–eye co-ordination

Basically, writing consists of a few lines: horizontal, vertical, diagonals to the left and right, and various portions of a circle. A child must be able to guide a writing tool in the necessary basic directions before being able to write efficiently. There are programs available to help children with poor hand–eye co-ordination, such as those of Haskell and Paull (1973b), consisting of graded booklets through which a child may work systematically. Colouring, joining dot-to-dot pictures and tracing also help a child to develop hand–eye co-ordination. There are pre-writing programs, humorously presented, consisting of cards inserted in a plastic folder on which the child writes with a special pencil, the marks of which are easily erasable (Philip and Tacey, 1987).

Subskill 4: memory

For children who find it hard to remember letters and how to make them, continued, regular practice and drill, on the lines suggested above, provide the most obvious remedy. A child with neurological impairment will need much more rehearsal of writing movements than will a normal child, and the teacher should be prepared for much slower progress. There are many games and activities to develop recall of letters. Examples are: Kim's game, using letters; writing letters on the blackboard and then rubbing one off and asking the children to write it down in their books; including letter shapes in other work, such as lino cuts, painting, mobiles and collages; building letters in wood and plasticine; sewing letters in felt; using jigsaw puzzles with letters fitting into a cut-out background; using typewriters; using wooden or plastic letters, getting the child to feel round them with eyes closed and guessing the letter; using stencils; making small size clay letters, firing and using them for necklaces and bracelets. It is also helpful to have many examples of letters in different colours and sizes. Now available are magnetic letters which can be attached and moved around on a whiteboard. Lego letters, which can be firmly fixed, can be helpful for children with poor hand control.

Left-handed writing

The handwriting problems of left-handed children can be considered at this point. Left-handed children often scribble from right to left before they start writing properly. Wedell (1973) observes that if they continue to do this when they start writing, mirror writing results. He suggests that the teacher can remedy this fault if it is noticed early and the child is told where to begin writing. One must, however, be very careful to assess that the child is left-handed and still not ambidextrous and in the throes of establishing hand dominance. Too much interference at this early stage may result in stunting the child's creative and experimental satisfaction in the activity of scribbling – the teacher should not be too anxious to teach!

Left-handed writers have other difficulties. They have to learn to push rather than pull the pen. As they write their hands may obscure the words they are writing and this may make spelling more difficult to master. To avoid this problem, some left-handed writers adopt a hooked hand position, writing above the line. Nowadays, attempts to make a genuine left-hander write with the right hand are strongly discouraged. It is easier for a child to overcome the difficulties described than to write with the non-preferred hand. Hooton (1976), however, has observed that occasionally children are found writing with their left hands for some social reason (for example, everyone else in the family does) or possibly due to mixed laterality (i.e. dominance of either right or left hand is unclear) and are experiencing difficulty in executing letters, when really they have right-hand dominance. In these cases a change of hand is advised at least for an experimental period. Close observation of a child's natural handedness in other tasks and tests for mixed laterality might reveal this possible source of trouble. Normally, however, left-handed writers adapt fairly easily to the English writing system. Cole (1939, 1946) and more recently Clarke (1974, 1975) have written about the problems of those who write with their left hand and make suggestions for this help based on an analysis of their difficulties. Three main points emerge from their writing concerning help for left-handed writers; the position of the paper, the grip on the writing tool and the nib of the pen (if one is used).

The paper should be placed so that the bottom right-hand corner is nearest the body. The pen should be held at least one or one-and-a-half inches up the stem so that the child can see what he is writing, without having to adopt an awkward wrist position. The nib of the pen should be broad, preferably with a turned up point or bulbous end. It is possible to have a nib cut reverse to oblique. Some ball-point pens are suitable for left-handers.

Writing styles

Various styles of handwriting and their suitability for the needs of handicapped children must now be considered. It must first be remembered that a child will always adapt a style of handwriting according to personality. Indeed, a whole 'science' has been made of studying character in handwriting, although we do not consider this a serious scientific pointer to personality.

Nearly all schools start children writing with manuscript or 'printing' style. The advantages of this style are that:

1. it most clearly resembles the printed word;
2. the straight line, the circle and spacing forms on which printing is based are more in accordance with motor and hand–eye–arm co-ordination of the young child than are the complex movements of cursive writing systems;
3. it is easily legible.

This style is usually abandoned at some point in the junior or middle school in favour of a joined or italic script because it is generally considered to be too slow for a child's growing need to write at length and speedily. The research evidence available does not support this general supposition. In the few published experiments (Hildreth, 1945) adults and also children in their teens, who have used only printed style, have written just as fast as those who used cursive script. It seems that children using printed scripts may be slower than those using joined scripts but by adolescence there is little difference in speed. More research on a wider scale is needed to verify this tentative conclusion, for we may be unnecessarily forcing children to learn two forms of script – a futile effort and a waste of time. This point must be considered in teaching disabled children, who have to be taught so many things which are easily learned by most able-bodied children that the time spent in formal learning must be planned to the child's greatest advantage.

For an adult, at present, a cursive script is socially more acceptable than a printed one as it suggests greater maturity in the writer. Marion Richardson (1975) method and style is one commonly used in schools because the style is clear and closely resembles printed forms. The disadvantages are that a few letters, such as b, f, p, z and x, have to be relearnt (although some teachers consider that a new form of b and p is an advantage as it reduces reversal error); letters with descenders, such as g, j, p, q, y, are not joined, and capital letters, which closely resemble printed forms, cannot be joined to the rest of the word. These two facts may compel a child to keep stopping and starting, which may hinder a child with poor perceptual–motor control or poor concentration. As it is an upright style, a child with a tendency to write with a backwards slope has no encouragement not to do this. On the other hand, if the Marion Richardson style is taught properly, according to the original teacher's manual, emphasis is placed on writing patterns, encouraging flowing penmanship and on the basic association between drawing and writing. Pleasing results can be obtained from this style.

For those who have difficulty in writing, a new style was produced by Mullins, Turner, Zawadski and Saltman in 1972 – the Model Script. This is effectively the printed characters joined together and it avoids the disadvantages of the Marion Richardson style, namely the lack of join in some lower case letters and the need to learn new forms of lower case letters.

As the new style emphasizes forward slant, it is more difficult to lapse into backward slant. Every word begins with a downstroke. Other similar styles have been produced in recent years (Alston and Taylor, 1987). The Nelson style of handwriting is gaining popularity. It also has patterns to practise, but all the letters are similar to those in print. Letters with descenders and odd letters like X, S and Z do not join. The link between print and joined-up writing is very close in this style, and it is claimed the transition from one to the other can be made quickly and easily. This should help physically disabled children.

Traditional cursive writing is still taught and can be very pleasing. As an art form it is effective. It is taught at a later stage than other forms because it requires more skills. Some remedial teachers maintain that a change from printed to cursive writing helps weak spellers and there is less confusion of letters. There is a movement to teach children cursive script from the beginning without going through the stage of teaching them to print. This is what was done in the early part of this century, when the school curriculum was, for most children, narrower than it is today and much time was spent on practising handwriting. The authors remain to be convinced on the advisability of this method for children with physical and/or learning difficulties.

In recent years italic writing has been introduced in schools. This has the advantage of resembling the 'printing' style so that children can adapt to it very early and easily. Well done, it is a beautiful art form. Poorly done, it is a mess. Children should not be started on this style unless their hand control is such that successful mastery of the style is certain. Italic writing also has the minor disadvantge of needing a special nib.

There is no reason why an enterprising teacher could not adapt a style for the individual needs of a pupil, incorporating the advantages of one style but avoiding its disadvantages. For example a child could be taught to put loops on the y, g, q and z of Marion Richardson script if a clear style were needed but the child found unjoined letters in a word distracting. An excellent short discussion of the general teaching of handwriting, including techniques of display, has been written by Dean (1968).

Alternatives

There are in schools a number of physically disabled children who do not possess the motor co-ordination necessary to use a writing implement effectively with their hands. Some are without hands or arms. Some children, for example a few of those affected by limb deficiency and some spastic children, are able to use their feet as alternatives to hands with which to write or draw. It is often found, however, that children with cerebral palsy, particularly those with athetosis, are unable to use any writing tool with hands or feet. A typewriter or other machine may be used if no other method of writing is possible. Careful assessment of manual ability should be made when a child has mastered some elements of reading, has had the opportunity to use brush or pencil and needs to be able to express his/her ideas in some form of writing. Despite his inability to write, Christy Nolan, the Irish author, won the 1987 Whitbread literary award for his book, *Under the Eye of the Clock,* with the aid of an adapted typewriter.

In recent years there have been enormous advances in information technology. The development of the electronic typewriter incorporating display, corrective devices and memory; the word-processor; the micro-computer with enlarged display and print-out are all examples of this. These improved methods of recording and output make the mastery of the traditional keyboard of greater importance than formerly.

A number of subskills are required to use a keyboard efficiently. These are:

1. ability to see and perceive the shape and orientation of the letters on the keys of the keyboard and the printed character once it has been typed. If a child needs to copy or work from a book, he/she has to be able to see the original material, the keys and the typed output;
2. sufficient hand–eye co-ordination to select the appropriate key and direct the hand to the desired key;
3. sufficient motor control to press the desired key;
4. adequate memory to learn and reproduce the correct sequence of letters to spell the words required.

With reference to item (1) above, the disadvantage of most keyboards is that the upper case or capital letters are written on the keys. This means that the child has to transpose from one form of character on the keys to another, i.e. the printed form, which is reproduced in the typewritten script. To help a child it may be necessary to cover the keys of a typewriter with the appropriate lower case letters until the child has become used to the machine. However, capital letters have to be learned. Some teachers of physically disabled children, however, have found that this transposition presents no problems.

Normally a child needs to be able to direct voluntarily a chosen thumb or finger to use a typing machine efficiently. It has been found possible, when a child has been able to use his/her head only, to fix a protruding attachment or 'beak' to a headband, and the child has been able to type using its head. The teacher and the physiotherapist or occupational therapist together should decide if a child needs a typewriter and of which kind. A physiotherapist can also advise exercises to improve manual strength and co-ordination which will aid writing and typing skills.

One school of thought, supporting the Peto method (described in Chapter 14), totally rejects the idea of any form of typewriters, and by means of carefully graded exercises systematically trains children to be able to hold and guide a writing tool. To be successful, this training must start when a child is about three years old and be followed rigorously for several years. In Britain, where the program has been tried experimentally in one or two schools only, it is difficult to judge its success.

For some children, even an electronic typewriter is useless and more sophisticated means must be employed. One major advance in electronic technology is the development of the POSSUM machinery. This can be used by severely disabled people to control their environment in various ways, for example, switching on the television and opening doors by electronic means using a controlled movement of any part of the body to do this. Part of the equipment is a large illuminated grid showing letters which makes it useful in schools with children with severe physical disabilities. This grid reflects either pressures from a joint or muscle or sucks and puffs from the mouth. A letter is chosen, a light is guided to the required point on the grid by a series of pressures or sucks and puffs, and when the light is allowed to stop at a letter, that letter is printed by an electronic typewriter in the normal way. The main disadvantages are that the process is slow and the user cannot always easily see what has been written.

Adaptations whereby whole phrases are written by one action are a welcome development. The concept keyboard enables children with very limited movement to touch an area on a board and whatever is written and recorded on that area is displayed on a computer screen and can later be printed.

The development of the micro-chip has enabled the invention of small hand-sized devices for communication by severely manually disabled people. The micro-writer, for example, is a small, portable device with a memory facility which can be interfaced with a micro-computer with all the peripherals. This differs from a keyboard machine as it is designed to be operated from the fingers of one hand in a 'chord' technique.

For physically disabled children, use of other mechanical aids such as cassette recorders in school can reduce the necessity for writing. It is particularly important that disabled children learn to express themselves verbally both clearly and concisely; speaking into a recorder will aid this. Practice in using the telephone in as many situations as possible is also essential for physically disabled children, as the telephone is a modern substitute for written correspondence. Replica telephones with connection wires can be bought in Britain from the Post Office.

Writing as an art form or craft can engender interest and give satisfaction to disabled children who may dislike other forms of art. This is a source of pride and pleasure to children to whom achievements are rare. Amazingly good results can be achieved by children who may have deformed hands but whose grip and fine motor control are good.

Little research has been done on handwriting in relation to physically disabled children. Anderson (1975), among other things, compared handwriting performance of spina bifida children with that of normal children. She matched her subjects for age, IQ and socio-economic status. She found that, on the whole, spina bifida children did worse on a handwriting test than did other children used as controls and that performance by spina bifida children on the handwriting test was more closely related to IQ and other perceptual–motor tests than it was for normal children. Children affected by epilepsy, muscular dystrophy and brittle bones may experience difficulties with handwriting. The effect of drugs, temporary loss of consciousness and weakened muscle control are factors which will affect hand control and speed of writing.

With the renewed interest of the education authorities in handwriting, we hope that this deficit in research will shortly be remedied.

9

Spelling

What is spelling? It is the use of conventional symbols as an aid to the reproduction of the spoken word. To spell correctly one must normally be able to hear speech, to have learnt the written form, retain that in one's mind and then recall and reproduce it accurately. Each of these processes involves complex actions and failure in any one of them will affect spelling performance. More will be said about specific difficulties later.

Most people, however, whether quick or slow-learning, able-bodied or disabled, find the spelling of English difficult. The main cause of the difficulty seems to be that English spelling is irregular, i.e. there is no correlation of either one-to-one sound/letter or sound/letter combination. There are historical reasons for this. Old English spelling in the tenth and pre-Conquest eleventh centuries was fairly regular and had two extra letters denoting the voiced and unvoiced 'th' sound. After the Conquest in 1066, Norman scribes, misunderstanding the existing convention, wrote English as best they could within their own convention, without the two extra letters, causing orthographic chaos. Added to the Norman French influence, down the ages there have been many influences on spelling: different dialects, including the effect of Scandinavian settlement in the North; anomalies caused by foreign printers and the effect of phonetic changes such as the Great Vowel Shift. This was a complex phonetic change which took place in southern England between the time of Chaucer and Shakespeare. Under certain conditions, some vowel sounds 'shifted', i.e. the sound of the vowel was made further forwards in the mouth thereby affecting pronounciation, while the spelling in many words remained the same. An example of this is BOAT (shifted) and BOAR (unshifted). Originally they were pronounced in the same way. Vocabulary introduced at the time of the Renaissance, based on Latin and Greek, and foreign vocabulary from trade and Empire, brought in fresh spelling conventions, which exist alongside native forms. These were incorporated into English spelling which was not standardized until the second half of the eighteenth century. Latterly there has been the influence of American spelling. The result of all this has been an interesting if apparently confusing orthography.

Nevertheless, as Albrow (1974) has pointed out, there is no necessity for writing systems to be related to phonology at all. The Chinese system is an example. In fact, the more recent the writing system, the more closely related to speech it is. For example, languages of the Amazon jungle recently translated are purely phonetic. Albrow has hypothesized that there are in present-day English fairly logical systems in spelling. By noting the environments in which symbols (i.e. certain letter patterns like ph, ch) have various correspondence, together with the grammatical and lexical status of the items concerned, regularities can be found in our writing system which may not be at first recognized (Albrow, 1974). The implication for teachers is that they should not tell children that a particular letter or sequence of letters 'spells' by nature a particular type of sound basically (e.g. 'a' represents the sounds in 'hat' or 'hate') and everything else is an exception, but rather that letters of the alphabet have many and varied jobs to do, each equally valid and important (Albrow, 1974). The child is therefore prepared to meet different combinations of the same letters and to try out alternatives of sound when meeting a new word; and is also ready to take context into consideration.

The idea, however, that the apparent irregularity of English spelling is a main cause for difficulty in reading and therefore writing, and the subsequent call for simplified spelling has a long history and dies hard. Does simplified spelling affect reading, itself a necessary preliminary of spelling? The National Foundation of Educational Research (NFER) wanted to see if children learning more regularly spelt languages made quicker progress in learning to read and write in their own language than those learning apparently irregularly spelt languages.

The National Foundation also wanted to see if the way in which a language was spelt was taken into account when deciding upon methods of instruction, and whether spelling had influenced these methods. Accordingly, education authorities and educationists, in more than 30 countries, chiefly European, were approached for information on reading instruction and achievement. (The results were, on the whole, inconclusive.) More recent research (Read, 1986) has revealed similar spelling difficulties in more regularly spelt languages than English. The NFER also examined other effects of spelling on reading in English. Six different junior–mixed and/or infant schools in London were visited, one girls' secondary modern school and three English-speaking schools in western Ireland. The schools were all in working-class areas. The schools chose the passages to be read. The researchers found that, on the whole, less regularly spelt words caused more difficulty than regularly spelt words. In another experiment, ten nonsense words were dictated to groups of children who were asked to write them down in their own way as if they were real words. It was found that children in general did not relate certain groups of letters (graphemes) with certain sounds (phonemes) irrespective of context (Lee, 1972). Obviously, much more evidence is needed before we simplify English orthography for educational reasons.

There has nevertheless been one attempt at regularizing English spelling and that is the Initial Teacher Alphabet (i.t.a.), an alphabet designed to help children to learn to read. It contains 44 instead of the usual 26 letters, to represent the 40 sounds in English. There is no q or x. An example of i.t.a. is:

“Whær ʃhall wee chauk?” askt peeter.
'Where shall we chalk?' asked Peter

What is the effect of this on children's spelling as contrasted with the effect on children's reading? Two questions arise:

1. Does i.t.a. with its sound/letter relationship facilitate spelling when children write in it?
2. Does it confuse or help children when they transfer to traditional orthography?

In a study by Warburton and Southgate (1969) the conclusion drawn from verbal evidence of teachers, advisers and schools inspectors who had dealings with i.t.a. as regards spelling were as follows:

1. Infant teachers and all knowledgeable visitors to the schools were generally of the opinion that the use of i.t.a. for writing had enormously simplified the task of spelling for children.
2. No infant teacher expressed the view that once they had made the transfer to traditional orthography, children who had been taught by i.t.a. were less able spellers than children who had used traditional orthography from the beginning.
3. The small amount of evidence on the spelling ability of junior children showed there was no clearly observed deterioration in the spelling of children who had learned to read and write with i.t.a. and later transferred to traditional orthography, although such a result had originally been widely feared (Warburton and Southgate, 1969).

How many of these children would have learnt to read and spell early anyway is unknown.

In recent years i.t.a. has largely gone out of fashion and is now rarely taught in schools. With the introduction in England and Wales of the National Curriculum (1989) and English being a core subject, it is doubtful that i.t.a. will return in popularity. It can, however, be taken as an example of simplified spelling.

The opinion of those whose work involves the teaching of spelling is important, but it must be supported by evidence before it can be considered seriously. Peters (1970) tested for spelling proficiency, by a standard spelling test and a diagnostic test, two groups, each of 69 eight-year-old children. One group was taught by a rigorous look-and-say method, the other an equally rigorous phonic method. She compared the results. She then gave the same tests to 115 children taught by traditional orthography and 115 taught by i.t.a. and compared these results. This experiment also gave evidence for the debate on whether phonic or look-and-say methods help or hinder children's spelling. The subjects were matched as far as possible for IQ, social and economic status, sex and age. She concluded that the use of no one method was superior in overall spelling achievement of children: however, differences of method or medium led to differences of perception which were reflected in the types of errors made.

Peters suggests that children who find spelling difficult and have been taught by look-and-say are restricted in their learning because they have visual but no rational reference: those taught by phonic methods are able to make a reasonable attempt at spelling a word which may well be a homophone (words pronounced alike but differing in meaning as hair, hare), while children taught by i.t.a. have a basic structure from which English spellings can be developed (Peters, 1970).

This research reveals important implications for remedial teaching. A teacher of remedial English would do well to find out the method by which a child has been taught and supplement it by other methods. If taught by look-and-say, try phonics: if by phonics, try look-and-say: if taught by i.t.a., try both. It must be remembered that most teachers teach children to read by an eclectic method rather than by a single defined means.

The question arises whether a child, having once learnt to read, needs specific teaching of spelling to achieve spelling success or whether it will be acquired on maturation: in the words of a teacher, 'with sufficient enrichment in the form of the spoken and read word (provided that this is sufficiently active, emotional and meaningful)'. In short, is spelling caught or taught?

As a result of her research in Cambridge schools, Peters selects the following as being possible teaching approaches to aid spelling: apart from talk, being read to, and reading, all of which engender interest in word forms, the essential elements to be taught are:

1. awareness of common letter sequences and the probabilities of these occurring;
2. the increase in the span of apprehension of letter sequences which necessarily involves:
   (a) the use of imagery;
   (b) certainty of formation of letters in writing;
   (c) swift handwriting.

Peters tested children in the beginning of their school year in junior schools in Cambridge for spelling by means of a standardized spelling test and a dictation test. She followed their progress and retested two years later. Peters came to the following conclusions:

1. Children with high verbal IQ and social and economic status scored initially better than less favoured children but over the two years the less favoured, by regular, systematic teaching and testing had more or less caught up.
2. The teacher's approach was of paramount importance: total time spent on spelling, regular marking of spelling errors, testing and learning tests, and drawing attention to combination frequency resulted in proportionate spelling progress. So did the practice of handwriting with a view to increasing speed.
3. Lists based on children's writing needs were more effective than published word lists.
4. Children whose teachers did not believe in specific spelling teaching progressed least or even retrogressed. (For further discussion see Peters, 1970.)

Peters was testing children simply for spelling. She did not examine creative writing. Some of the most interesting written work done by children in the eight-and nine-year stages will have very poor spelling, for it is often the quick reader who has raced ahead in the infant stages and has much to tell who is not going to accept a brake being put on his/her need for self expression. An example of lively writing by a boy describing a visit to a fair ground: '. . . then I went on the octopuse which is licke a sorspen lid that has just finisht topaling.' (Then I went on the octopus which is like a saucepan lid that has just finished toppling.)

It is our feeling that although a child should be encouraged to be adventurous with words and not be afraid of being wrong, it is unkind to let a child continue to think that incorrect spellings are correct. From children's writing, word lists can be evolved and used successfully, as Peters indicates. Moseley (1974) from his research puts forward the view that ability to master the full range of spelling conventions is largely independent of vocabulary development.

A study by Personke and Yee (1971) comparing spelling achievements of matched Scottish and American children showed that the Scottish children performed significantly better, especially in the lower range of ability. The reason was thought to be a more formal and direct approach to spelling. Personke and Yee have also produced a model of the spelling process, which many teachers find helpful.

It seems therefore that children can be helped to achieve spelling success and that it would be profitable to try to help children who have special difficulties.

There are numerous books and schemes now published for helping to teach spelling (Todd, 1982). Most of them concentrate on word lists and spelling rules, and provide activities for practice and memorizing them. A few involve parents (Nichols, 1980; Jeffs, 1985). Computer programs have been devised to help teach spelling. (There are now programs which correct spelling recorded in a word-processor but they relate only to American English.) Research has shown, however, that mastery of sound-to-letter spelling rules, though basic to spelling ability, is not by itself sufficient to make a good speller. Alone it can bring one to only a moderate level of achievement (Frith, 1980). One needs to acquire sufficient knowledge of language to be able to recall words letter by letter.

To spell one must be able to read. To do this one must have adequate visual perception to distinguish between the different letters of the alphabet. This is what brain-damaged children (for example, those with cerebral palsy) frequently cannot do. It has been mentioned that some brain-damaged children find it hard to distinguish between figure and background. Others cannot reproduce shapes or patterns (Vernon, 1961). All these limitations in perception will be reflected in difficulty in perceiving the lines and curves which constitute the printed word.

Certain types of brain damage in adults have been shown to affect ability in previously good spellers (Kinsbourne and Warrington, 1964). Different types of brain damage have been shown to produce different types of error. Some patients suffering from what was apparently a disorder in language functions made different errors from those who had difficulty in processing information in spatio–temporal sequences (i.e. putting things in the right order). From this it follows that children with certain types of brain damage may have difficulties in processing information which will be reflected in their spelling.

One useful diagnostic test of language difficulties is the Illinois Test of Psycholinguistic Abilities. Administered by trained psychologists, it can be used for children from ages 2 to 10 years. The revised ITPA consists of 12 sub-tests covering the three main abilities needed for language usage, namely decoding (receptive process), association (organizing process) and encoding (expressive process) (Kirk *et al.*, 1968). It is particularly useful for diagnosing language difficulties in brain-damaged children. From the diagnosis, remedial programs can be planned. Hart (1973) carried out an ITPA remedial language program on 18 children. Pre-testing scores showed a mean retardation of three years in language development. After seven weeks the experimental group made an average gain of 13 months in language and 9 months in reading. The control group made 'only normal' progress. When the control group was given language training, identical gains in lanaguage age were achieved. Hart argues that the ITPA's claim 'to provide a diagnostic instrument which leads to clues for remediation' is valid.

Here are a few examples of children's work showing their difficulties with spelling:

Child A
Aged 14. At normal primary school up to 11 years.
Speech problem. Hemiplegic.
WISC Verbal 87. Performance 55.
Original work typed.

In 1973 we had kinkjan was it offer and the magers sein that the man who was in nueas and he was or the way out of course on the shep to the couns of the Austion nea Path. Back in the Amaers the was a sash paty to see if the man was near the pordey of Amaers and the costin

Corrected and revised version
In 1973 we had a message in the office. It was Kojak's office and the message said that the man was in New York and he was on the way out of the country on the ship to the country of Australia, near Perth. Back in America there was a search party to see if the man was near the border of America . . .

Comment
The boy is muddled in his story and his spelling. His speech difficulty is reflected in words like Kinkjan – Kojak, offer – office, Austion – Australia. There are sequencing errors: magers – message, and in the order of the first sentence. In this case a program based on the results of an ITPA test might be appropriate.

Child B
Aged 10. Athetoid. Speech Problem.
WISC Verbal 108. Performance 71.
Original work typed.

wesn a poner timethere was a squirr it was bron on it lived up a rev old tree the squirr leve nest he wesn aman cam wif a gun the squirr sed dont shoot me acoos i woot shoot you sed the man you are a derd little squirr

Corrected and revised version
Once upon a time there was a squirrel. It was brown and it lived up a very old tree. The squirrel loved nuts. (He) Once a man came with a gun. The squirrel said, 'Don't shoot me!' 'Of course I won't shoot you,' said the man. 'You are a dear little squirrel.'

The trip to the aquarium
. . . wen we wnt in it wos drck it hat little lis in it we cod hear the pims rarth like the typewrit . . . i hlop i go a gen one day it is cyit therer.

Corrected and revised version
When we went in, it was dark. It had lights in it. We could hear the pumps, rather like the typewriter . . . I hope I go again one day, it is quiet there.

Comment
If one is familiar with the Devon dialect, one can understand this. The boy's speech problem is reflected in the omission of the ends of some words. There are also errors in sequencing: next – nuts, rev – very. These pieces were typed so it is possible a few errors were made by hitting the wrong keys. Many words are spelt phonetically, in the way he would say them. 'acoos', wif, a poner.

Child C
Aged 10. Had home teacher previously. Totally dependent. No speech. This was done (the original) with a 'beak'.
Original work typed.

Jack and the Beansturk
Jack woas all a lon with his Mummy. they did not have einy muney. hes Daddy was ded. They had a cow. Jack sid hes Mummy we will have to sel uer caw. Jack tok the caw to market. on the way to market he bumped in to a man. the

man sid where are you going wer that caw. Jach sid I am going to maret with it. if i gif you sum beans they are magıc beans. He took thim home. his mummy took the bens and threw thime out of the window. In the moren they bekam a benstork. Jack went on it. Jack climde and klimde up to the top. when he got there he saw a road.

Comment

This boy is intelligent in spite of his disabilities. It is easy to understand what he means. Many words are spelt as he would understand they would be said – klimde, sum, ded, muney, einy, bekam. It is possible that with systematic spelling instruction, this boy's spelling would improve considerably. There are no sequencing errors and he has the sequence of the story correct.

There is evidence that in most people the left hemisphere of the brain is used for language. It follows, therefore, that damage in this part of the brain may affect language and subsequently spelling, especially if this damage has been caused by accident at an age when language functions have already been established. Although recovery of speech functions in infants with brain injury is greater than in adults, learning disorders and retardation in intellectual development often follow. If brain damage occurs at an earlier age compensation may be established and language functions served by the right cerebral hemisphere. Marcel (1980) has described certain spelling errors made by patients with left hemisphere damage. Similar errors are made by children retarded in reading and many adult illiterates.

The evidence that there are physiological sex differences in parts of the left hemisphere, certain key areas for language function and laterality for language being generally better developed in girls than in boys, has been discussed previously (Buffrey and Gray, 1972). This may help to explain the relative superiority of girls over boys in certain aspects of the use of language, such as the verbal parts of intelligence tests. It may also explain why more boys than girls need remedial help in reading and spelling.

Present opinion tends to consider theories linking spelling disability to inadequate functioning in parts of the brain, without implying any structural damage, change or abnormality.

Just as people can and do vary greatly in physical stature and consequently in physical ability, so they can vary in sizes, shapes and organizations of the different parts of their brains, with the consequent differences in levels and patterns of cognitive, i.e. mental abilities (Nelson, 1974).

The best-known spelling disorder is commonly called 'dyslexia'. Much has been written on this subject and many differing opinions have been expressed varying from the assertion that dyslexia is a form of brain damage, to the rebuff that it is 'a disease of the middle classes' and 'exists only in the minds of over-anxious parents'.

Whether there is medical evidence for its existence or not, there do seem to be a number of children, otherwise intelligent, to whom the written word means nothing and whose attempts to reproduce it are highly bizarre. These children are not emotionally disturbed or suffering from any recognizable brain damage, the presence of either of which might help explain their difficulty. One can understand, for the spelling of 'saucer', how a child might write 'sauser' or 'sorcer', but surely not 'scaed' and 'sloy' and 'spiendce'? (Peters, 1970).

Vernon (1970) suggests that there are two types of dyslexia: the first is a disorder of language, possibly some form of dysphasia (impairment in speech); the second and more interesting type is, according to Vernon, characterized by some impairment of visual perception and memory. Children of the first type have spelling retardation accompanied by reading retardation, tend to have histories of delayed speech development, weaker verbal than non-verbal abilities, and make the sort of spelling errors which are consistent with language dysfunction (e.g. phonetic inaccuracies of the type shown to characterise the spelling errors of adult dysphasic patients). The second type of child has a spelling retardation but adequate reading ability. These children do not have a significantly lower verbal IQ than performance IQ on the WISC test and they make significantly fewer phonetically inaccurate errors in their spelling than do their contemporaries with reading retardation. Of the second type, the causes of difficulty are still largely a matter for conjecture.

One difficulty seems to be in perceiving the differences between letters, especially b and d. There is also difficulty in sequencing letters, for example 'asw', 'saw' and 'wsa' are interchangeable; possibly some fault in the child's complex memory system causes error. Perhaps the child is scanning incorrectly.

Those children who have difficulty in reading as well as spelling often find it hard to relate letters to sound. Crosby and Liston (1968) advocate much time spent in letter discrimination, with a strong emphasis on phonic training for children with difficulties in perception and relating sound to letters. This method was used by one of the authors with a girl of 13 years who, although she otherwise seemed of average intelligence, was backward in reading and whose writing, i.e. spelling was nonsensical. Using Schonell's spelling list, and by going right back to the beginning, the girl began to make slow but steady progress in reading and spelling. This emphasis on phonics would not be advisable, though, with a child who had difficulty in sequencing, i.e. putting letters in correct sequence. In such a case a more visual approach is necessary.

Cotterell (1974), who worked for some years at the Word Blind Centre in Britain, advocates the following teaching principles for helping children with spelling difficulties. Many of them follow on from the findings and experience of other writers mentioned in this chapter.

1. Whether a child's weakness is in visual or auditory recall it is a good idea to take the learning off the weak 'rote' memory and place it on the ability to reason.
2. No word that follows an expected pattern needs to be committed to memory as it can be worked out.
3. Long words are not to be feared as they can be divided into short manageable bits (syllables).
4. It must be understood that every word and every syllable always contains at least one vowel (except when y is used as a vowel as in by, why, cry).
5. Words should be thought of as a collection of sounds and syllables rather than separate letters. But alphabetical spelling, i.e. using the names not sounds of letters, is useful to help the weak visualizer master irregular words: in fact, as the child grows older, resorting to this technique often naturally circumvents the problem. If taught as suggested by Albrow (1974), the child will have been helped in his/her attempts.

6. To establish an association between speech and symbols it is all-important to train a child to vocalize (read it aloud) while writing. This helps avoid syllable omission.
7. Crossing out a complete word needs to be tolerated because it is always best for a word to be written as a whole and not crossed out in the middle with letters inserted. The latter results in a distorted picture and 'feel' of the word.
8. Teaching of the phonic structure of language needs to be systematic with a certain degree of overlearning and reinforcement through writing. Words containing like digraphs, prefixes and suffixes need to be taught together so that they support each other and aid recall.
9. When learning a difficult word, a child should be trained to look at it, cover it, and then write it from memory, vocalizing while writing. If the word is used in a sentence learning becomes meaningful.
10. A child should be trained to enter a word in an alphabetically indexed pocket notebook and to underline the 'tricky' part of the word that caught him/her out. It is then available for future reference. Encouragement should be given to devising mnemonics, as a verbal tag is frequently recalled more readily than the spelling of a word.
11. Many bad spellers find knowledge of the spelling rules helpful. This reduces the learning load as rules govern hundreds of words. Every teacher should be familiar with the rules so that they can be introduced as the spelling arises.

As well as the above-mentioned difficulties, poor auditory perception hinders accurate spelling. Often a clue to this imperception is given in a child's speech. A child in one of the author's experiences had suffered a hearing loss as a result of juvenile rheumatoid arthritis when she was learning to talk. The loss fluctuated for some years with the intermittent nature of the illness. At the age of ten she had only a slight resultant hearing loss but a marked speech defect. In her writing she persistently omitted the ends of words and confused certain sounds. A special speech therapy program was advised and devised, to be carried out by the teacher. Slowly but surely both her speech and her spelling improved. Here a knowledge of the child's medical history was essential in prescribing remedial work.

Cromer (1980) has analysed and compared spelling errors made by deaf and receptively aphasic children. Dodd and Hermelin (1977) however, have demonstrated by their ability to lip-read nonsense words that profoundly deaf children can develop a phonological code.

To aid remedial work it is essential to know what kinds of mistakes children make. Livingston (1961) tested 125 children aged 9–10 years using Schonell Regular and Irregular Word Lists and Schonell Graded Dictation Tests and found the rank order frequency of errors to be as follows:

1. Confusions – dimet (dynamite), colering (colouring)
2. Omissions – grond (ground), plese (please)
3. Insertions – takeing (taking), warter (water)
4. Transpositions – twinkel (twinkle), palying (playing)
5. Single for double – stoping (stopping)
6. Double for single – slopping (sloping)
7. Homophones – red (read), led (lead)
8. Perseveration – perpersevseveration

Glavin and de Givolamo (1970) compared types of spelling errors of 'emotionally disturbed' children with those of 'normals'. In two investigations both groups were matched on age, IQ and socio-economic status. In the first investigation the disturbed children made more errors than the normal controls. In the second study a different pattern of spelling errors between two subgroups ('conduct problem' and 'withdrawn') of emotionally disturbed children emerged. 'Conduct problem' children refused to attempt spelling more often than the 'withdrawn' children. The latter group reproduced significantly higher numbers of words with 'unrecognisable' spellings than children with conduct problems.

As well as Schonell's Word Lists and Dictation Tests, which are still a good guide to what can be expected of a child at a certain stage, Daniels and Diack's (1964) Graded Spelling Test is also useful. Peters (1975) has published a set of diagnostic dictation tests from which one can plan remedial help. There are many spelling programs now commercially available based on spelling rules and patterns. The Aston Index and Quest Programs provide assessment, diagnosis and remedial programs for children showing difficulties in expressing themselves in writing.

In our experience, children who are chronically sick but of average or above intelligence are often weak in spelling and make mistakes several years later than one would normally expect.

The children have had interrupted schooling and often seem to misapply spelling rules which they have only half understood, e.g.

Spelling	**Correct Form**
noes	nose (transposition)
thay	they (confusion)
mornning	morning (insertion)
sum	some (homophone)
don	done (omission)

These mistakes were made by children of 11, 12 or 13 years who had good average intelligence.

Sometimes these children write as they speak, having realized that there is some letter/sound correspondence, but in our opinion they lack the experience of seeing the word in its written form. For example:

Spelling	**Correct form**
clectid	collected
Satday	Saturday
dressd	dressed
finly	finally

These mistakes also were made by children of the lower secondary stage.

Dialect is another important factor for many children. If regional dialect, speech defect, brain damage and missed schooling are added together, it is not surprising that many children with physically disabling conditions have severe problems with spelling.

The lack of speed in handwriting which Peters found to be a significant feature of spelling success (if it is the cause of poor spelling rather than the effect) may be a source of spelling difficulty for physically disabled children. In writing a word, a child who is slow seems to lose the image of it in his/her mind. A painful condition such as juvenile arthritis (Still's disease) will slow down a child's writing speed. This point prompts us to look at methods of communication, such as typewriting for children (such as those affected by cerebral palsy, who are unable to write manually or can only write very slowly). If means of expression on a typewriter or POSSUM machine is too slow, spelling will probably be affected. Delayed feedback leads to inefficient learning according to operant learning theory. These points should be remembered and considered carefully in deciding whether a child should be given a typewriter or not. Attempts should be made to increase speed of communication and advances in information technology such as word-processors and microwriters are very welcome.

Partially sighted children often find difficulty in spelling. This may be because of the lack of visual feedback, and hence the child's inability to retain an image of a word in his/her mind. Here again modern technology is proving invaluable with developments such as closed circuit television. With this apparatus any writing can be displayed clearly enlarged on a screen so that a child can have the visual reinforcement of language so often previously lacking. The device can be used to aid a child's reading or his own writing. In addition, remediation on the lines that Cotterell suggests (1974) is often helpful for partially-sighted children.

In recent years the relationship between reading and spelling has been further explored (Frith, 1980; Jorm, 1983; Read, 1986). It has been shown that, though proficiency in a child's reading is often reflected in spelling, this is not always the case. A different set of skills is required. Interest has been shown in understanding the strategies needed for correct spelling. These are divided roughly into two groups – visual and phonological. Both are needed for spelling. Proficiency in either one exclusively leads to limited success. At different stages of language development, each is needed. Poor spellers often remain predominant in one approach. We know a little more about at what age and to what extent in what circumstances which strategy is most effectively used (Frith, 1980; Read, 1986). Our knowledge of the spelling process is growing but precisely how one learns to be a good speller remains a mystery.

National Curriculum (1989)

In England and Wales, spelling has been included as part of the English requirement of the National Curriculum (1989). Four Levels of Attainment are set out specifically for spelling. At Levels 5, 6 and 7 spelling joins with handwriting in presentation. Pupils are assessed from the basic Level 1, where they should be able to:

1. Begin to show an understanding of the difference between drawing and writing, and between numbers and letters.
2. Write some letter shapes in response to speech sounds and letter names.
3. Use at least single letters or groups of letters to represent whole words or parts of words.

Pupils learn through the various levels of 1–5 how to spell monosyllabic words, recognize word patterns, spell polysyllabic words, use correctly regular vowel patterns and common letter strings, become aware of word families and their relationships, use dictionaries and computer spell checkers.

At Level 6, pupils should be able to recognize that words with related meanings may have related spellings, even though they sound different (e.g. sign, signature); recognize that the spelling of unstressed syllables can be often deduced from the spelling of a stressed syllable in a related word (e.g. manager, managerial).

At Level 7, pupils should be able to spell (and understand the meaning of) common roots that have been borrowed from other languages that play an important role in word-building (e.g. micro, psyche); recognize that where words have been borrowed in the last 400 years, there are some characteristic sound–symbol relationships that reflect the word's origin (e.g. ch in French words like 'champagne', ch in Greek words like 'chaos', and ch in long-established English words like 'cheese'); check final drafts of writing for misspelling and other errors of presentation.

If pupils attain Level 7 by the age of 16-plus, the statutory school leaving age, they will be well grounded in the knowledge of the history of the language and adept in its usage.

Spelling is required nationally to be specifically taught. Many of the techniques suggested in this chapter are laid down in the guidelines for programs of study for 'helping children to master spelling conventions'. These are encouraging children to learn to spell words they collect and use themselves, the encouragement of visual memory, and the 'look, cover, write, check' technique. The use of spell-checker programs is advocated.

The National Curriculum (1989) was laid down in 1989 and the first cohort of children listed in 1991. It will be interesting to see how it affects the school population in the coming years. Technological aids are acceptable for each level of attainment for those who physically depend on them. It will also be interesting to see how far physically disabled and neurologically impaired pupils can progress without being 'disapplied', or the curriculum modified when there is an all-out attack on spelling and presentation in all schools nationwide.

Part Four

The organization of education

The last part discusses the philosophy behind attempts to educate disabled children, briefly traces the history of such education and describes the present provision for this, particularly in England and Wales. A description is given of conductive education, a special method originating in Hungary of educating severely physically disabled children. This incorporates many of the ideas discussed earlier in the book. A chapter is included describing briefly the situation in the USA, followed by a discussion of various influential American educationalists and psychologists. The education of the disabled in Sweden and Australia is also included as these countries with small populations have developed their resources in an interesting way.

10

Background history of special education

Until the eighteenth century people who would now be referred to as 'disabled' were regarded as some of nature's mistakes and were left to the care of hospital or church. In the late eighteenth century, however, from interest in the earlier work of the English philosopher Locke, a kind of intellectual curiosity about the disabled was aroused. In his *Essay Concerning Human Understanding*, Locke put forward the view that the mind possessed no innate ideas and that knowledge was derived through the senses. Locke argued that the way ideas were formed was essentially an inductive one, and that the process of learning was by observation and experiment, and through the application of stimuli to the senses. In the middle of the eighteenth century, the philosopher, writer and educationalist, Jean Jacques Rousseau, stressed the curiosity of the individual child as the source of learning, and prompted a new awareness of the child as a subject for scientific and intellectual study. Rousseau maintained that education should be based on the nature of the child, not on the requirements of an artificial society.

The influence of both these men was seen in the work of a French ear specialist, Jean-Marc Gaspard Itard (1775–1838) who studied a severely disabled child, Victor, and this pioneering study marked a growth in the educational treatment, as opposed to the custodial care, of disabled people. The intellectual curiosity of medical practitioners was presented with a challenge, hitherto unrecognized, and a tradition established from Itard can be seen in the individual studies, practice and research of doctors, teachers, educational administrators and educational psychologists.

Itard made a detailed study of Victor, 'the Wild Boy of Aveyron', and presented his findings to the French Academy in 1801 and 1806. The boy, a wild, deaf and dumb 'idiot' was discovered at about 11 years of age, in the forests of Aveyron, incapable of all but the most primitive animal responses. He had lived on acorns and berries and had been unexposed to any form of human society.

Itard took him into his care and began to train him systematically, using a technique of reward and punishment and of sensory stimulation. He attempted to socialize Victor, extend his concepts and ideas, and his awareness of people and events. He taught him language and gave him physical exercise, with the result that 'the biting, scratching boy' began to make some use of his senses, could remember, speak, write and count, though he could never be termed 'normal' as Itard had hoped he would.

The French Academy commented:

> The pamphlet of Monsieur Itard contains the exposition of a series of extremely singular and interesting phenomena, and fine judicious observations, and presents a combination of highly instructive processes, capable of furnishing science with new data, the knowledge of which cannot but be extremely useful to all persons engaged in the teaching of youth.

The important link which is made between science and education in these remarks, the notion that data could be accumulated which would be relevant in more than this one extraordinary case, the idea that the findings of a specialist could be of use to teachers, and above all the understanding that the skills of one discipline could interact with another were the origins of the twentieth century multidisciplinary concern for the disabled. The disabled were elevated from their inferior position of a minority group to one of increased importance.

11

England and Wales

In Britain the practice of caring for rather than educating the disabled has had deep roots. Until the late nineteenth century religious and charitable bodies predominated, establishing institutions and, in some cases, schools. A tradition of doing things cheaply prevailed, generated by the Poor Law, together with the notion that the poor and the disabled were so by virtue of their inherent wickedness. Men with noble intentions, like Thomas Cranfield the reformed dissolute soldier, John Pounds the crippled shipwright and the young medical student Thomas Barnado, attempted the redemption of delinquent and physically ill children who had been sold in pledge to their employers. They took these seven-year-old waifs from 16 hour days in tobacco or pin-making factories into cramped, airless classrooms where instruction in Christianity and 'the three Rs' for equally long hours was the order of the day. These 'Ragged Schools' and the notorious private schools at which Dickens directed his pen in Nicholas Nickleby were the educational norms for the poor and the unfortunate. The doctrines of 'self-help', of not pampering the children and of encouraging them to fend for themselves were often taken to an extreme. Dickens said of his representation of these schools, 'Mr Squeers and his school are faint and feeble pictures of an existing reality purposely subdued and kept down lest they should be deemed impossible.' Such treatment inevitably associated the disabled in general with a tradition of 'second best'.

The industrial revolution and social matters, like the fight for the right to vote at the beginning of the nineteenth century, occupied the nation to the exclusion of any major developments in education. It was not until 1870, with the advent of universal elementary education in Britain, that children with physical and intellectual disability, malnutrition and debility began to be noticed within the ordinary schools. It soon became apparent that there were some children who differed from their fellows by virtue of poor sight or hearing, physical or mental deformity, malnutrition and general ill health, and that the ordinary schools could not cater for them. It was then that the notion of education for the disabled began, but only as an afterthought in the wake of education for the normal child.

From 1895 onwards schools for what were termed 'defective' children were established, these children being defined as having imperfections of body or physiognomy, abnormal neurological responses, poor physical condition due to illness and poor nutrition, or mental dullness. Other categories were 'imbeciles' (children who, due to mental defect, were unable to be educated and become self-supporting) and the 'feeble-minded' (children who were unable to receive ordinary education but who were considered to be above imbecile standard). Entry to these schools was decided by a physical examination made by a doctor. As a rule conditions within the schools were poor because of overcrowding, lack of discipline and poorly paid staff employing inappropriate traditional teaching methods. This contrasts with Itard's ideas which could apply equally well to disabled and 'normal' children.

It is worth noting that in Britain as elsewhere in Europe, the blind and the deaf had been receiving education for over a century, largely through charitable organizations.

The neglect of the intellectually disabled and the very cursory attempts at educational provision for them at this stage need some explanation. The influence of Darwin's *Origin of the Species*, propounding the theory of the survival of the fittest, may have raised fears among the Victorians of the degeneration of the human race through the 'unnatural' selection of its weak and deformed members. Provision and care for these 'mistakes' in nature was interfering with and unbalancing the natural processes of human development. Indeed, Darwin's cousin, Francis Galton, advocated the segregation and sterilization of the intellectually disabled. His equation of eminence with intelligence, and his refusal to consider the environmental influences upon mental ability may be contrasted with the attitude and practice of Itard. Galton's contemptuous and cruel descriptions of even the mildly disabled as 'polluters of the noble stock of humanity, too silly to take part in general society but easily amused with some trivial, harmless occupation' was powerful discouragement for the already limited support for the education of such children. The long dark period of institutional and custodial care for the intellectually disabled began with the ideas of Galton.

Abroad, however, the disciples of Itard, Seguin, Montessori and Binet were displaying a robust optimism about the modifiability of intellectual disability that was finally to exert an impact upon the educational philsophy of that period. Seguin, for example, pleaded for 'the most rapid evaluation of the lowest and the poorest by all means and institutions, mostly by free institutions' and he advocated a social application of the principles of the Gospel in this matter. Binet protested 'against the limited pessimism' of the Darwinian and Malthusian attack on the perfectibility of human society. He established classes for intellectually disabled in which 'mental orthopaedics' in memory, logic, verbal attention and other related areas were offered and its effects systematically evaluated. Maria Montessori, herself a doctor, recognized that the needs of the disabled with whom she worked were pedagogical, not medical. She devised her own system based on the writing of Itard and Seguin, trained her staff in these methods, and, encouraged by her success with the disabled, applied her methods to ordinary children. The beginnings of an overlap in the methods of teaching for the disabled and the ordinary child here represented another powerful move towards the integration as opposed to the segregation of the disabled from the rest of the community. Indeed, the innovations derived from work with this minority have given teachers working with ordinary children greater insights.

The twentieth century in Britain saw the establishment of what we now call 'special education', based initially on the German model. The English elementary schools still contained in the standard classes a wide variety of children, some of ordinary ability, some partially sighted, some 'imbeciles', some delicate or physically disabled. In varying degrees these children truanted, misbehaved, were neglected and learnt very little. In Germany, however, the authorities had begun to provide for children who failed to progress after two years in the ordinary school. These children were seen by the head teachers of the ordinary and 'special' schools and by a doctor. The intellectually weak, who were poorly endowed in memory, perception and reason were admitted into the special school. The chronically disabled were not. In these schools, timetables were fairly free, much manual work was done and training for a useful activity was the main aim. In Britain, Alfred Eicholz, an inspector appointed to work in the field of special education, drew up some important recommendations in 1899 concerning disabled children, and anticipated the era of administrators and legislators in this field which culminated in the 1944 Education Act, a milestone in the history of education in England and Wales.

Eichholz defined three categories, 'the mentally deficient, the physically defective and the epileptic, and the physically and morally healthy' who were nevertheless retarded. Three suggestions were made. The first group should attend schools in the country where farm work was the main activity and the possibility of doing harm was reduced. (The moral inferiority of the mentally deficient was still universally believed.) The second group should attend at a healthy residential site, where good diet and medical supervision could be provided, and the last group should attend special day schools and return to the ordinary schools once their retardation had been overcome. Attendance at these schools would be from seven to 14, or 16 if wished, and would be compulsory. The very mildly physically disabled and epileptic were expected to attend ordinary schools. In the same year, a Bill in Parliament made the care of defective children necessary but not compulsory 'due to the difficulties and expenses of carrying out such care,' and by 1909, 133 out of 328 local education authorities had taken up their responsibility.

This period in the early twentieth century saw the provision of school meals and the creation of the school health service. These were some results of examining the many unfit recruits called up for service in the Boer War. The examination revealed an undernourished population.

It was not until 1944 that legislation specifically for the disabled was drawn up. Local education authorities now had to educate all children in accordance with 'age, aptitude and ability'. Any children suffering from a disability of mind or body were to receive special education. Special education thus became part of every local education authority's responsibility and not a separate requirement.

The 1944 Education Act defined eleven categories of disability. Special schools were to provide for separate disabilities, namely deaf, partially hearing, blind, partially sighted, educationally subnormal, physically disabled, maladjusted, epileptic, speech defects and delicate. (The severely subnormal did not become the responsibility of the local education authority, instead of the health authority, until 1971. A number of local authorities, however, had already made good provision before 1971). Provision was made for special education to take place outside special schools in separate classes in mainstream schools. Children in long-term hospital care were also to be educated. In all, an attempt was made to suit education to the individual child's needs.

As a result of the 1944 Education Act a system of special schools was set up, particularly in areas of high urban population, such as London. Many schools were generously staffed and financed and so local education authorities (LEAs) were reluctant to dismantle the system in later days when educational thinking had changed. Smaller, rural LEAs would send their pupils to schools established in more populous areas. This often involved residential schooling or travelling long distances.

There has always been a tradition of independent schooling in Britain for a minority of children, often involving boarding education. (The great 'public' schools such as Eton were mostly residential. Many famous schools were originally charitable foundations.) Parallel to the development of LEA-sponsored schools, there evolved after 1945, a number of schools founded for specific disabilities by new charitable organizations, such as the Spastics Society and the Association for Spina Bifida and Hydrocephalus. The pattern of physical disabilities was changing. More children with congenital and neurological disabilities, such as spina bifida and cerebral palsy, were entering the school population. Previous conditions caused by disease, such as poliomyelitis and tuberculosis, were disappearing. Often these new schools were set up in large houses in rural settings as spacious properties became available after World War 2. Special schools of all types which had been situated in inner cities, moved to the countryside. LEAs often paid the fees for disabled children to attend independent schools specializing in a particular disability. The system continues today. The educational philosophy justifying this was that disabled children needed fresh air and space; that boarding education made them independent; that children's specific needs could be best met if those with a particular disability were educated together.

Unfortunately, one result was that schools became isolated and, although much good work was done, all types of disabled children were cut off from the rest of society. The independence that children gained from living away from home was balanced by the lack of friends in their local community on their return, and the community's consequent reluctance to accept them as adults.

Interest was shown in Britain's special schools for the physically handicapped by the rest of the world, especially by those countries which were setting up systems of their own in the wake of independence from colonial rule. However, in spite of dedicated teachers, good facilities, physiotherapy, speech therapy, small classes, adapted buildings, little emerged as specifically appropriate educational methodology for motor and neurologically disabled children. The advances made by medical research were not being equalled by educational advance. What was being offered in many special schools was a watered-down version of mainstream teaching, often with reduced breadth and depth of curriculum. No modern Itard emerged. In British schools for the physically handicapped there developed no equivalent to the approach of conductive education being pioneered in Hungary. Even in special schools, the emphasis was often on the children's physical need, with many interruptions for various therapies, rather than educational attainment and critical evaluation of teaching methods. In the whole country only one postgraduate course was established to train teachers of physically and neurologically impaired children.

The immediate drawbacks of the 1944 Act, as regards special education, were the disruptive effects upon a child's education that moving between mainstream and special schools entailed, the frequent mis-categorization of children, insufficient provision by mainstream schools for special classes alongside regular classes, a still predominantly medical rather than educational reason for referral to special schools, and insufficient aftercare for the special-school-leaver. These issues, among others, have occupied administrators and educationalists in the last few decades.

It came to be argued that the categories of disability laid down by the 1944 Act needed modification, and that a wider category, based on learning disorder rather than medical definition, should be adopted. Children suffering from a variety of disabilities which would require a common education rather than medical treatment would then be grouped together. Evidence has shown that there is considerable overlap between disabilities, for example, over half of the cerebral palsied children have IQs below 70; there is considerable overlap between 'educational subnormality' and 'maladjustment', and the survey carried out on the school population of the Isle of Wight (Rutter *et al.*, 1970b) indicates that one in four children with a disability has additional disabilities. All practising teachers, doctors and educational psychologists will testify to the difficulties of categorizing children, with whom they work, under one single disorder. The advent of comprehensive education as an ideal and then a working reality also had its effect on the concept of special education. The 1944 Education Act reflected the thinking that children could be selected into different groups and educated accordingly in different types of schools: grammar, technical, secondary modern and special. With the British genius of arranging hierarchy, the public came to think of schools in that order of precedence inserting 'public', i.e. placing independent schools at the top and placing special schools at the bottom. This philosophy became outdated and it became less and less easy to justify separate education systems for minorities of all kinds, including the disabled and those with special educational needs.

Parents came to demand a greater influence in deciding how and where their chilren should be educated. The 1980 Education Act obliged schools to publish detailed information on their general school policy, discipline and examination results. School governing bodies were to include a proportion of parent governors. This Act paved the way for greater parent participation in special education. Voluntary organizations, some now long-established, wanted their contribution to be officially recognized and utilized. The unevenness of provision for 'handicapped' children over the country as a whole was constantly being deplored. Increasingly, intervention and support at the pre-school stage was being demanded.

The Warnock Commission was established in 1974 to report on special education in England and Wales. It produced its report in 1978. It made 250 recommendations introducing new concepts in education law. The report provided the basis for new legislation both in terms of philosophy and practical measures. The resulting 1981 Education Act amended key sections of the 1944 Education Act and became the central law governing special education in England and Wales. In 1983 it was supplemented by a set of Regulations which were concerned with the conduct and recording of assessments. Additionally Circular 1183 *Assessments and Statements of Special Educational Needs* was issued in 1983. (In Scotland similar legislation has taken place to ensure uniformity in the United Kingdom.) The 1981 Education Act came into force in 1983 (Cox, 1984). The government provided no extra resources to finance its implementation.

The 1981 Education Act can be briefly described under four headings.

1. **The concept of special educational need**
   Under the Act a child is deemed to have special educational needs if he or she has 'a learning diffculty which calls for special educational provision to be made.' Children have a 'learning difficulty' if they have significantly greater difficulty in learning than the majority of children of their age or if they have a disability that either prevents or hinders them from making use of educational facilities generally available to children of their age. Special educational provision is defined as 'educational provision which is additional to, or otherwise different from, the educational provision made generally for children in schools maintained by the local educational authority concerned'.

There is a subdivision of children with 'special educational needs.' One group remains the responsibility of the school. In practice these are roughly 18% of disabled children as mentioned by the Warnock Report, who were in mainstream schools anyway. The other group, roughly 2% who were mostly in special schools or special settings, are the responsibility of the local education authority who has 'to determine the special educational provision that should be made for them.' There is relatively little said about the first group. Schools are charged to 'use their best endeavours' to provide an appropriate education for them; teachers must be told about the special educational needs of their pupils and made aware of the necessity of providing for them. The second group must be formally assessed according to carefully laid-down procedures and the results communicated with similar strict adherence to rules.

The local authority is responsible for ensuring that all children with special educational needs are provided for at nursery school age, whether formal procedures have been invoked or not. Formal assessments can be started when a child reaches two years of age.

The concept of special educational need is important because the shift is from medical to educational criteria. A far larger proportion of children, hitherto ignored in legislation, have been included. Nursery provision is now legally deemed necessary for children with special needs.

2. **Provision in mainstream schools**

The mainstream school is declared to be the normal place of education for all pupils except in special circumstances. For those pupils attending the mainstream school, there is a duty placed on the school authority to ensure that 'the child engages in the activities of the school, together with children who do not have special educational needs'.

There are some exclusion clauses. The conditions are that account has been taken of the views of the child's parents and that educating the child in a mainstream school is compatible with:

(a) he/she receiving the special educational provision he/she requires;

(b) the provision of efficient education for the children with whom he/she will be educated; and
(c) the efficient use of resources.

3. **Identification and assessment**
For children whose educational provision remains the responsibility of the school, assessment should take place within the school, bringing in external specialists if necessary. Parents must be involved and informed at every stage. It should be an ongoing process designed to formulate class-teaching and monitor progress.

Where it is likely that the local authority will have to make special educational provision, a formal assessment will have to be made. This is done with very strict guidelines and will involve input from the school, medical, psychological and, where relevant, specialist sources. Parents are actively involved at every stage. If necessary, a Statement of Special Educational Need must be made which will specify the child's educational needs in detail and the provision made to meet those needs. Parents have the right to initiate the assessment procedure.

If there is disagreement, parents have a right of appeal to the Secretary of State for Education.

4. **Statements**
Local authorities are required to review the Statement every 12 months and inform parents of any changes made. If a pupil is still the subject of a Statement of Special Educational Need at the age of 14 years, a further assessment must be conducted when the child leaves full-time education.

The 1981 Education Act marked a milestone in special education. The whole emphasis of categorizing children and designating where they should be educated has altered. Parents have a positive, legal role to play. Voluntary organizations are brought in for advice. A multidisciplinary approach to assessment is assured and Statements of Special Educational Need are legally binding. Regular review is compulsory. Nursery education must be provided.

Local education authorities reacted at differing speeds to the new legislation and much remains to be effectively implemented. The lack of provision of extra resources has been a strong bone of contention. Nevertheless, children with special educational needs have legal backing for receiving a better deal than many received before the 1981 Education Act

DISCUSSION ON PRACTICAL IMPLICATIONS OF INTEGRATION

Pre-school provision for all children, as well as those with special educational needs is, in 1991, still patchy. There needs to be a great expansion of facilities. Some authorities have nursery schools which children with special educational needs are encouraged to attend. Some remaining schools for physically disabled children have nursery departments for assessment, as well as education. To quote the Isle of Wight survey (Rutter *et al.*, 1970b):

> Free play and an opportunity to experiment are valuable but on their own they are of little use to children who have not yet learned how to profit from such opportunities . . . Nursery schools must make deliberate efforts to provide 'specific' training which is appropriate in relation to the children's handicaps, whatever they are.

Which school?

Once disabled children have reached school age, it must be decided if it is possible to provide adequate facilities and sufficient support for them to attend their local school. If not, they may have to go to a school with more resources, further away.

Many factors determine the successful placement of a child.

1. **Practical consideration**
   It must be considered whether the child will be able to cope with the physical environment of the school – stairs, distance between rooms for lessons and moving about in

the classroom. Many questions must be asked. How much adaptation to a building is required? What special equipment and furniture must be provided? If the child is in a wheelchair, are the corridors and doors wide enough for it? Are there ramps? Does a lift exist or can one be installed? If not, can special facilities be provided without reducing provision for other pupils? If the child has spina bifida and attendant incontinence, problems will arise in a mainstream school unless special provision is made for toilet arrangements, both by way of extra toilets and staff to cope.

Has the child the physical ability to write and draw? If not, what other means of communication should be provided? Are facilities such as speech therapy and physiotherapy easily available or will much valuable time be lost from school in procuring them?

Would the provision of a welfare assistant enable the child to overcome physical problems?

2. **Personality and intelligence**

   If a child has a high IQ, and does not have personality problems, physical difficulties can usually be overcome. Many physically and neurologically impaired children, however, are by the nature of their disabilities, likely to have learning difficulties. It may well be that, unless there is remedial teaching help in some form, a child will be unable to cope in a normal-sized class in a mainstream school, and thereby encounter emotional difficulties. An anxious or withdrawn child may find it hard to settle happily in a large school, and may need extra adult support. Other members of the class should not be allowed to suffer if a child is disruptive or hyperactive, nor must a child be allowed to take up an undue proportion of a class teacher's time.

3. **Teachers**

   If a physically disabled child is to be placed in a mainstream school, the teaching staff must be properly prepared, and have access to advice and help from a specialist teacher of the disabled. Special equipment, if necessary, should be available for the class teacher who, above all, should be happy about receiving the child into the class. Few teachers in mainstream schools have had training in teaching children with physical and neurological disabilities. In-service training is necessary.

Special departments within a mainstream school can provide the right balance between integrated and special education. Children can attend the optimum number of regular class lessons, according to their ability. Relationships between the head teacher, department teacher and other school staff must be harmonious for this form of special educational provision to be successful. Nowadays in-class support is preferred to withdrawal, if possible, as this is more conducive to true integration.

4. **Special schools**
   Special schools, catering for children with physical and neurological impairment, are having to rethink their role in the education system. There will always be a few children who will need full-time support in a specialist setting. The schools can be adapted to become valuable centres for resources and expertise. Outreach services to mainstream schools can be developed. Special schools have proved that they can educate severely disabled children. They must now look forward to taking part in future developments in special education, in new and exciting ways.

   The National Foundation for Educational Research commissioned a survey of current practice on integration of children with special needs. For further reading see Hodgson *et al.* (1984), Hegarty (1987), Norwich (1990).

New legislation

In recent years there has been much legislation in Britain concerning the organization of education and the rights of children. Although it is too soon to see the effect of it all, there are a number of significant factors which might affect disabled children. A brief discussion follows of the most significant developments affecting children with special needs.

THE EDUCATION REFORM ACT 1988

National Curriculum (1989)

Every child, unless 'disapplied', must follow the National Curriculum (1989). Three subjects constitute the 'core' curriculum – English, mathematics and science. There are seven foundation subjects: history, geography, technology, physical education, music, art and later, a modern foreign language. There are four key stages, each of which has ten levels in a series of attainment targets, for every one of the ten subjects included. The three core subjects have standard attainment tasks (SATS) to be administered nationally when children reach certain stages in education – key stage 1 – end of year 2 (when most children have reached 7 years of age); key stage 2 – end of year 6 (11 years of age); key stage 3 –end of year 9 (14 years of age) and key stage 4 – end of year 11 (16 years of age). The last is to be merged with public examinations. Teacher assessment forms a large part of the assessment procedure. The National Curriculum (1989) will have an effect on disabled children both in mainstream and special schools.

Special schools are being forced to examine their curriculum. Some children with profound and multiple learning disabilities (PMLD) will be perpetually 'working towards key stage 1'. To avoid an exercise in absurdity, by trying to fit in basic activities to an attainment target, schools which have not done so already, are working out pre-level 1 stages and attainments, often within a group of other special schools working with similar children.

Standard attainment tasks are having to be modified. Groups of teachers are coming together nationally to do this, for example, those who teach visually impaired children have formed a committee acceptable to the body setting SATS nationally to achieve nationwide comparability of modifications for blind pupils.

Disabled children should have access to a full curriculum. The lack of this has been a criticism of the system in the past.

The negative aspect is that children may be forced into inappropriate activity such as sitting through lessons which are meaningless to them for the sake of appearances. Also, children with special needs may be forced to work at a pace not suited to their capabilities.

Local management of schools

The power and authority of the local education authority, the mainstay of English education, is being eroded. All but a small percentage of the financing of schools' budgets has been devolved to the schools themselves so that the headteacher and governors of each school can decide on staffing, equipment, maintenance, etc. This may militate against integrating disabled pupils, as they are costly in terms of staffing and adaptation and equipment if the integration is to be successful. On the other hand, enlightened headteachers and governors will not be held back in their spending on what they consider as beneficial to all the children in their school by including and properly supporting disabled children.

Peripatetic services may eventually have to be 'bought in'. This could go two ways. These services will have to look at what they are doing – no bad thing – and 'sell' themselves. Schools may, however, go ahead with inappropriate schemes without proper, informed advice, in the so-called interests of economy. Essential services to disabled children should not be subject to mere market forces.

Grant-maintained status

Schools may, with the permission of the Secretary of State, opt out from local educational authority control and become funded directly by central government. This may have the effect of excluding children with special needs because of their expense and 'lack of status'. Grant-maintained schools will compete for pupils with local authority schools, especially as it is now compulsory to publish public examination results, aims, activities and achievements.

Reform Bill

This Bill would allow state schools (and independent schools for pupils with special educational needs), to appoint their own inspectors. 'Recognized inspectors' would have to be approved by a reorganized Her Majesty's Inspectorate and could include people not connected with education.

It is important that those concerned with children with special needs voice their concern that such children are not rejected by schools; that their needs are met within schools, and that inadequacies are not 'covered up' by an inspectorate not fully experienced in and aware of the techniques which teaching these children requires. In fact, there might well be a case for establishing a special inspectorate for children with special needs.

Children Act 1989

In October 1991, the Children Act, a most far-reaching piece of legislation for the welfare of children, came into force. Provided that it is properly implemented (in spite of lack of funding like the 1981 Education Act), it should benefit children in all aspects of life: family affairs, procedures in courts of law, social welfare and educational provision.

The paramount consideration is the welfare of the child. Parental rights and responsibilities are also delineated as never before. Stress is laid on partnership with parents and the various official bodies.

One benefit of the Act should be the closer co-operation between social and educational services in providing facilities such as pre-school placement, care in after-school hours, provision for care in school holidays, matters arising with residential schooling, and other services for 'children in need'. Many children with special educational needs will be included in that group, especially if they have severe motor and neurological impairment.

Conclusion

There has been much legislation in the 1980s beneficial and helpful to children in Britain. In addition, the 1990s will see greater involvement in the expanding European Community. This, with the cross-fertilization of ideas, should bring even greater enlightenment as to how we can best educate all children, and those with special educational needs in particular. It is incumbent upon the educators of Britain to make the most of the opportunities now available.

12

United States of America

In the USA, children who, in Britain, are usually referred to as 'handicapped' are called 'exceptional', a term which includes gifted children. An exceptional child is defined by Kirk as 'that child who deviates from the average of normal child in mental, physical or social characteristics to such an extent that he requires a modification of school practices or special educational services in order to develop to his maximum capacity' (Kirk, 1962). This, however, is not a legal definition.

The relationship between local, state and federal powers in educational matters must be understood before one can appreciate the diversity of American special education from state to state as well as understanding the role which parents have played and are playing in the development of this special education. Variations occur not only between state and state but also between different localities in the same state. Generalizations cannot be made for the country as a whole except from the effects of specific pieces of federal legislation.

In 1642 the governing bodies of the Massachusetts Bay Company announced that each of its towns should select men to be responsible for seeing that members of the company were able to read and understand religion and the capital laws. In a few of these towns free schools were built and funds collected for the salaries of the schoolmasters, thereby establishing an historical precedent of local control in education. This local responsibility was well established by the time the Federal Constitution was adopted and each separate state then, as now, reserved the power to control the education of its young people.

Each state, through its constitution and/or laws, lays down

the powers of local government agencies. Each local educational agency then enforces those special powers and other powers necessitated by them. The federal government is unable to usurp the responsibility of the state for educational matters, although it is able to withold federal funds until a state has complied with certain minimum federally legislated standards.

It was not until 1867 that a federal Office of Education was established, and even then its function was limited to collecting information about and promoting the cause of education. The Office of Education has increased its powers over the years, slightly reducing local autonomy, and its functions now include the collection and dissemination of information, financial assistance and special studies and programs. Although theoretically the states are still independent in educational matters, they defy the federal government at the risk of being denied access to substantial financial funds and assistance.

For exceptional children the state or the local education authority provides a cost per child, per teacher or per classroom over and above the cost for each of those things for non-disabled pupils. This is primarily because special education inevitably demands a lower pupil–teacher ratio and is therefore more costly.

In pre-revolutionary America, people with psychiatric disorders and associated aggressive tendencies were considered to be criminals, and those without violent tendencies treated as paupers. People suffering from mental retardation were placed in one of three settings:

1. Confined to their own homes, with partial community support.
2. Placed in poorhouses.
3. Sold by auction to bidders who would maintain them at minimal public cost in lieu of work undertaken by the retarded. This latter practice ceased as a result of public outcries.

Before 1800 there was no provision for exceptional children in America; the mentally retarded were regarded, as they were elsewhere, as ineducable and were hidden away or left to their own devices (as was the 'village idiot' in Britain). As has been mentioned previously, Itard's contribution to the education and training of exceptional children arose directly from his inspirational work with the unfortunate 'wild boy of Aveyron'. Itard's influence was strongly felt by special educators in the early 1800s in the United States. Two outstanding workers were Thomas Hopkins Gallaudet who, in 1817, established the first school for the deaf on 'Asylum Avenue' in Hartford, Connecticut, and Samuel Gridley Howe, a physician, who founded the Perkins School for the Blind in Watertown, Massachusetts, in 1829.

These schools offered training but the 'care' aspect was also important; often disabled people spent their lives in these institutions. As early as 1871, however, Samuel Gridley Howe who had become a political and social reformer, envisaged the decline of the use of residential schools and a trend towards integrating exceptional children into the 'common' schools with 'common' classmates.

Another notable special educator was Edward Seguin, Itard's outstanding disciple and student. There was close collaboration between Gallaudet, Howe and others which led to the publication of Seguin's book, *Idiocy and the Treatment by the Physiological Method* in 1866.

During this period the impetus for setting up institutions for the mentally retarded was given recognition when Seguin became president of the Association of Medical Officers of American Institutions for Idiotic and Feeble-minded Persons. This organization was later named the American Association on Mental Deficiency, and is currently the American Association of Mental Retardation.

In the early 1900s the movement towards special classes in the public schools began. (In this section the term 'public' school is used in its American sense as 'one financed by public funds'.) This was brought about largely by the representation of parents on public school boards and it was recognized that children should be educated as close to their homes as possible.

The unscientific views of an influential psychologist, Henry Goddard, who 'traced' five generations of the Kallikak family's legitimate and illegitimate lines led to the most unfortunate consequences for generations. Goddard claimed in 1912 that the descendants of the legitimate line of the Kallikaks produced people with distinguished careers who were endowed with superior gifts and intelligence. On the other hand, the offspring of the illegitimate union were mainly of defective moral and intellectual make-up. Such views prompted the gravest fears among the law makers in several states and led to laws being enacted to sterilize 'mentally retarded and criminal people'.

Fortunately, the segregation of mentally retarded people was accompanied by the demand for special education programs and the need for special education teachers to help these people. It was during this period that the first special education college programs were established. The growth of towns, making the population less scattered, meant that special units could be more locally based. The number of public school programs for exceptional children has increased intermittently since then. The most dramatic progress has been made regarding educational provision, research and legislation on behalf of exceptional children in the 1960s and early 1970s.

In the 1960s provision was made for graduate fellowships for training people for a career in teaching retarded children (Public Law 85- 926) and for funds for preparation of teachers of the deaf (Public Law 87–276). These two laws set the scene for great advances in legislation for the education of exceptional children. By 1968 two Public Laws, 88–164, Title 111 and, as amended, 89–750, Title VI, provided federal funds to educational institutions for training personnel in special education, financial assistance to those being trained and direct aid to states for their special educational programs. Federal funds continued and were increased for research and experimentation. Many other Public Laws have provided funds which may be used for special education; for enterprises as diverse as libraries, captional films for the deaf and community health centres. Every Congress since the Eighty-fifth has passed laws benefiting exceptional children in some way.

Parental pressure groups were partly responsible for forcing this legislation to be passed. The success of the civil rights movement also had the side-effect of encouraging minorities, including those concerned with exceptional children, to push for amelioration of their legal position. The membership of societies working on behalf of exceptional children increased greatly in the 1960s. These had strong parental support. An example is the Council for Exceptional Children, one of the major professional associations. In 1963 membership was approximately 16 000. By April 1973, membership had grown to 48 000.

In 1970, President Nixon signed Public Law 91–230 – the Elementary and Secondary Education Acts, 1969, the Education of the Handicapped Act – which was to combine new legislation and existing legislation within a single statute. This new law covered such things as administration at federal level, financial and advisory provision for the states, training personnel to work with exceptional children, research and special programs for children with learning disabilities.

The next decade saw a tremendous increase in new provisions for exceptional children at state level. In some states the compulsory attendance laws had become the 'non-attendance laws' as the exclusion clauses were used against disabled children. Examples are: 'children with bodily or mental conditions rendering attendance inadvisable' (in Alaska), exclusion may occur (in Nevada) when 'the child's physical or mental condition or attitude is such as to prevent or render inadvisable his attendance at school or his application to study'.

The legality of denying an education in public schools for some exceptional children has been challenged increasingly in the last few years. This challenge has been based on the Fourteenth Amendment to the US Constitution which guarantees to all the people equal protection of the laws. The first significant achievement in the right to education for disabled children's movement was the outcome, in 1971, of the lawsuit brought against the Commonwealth of Pennsylvania by the Pennsylvania Association for Retarded Children (PARC) and 13 mentally retarded children. The state had failed to provide access to a free public education for all retarded children. The court ruled in the plaintiffs' favour and, among other things, it was decided that by September 1972, all retarded children between the ages of 6 and 21 were to be provided with a publicly supported education. Similar lawsuits with comparable rulings followed in other states.

The PARC suit revealed the arbitrary way in which decisions about exclusions had been reached. Provisions were made for true representation of the parents or guardians in decisions about categorizing the children. Provisions were also made for informing parents about the available services and alternative forms of education for exceptional children.

In 1972 a major challenge was launched against the Board of Education of the District of Columbia as a result of the PARC case, on behalf of seven children with disabilities. The celebrated Mills lawsuit, as it came to be known, resulted in Judge Waddy handing down a ruling that all children with a disability were entitled to publicly supported education, and that such a right was guaranteed by law.

The PARC and Mills rulings were not merely landmark decisions, but laid the foundation for subsequent legal challenges and safeguards that confirmed the rights of all disabled children to appropriate education and training. Since 1974, parents have had the right of access to any school records kept on a child. Generally in the USA parents have been much more dominant in all educational matters than they have been in Britain. Parents have often been behind many of the advances in the provision for exceptional children. The British Parent–Teacher Associations (PTAs) are much less powerful than their counterparts in the USA. It must be remembered, however, that a parallel growth on a smaller scale of societies for various groups and categories of disabled children, largely originating from parents, took place in Britain in the 1960s, as it did in the USA.

Another area of controversy in recent times, in the USA as in Britain, is 'labelling' or putting exceptional children into categories. Similar arguments have been put forward against the existing categories in the USA as against those in Britain which have been discussed earlier. 'Labelling' cannot be altogether abolished but must be as accurate as possible. It has happened in the USA, as in Britain, that children from minority racial groups have been designated as mentally retarded when, in fact, their learning problems have stemmed from language and cultural differences rather than lower innate ability. Wrongful 'labelling' also has been the subject of litigation, as in the case of nine Mexican-American pupils aged 8–13 years, heard at the District Court of Northern California in January, 1970. They successfully contested that they had been wrongly 'labelled' as mentally retarded, and the tests were considered to have been unfair. Revision of testing procedure for minority groups was ordered.

Parent groups seek federal recognition for the particular disability in which they are interested because federal financial assistance may be given as categorical aid. This means that funds are earmarked for the education of children with a particular category of disability. Federal aid can be given as general aid or categorical aid. Educators in special education tend to favour categorical aid as these funds will find their way directly to disabled children without being siphoned off to regular education. On the other hand, funds specified for one kind of disability cannot be used for another, for example, funds for the mentally retarded cannot be used for the deaf or children with learning disabilities. There is a 'wastebasket' category in which handicaps not included in the primary categories (auditorily disabled, visually disabled, mentally retarded, physically disabled) can be put. These minority groups have to compete with each other for the funds allotted to the 'wastebasket' category. It is therefore preferable to have a disability recognized, hence the effort to put categories such as 'learning disabilities/behaviourally disordered' into a legal framework.

The legal struggles that were described earlier, as well as the historic passage of the enactment of Public Law 94–142, otherwise known as PL94–142, proved to be of the greatest importance in the modern special education scene.

Of all formative American legislation, the following two Acts have been of outstanding importance for special education:

1. Section 504 of the Vocational Rehabilitation Act of 1973;
2. PL94–142.

Section 504 of the Vocational Rehabilitation Act is similar in design and application to the Civil Rights Act of 1964, which repealed racial discrimination in the United States. PL94–142 was a great advance in removing legal educational impediments placed in the path of disabled people.

Joseph Califano, Federal Secretary of Health, Education and Welfare, declared in 1977:

> The 504 Regulation attacks the discrimination, the demeaning practices and the injustices that have afflicted the nation's handicapped citizens. It reflects the recognition of the Congress that most handicapped persons can lead proud and productive lives, despite their disabilities. It will usher

in a new era of equality for handicapped individuals in which barriers to self-sufficiency and decent treatment will begin to fall before the force of law.

Section 504 led to the historic enactment of PL 94–142 which promised specific educational opportunities for handicapped children.

PL 94–142 has had a profound effect on the service providers. There is a wide range of provisions in the Act and it includes some of the following key features:

Due process: This gives parents safeguards in crucial matters of assessment and educational placements, as well as consent for testing.
Least restrictive environment: This requirement means that children with disabilities are to be placed with non-disabled children as far as is practicable.
Non-discriminatory assessment: The object of this provision is to ensure that appropriate and culture fair tests are administered for placement purposes.
Individualization: The main feature of this provision is that children in receipt of special education must be working to an individual program based on the findings of an appropriate assessment, and that this be subject to review.
Confidentiality. This refers to safeguards about access to children's records and the protection of confidentiality.

Recently, further significant changes in legislation affecting people with disabilities have taken place. The US Congress passed US Public Law 100–46 (1987) to 'promote independence, productivity and integration of persons with developmental disabilities'. A strong focus on an individual's 'competencies, preferences and personal needs' rather than a consideration of the limiting effects of disability characterizes the mood of the legislators. Congress offers families the opportunity to make decisions about the futures of their disabled members themselves, rather than accept without questioning the programs provided by service providers.

The Americans with Disabilities Act (1990)

In 1983 President Reagan proclaimed that America would

celebrate a 'decade of Disabled Persons' during 1983 to 1992. The following goals for the decade were set:

1. to expand educational opportunities;
2. to improve access to housing, buildings and transportation;
3. to expand employment opportunities;
4. to expand participation in recreation, social, religious and cultural activities;
5. to expand and strengthen rehabilitation programs and facilities;
6. to reduce the incidence of major disabling conditions through biomedical research;
7. to reduce the overall incidence of disability by expanded accident and disease prevention;
8. to minimize the effects of disability through the increased application of technology; and
9. to expand the international exchange of information and experience to benefit all persons with disabilities (Steer, 1991).

It was clearly recognized that the major obstacle to achieving the twin goals of equal opportunity and full participation of disabled people was a problem of discrimination. Eventually, the severity and pervasiveness of discrimination was finally removed when President Bush, on 28 July 1990, signed the Americans with Disabilities Act (ADA). This legislation offered disabled people equal rights, protection in jobs, public accommodation, transportation and services similar to those guaranteed to minority groups, women and elderly people.

Psychology and philosophy

The early American educators were influenced by European thinkers, psychologists and educators. It was not long, however, before the USA made its own contribution and Europe was receiving ideas back from the USA. Development of easier and quick communication between the countries helped to make the exchange of ideas possible. A discussion follows of a few notable contributions relating to children with motor and neurological defects.

American psychologists of the first half of the century made a significant contribution to psychological theory and, in particular, to learning theory. Among these was Edward Thorndike of Columbia University, who was the foremost proponent of connectionism, a type of stimulus–response view of learning. Edward Tolman of the University of California, who considered himself a behaviourist, made a special study of 'insight' in rats. Tolman also engaged in lively debates about learning with Edwin Guthrie of the University of Washington in Seattle. Clark Hull of Yale University was another member of the illustrious set of psychologists who presented his particular view of behaviourism in a brilliant series of experimental papers and books.

British and American notions of intelligence developed along different lines. The British favoured the concept of 'g' or general intelligence and developed a hierarchical model of intelligence. The American notion, exemplified by Thurston and Cattell, was that different skills and aptitudes were not hierarchically organized from 'g' and could therefore be tested separately.

The British and Americans have held similarly divergent views of the concept of personality – the British having a hierarchical notion and the Americans a more separatist one, as is shown by the two personality tests (Eysenck and Eysenck, 1964; Cattell, 1965). Mental testing and personality testing have flourished in the USA more than in any other country. Some of the more widely used tests have been mentioned in previous chapters. Binet's test of intelligence has been modified (Terman and Merrill, 1960) and other intelligence tests standardized (Wechsler, 1949). A battery of neuropsychological tests has been developed to assess the strengths and weaknesses in children with motor, perceptual, intellectual and neurological impairments. The information obtained from these diagnostic tests of intelligence, sensory functioning and integration, body image, memory disturbance, language, etc. has often been used to design remedial programs for children.

Kephart's contribution

Before he produced *The Slow Learner in the Classroom* (1971), Kephart had worked with Strauss and, indeed, many of his insights come from his earlier work. He was also influenced strongly by the theories of Piaget and Hebb. In his book,

Kephart discusses children who are presenting learning difficulties and who need help to overcome them but who have no serious physical disability or obvious neurological damage. Kephart maintains that these children's problems stem from inefficiency in perceptual–motor skills. These perceptual–motor problems are mainly physical. They are often made worse, however, because children living in the modern environment are not required to develop the skills, such as eye–hand co-ordination, form perception and intersensory integration, which Kephart considers basic to academic learning. He has worked out ways of developing these skills. Kephart emphasizes that it is necessary to develop basic skills in their natural order of sequence. He says, 'training is easier if it is begun with the most basic area of performance in which the child is weak'. A number of tests, which have not been standardized, are described. These detect deficiencies and are used to monitor progress in overcoming them.

Kephart stresses the effect of movement on perception and perception on higher thought processes. He also emphasizes the part played by feedback in perception and the interplay between motor learning and perceptual learning. It is only through exposure and practice that perceptual–motor skills develop. Such things as practice in writing and drawing on a chalkboard, walking along beams, balancing, playing with balls and tracing templates are used in his remedial program. Music is used extensively to encourage listening skills, rhythm and co-ordinated movement. Intersensory integration in the form of auditory motor skills is developed by musical games.

Kephart discusses what he calls 'splinter' skills, which are skills that have developed in advance of more basic ones. These skills, therefore, are not generalized and are of little value. Kephart maintains that teaching skills which can be generalized is of paramount importance: teaching a specific task has to follow later. He therefore first concentrates on such things as broader aspects of 'body image' – knowledge of parts of the body, laterality and directionality.

We can see that many of Kephart's ideas have been discussed earlier in this book. In the USA, classrooms have been set up to enable teachers to follow Kephart's programs. In Britain, Kephart's ideas have not been put into practice systematically on any large scale. Kephart has been criticized

(Cratty, 1972) for his poor grounding in neurophysiology and questionable motor assessment technique. His ideas have, however, influenced thinking in special education in the last two decades.

Grace Fernald

Grace Fernald's kinaesthetic techniques for teaching children with visual and auditory disorders are well known to those working in special education. Fernald anticipated many current ideas with her insight into learning difficulties and with her methods of overcoming them. She believed that children should first read their own stories rather than those adults had written for them. (This approach has since been incorporated into reading schemes such as *Breakthrough to Literacy*.) She thought that children's interests and ideas should dictate the content of their reading and writing. She also thought that continual success is essential not only for learning to read but also for other forms of learning because failure causes emotional stress which hinders progress.

By Fernald's method, a teacher has first to find some means by which pupils can be motivated and guided to write words correctly. They then read a printed copy of their own words and, finally, will read other material. A fuller description of the method appears below.

At first, a child chooses a word which is written in enlarged script on a card. The child then traces the word with the finger, enunciating at the same time. The process is repeated until the child is able to write the word as a whole unit, on its own, from memory. The card is then filed. The child then has to try to use the word in a story. At first the stories consist of a few words only, but they increase in length over a period of time. In the next stage, tracing is omitted and the child looks at the word, speaks it and then continues as before. Now the words are no longer in specially large script. Word cards are not used in the third stage. The child looks at the printed word, speaks it and writes it while saying it. At this stage the child shows a desire to read from books. The child is allowed to read whatever it likes, and is told words it does not know. When the child finishes reading a passage new words are looked at again and written down. All words are later revised.

In the fourth stage the child is taught to recognize new words from their similarity to words or parts of words already known. During this stage Fernald did not read to the children and she asked parents not to read to them either.

Fernald's ideas and methods, although still useful for a fresh approach in remedial teaching, have been incorporated into present-day regular teaching techniques. Her emphasis on success, interest and learning in small sequential steps incorporating motor activity is thoroughly in accordance with modern thinking and was a considerable contribution before many had begun seriously to consider learning disabilities (Fernald, 1943).

Skinner's contribution

Skinner was not only one of psychology's most distinguished figures but one of the leading educationists of this century. His particular contributions to special education were the introduction of an effective technology of teaching (program instruction), teaching of self-management skills and the use of motivational techniques. He will long be remembered for the way in which he replaced the despair, which generally characterized the education and training of disabled people, with optimism (Skinner, 1968).

Skinner's approach can best be explained by reference to his work and experiments with animals and humans. The conditioning technique (operant conditioning) he used is described below.

Skinner built a 'Skinner box' containing a lever which, when pushed, released a food pellet. A hungry rat was placed in the box and the rat by chance pressed the lever and so obtained food. Gradually the rat realized that food followed the lever-pressing and it pressed the lever when it wanted food. The formula is

Stimulus (S) (desire for food)	→	Response (R) (rat pressing lever)	→	Reinforcement (food pellet)

This and similar procedures are called operant or instrumental conditioning, the rat's behaviour or response being operant or instrumental in obtaining reinforcement or food. This is essentially a learning procedure. The best results are obtained if the delay in reinforcement is small. Skinner showed that rats entering a correct goal box in a T-maze who were rewarded immediately performed better than those whose reward was delayed. Extinction occurs, i.e. the subject fails to respond if reinforcement is discontinued. The rat will give up pressing the lever if there is no reinforcement, i.e. the food ceases to appear. However, spontaneous recovery or renewed response will be shown after there has been extinction, followed by a period of rest; a rat will respond anew with the lever.

Skinner found that rats can show discrimination in their response according to the stimulus. If food is presented in the Skinner box only when a light is on when the lever is pressed, rats learn to press the lever only then. Reinforcement can be made 'partial' and can be regulated by such means as fixed ratio (reinforcement every fixed number of trials) or fixed interval (reinforcement every fixed interval of time). Pigeons peck so hard at a disc to obtain food at a fixed ratio that their beaks become sore. It has also been shown that larger rewards result in greater learning.

Operant conditioning shows that secondary reinforcement is effective. This is any stimulus which reinforces because of its associations with an original reinforcement. For example, a rat in a Skinner box may be conditioned to respond with a tone followed by food. Gradually the tone and the food are witheld, resulting in extinction of the animal's response. After a time the rat will press the lever for the reinforcement of the tone, even if the food is witheld.

These animal experiments, demonstrating learning in its simplest form have given insight to human learning. As a result of his work with animals Skinner developed linear programs, putting them into teaching machines. In linear programming, material to be learnt is broken down into small sequential steps. Each step has to be mastered before the pupil proceeds to the next. As the steps are so small, reinforcement (reward by means of obtaining the correct answer) is frequent and consequently learning is steady and fast. All kinds of developments and variations have followed from Skinner's work. Examples are branching programs originally in teaching machines and workbooks, now incorporated in educational software for micro-computers. In these, 'learning steps' are made larger than in linear programming and if one gives the wrong answer the learner is directed to a 'branch' which covers the point of difficulty in greater detail. Other examples are graded work books and work cards. The aim for these teaching aids is to enable a child to work at its own pace and to free the teacher from routine work for work which needs personal and individual attention. The notion of continual success is especially important for disabled children who may easily become discouraged. As many children who are disabled miss schooling for reasons of health or treatment, means whereby they can work on their own are to be welcomed.

Skinner's work has had the general effect of emphasizing to educators two main points, namely the importance of positive reinforcement (i.e. reward in the form of success and constant praise for even small achievements) and the frequent necessity of 'breaking down' a learning task into small sequential steps. If a child is failing at a task it must be analysed into even smaller components, each of which the child can master. Many disabled children fail because tasks demanded from them, although fairly easily mastered by non-disabled children, are too great for the disabled child without being analysed into a series of simpler tasks.

One result of Skinner's work has been the development of behaviour modification, whereby a pupil's unacceptable social behaviour is altered to make it more compatible with that of the social environment, e.g. the class at school. This is done by making a careful study of:

1. the behaviour to be modified;
2. the reinforcement which the child considers to be positive;
3. the stimuli causing the unacceptable behaviour

A program is worked in which acceptable behaviour is suitably rewarded and unacceptable behaviour is ignored. This is a very simple exposition of a procedure which merits a fuller explanation than we have space for here. Critics of behaviour modification maintain that, although the symptoms of unacceptable behaviour are treated, its cause is not.

Conclusion

The provisions of Section 504 and PL94–142 have brought about tremendous changes. They put great pressure on schools to change their special education service systems.

Although it is difficult to make generalizations in so large and varied a country, it is generally true to say that the trend is towards integrating, where possible, exceptional children into regular classes. Use is made of special resource rooms and specialist staff who are either on the school staff or are peripatetic. To enable children in hospital to receive an education, there are hospital schools and teachers attached to hospitals, as in Britain. Many more directors of special education have been appointed at local and state level to co-ordinate services and give advisory help. In recent years there has been great expansion in the number of training courses for teachers of exceptional children.

Many new and exciting developments in educational philosophy, remedial programs, psychological testing and legislation have originated in the USA. With humanity's ever-increasing ability to communicate worldwide, people everywhere can benefit from such a rich source of originality and ingenuity.

13

Australia

To understand Australian educational provision it should be borne in mind that Australia is a continent more than three-quarters the size of Europe, with six sovereign States, and two mainland territories (Northern Territory, Australia Capital Territory) which are the direct responsibility of the Australian Government. In 1989 the *Australian Year Book* indicates 70.5% of the total population were living in National capital cities and Darwin and four major cities with populations of 100 000 or more. The remaining 30% was spread out over the whole continent. The geography and demography of Australia have a significant bearing on its education service, including special education provision.

Education in Australia is compulsory from six to 15 years (to 16 years in Tasmania), although education is provided at lower and higher age levels. Most Australian children begin school in the regular schools at about five years of age and stay on beyond 15 years in increasing numbers. Approximately 21% of children are enrolled in non-governmental schools; denominational, private schools and schools conducted by voluntary organizations for disabled children. Other agencies also contribute to the development and maintenance of services for children with special needs. These include such professional groups as the Australian Association for Special Education and three levels of tertiary educational institutions which have a role in providing inservice and continuing education. Non-governmental schools receive government financial support mainly on a basis of need. Education in all government schools is free; fees are usually charged in non-government schools.

The administrative centres are in the State capital cities; however, a policy of decentralization on a regional basis has been spreading throughout Australia since the 1950s. New South Wales, for example, has 11 regions, each with regional offices, a director and staff with a growing responsibility to the central administration for the organization, administration and delivery services in education, including special education (Drummond, 1978).

Australia has been providing special education to disabled people since the early colonial days and the current level of service provision, while not adequately providing for all groups, would rank highly among developed nations. However, any description of the nation's special education services must take into account the seemingly contradictory concepts of homogeneity and diversity.

Because education and special education are the responsibility of each individual State and Territory, both the philosophy and the service provision have been shaped by the differing geographical, demographic, multicultural and political influences which exist or have existed in each region. Queensland and Western Australia have had to deal with their vast distances and dispersed populations. Tasmania has built a system based on its relatively small population. Victoria and New South Wales have developed systems to cope with multicultural populations of four to five million people. Consequently, there is no single Australian special education service, but rather eight diverse solutions to the problem of catering for disabled children and adults.

Service is provided in many forms, ranging from the residential schools for severely disabled students, through day special schools, to special classes in regular schools. In many situations, resource teachers and aides are provided to assist children integrated into regular schools; in other situations these children are visited by itinerant (visiting teacher) specialists. Some States provide residential accommodation for isolated children. Some States provide education in maximum security prisons.

Service is provided for children who are intellectually disabled, hearing and visually impaired, physically and orthopaedically disabled, deaf and blind, hospitalized and specific-learning disabled. Service is also provided for children who are wards of the State declared by the courts to be delinquent, attending psychiatric hospitals or clinics, or who evidence behaviour disorders in regular schools. Special education staff in some States also staff prison and youth training centre schools. In addition to these more specialized facilities, special educators in some instances working from regional school support centres assist slow learners and children with reading and mathematics problems in regular schools. Some States also provide remedial gymnasiums for children with serious motor problems.

While there is diversity in the type and form of service provision, there is a shared belief across the States and Territories that the rights of disabled people must be upheld. There is a growing awareness that disabled children are entitled to appropriate education, training and care, and that formal education should take place, wherever possible, in their local school in the company of non-disabled peers.

The impact of this philosophy, now almost universally termed integration in the educational system, or normalization (or deinstitutionalization in the previously health-dominated mental retardation field), has led to a questioning of traditional policies and practices.

To understand the major concerns raised, it is useful to examine the historical antecedents of Australian special education. The earliest providers of service were the charitable organizations which established the King's Orphan School in Sydney as early as 1828 and schools for the blind and the deaf in Melbourne and Sydney during the 1860s. The 1930s and 1940s saw the emergence of the spastic societies who also catered for children who had contracted poliomyelitis. During the late 1940s and 1950s, voluntary groups established day programs and facilities for intellectually disabled children, and this pattern continued with interested people establishing facilities for low-incidence groups, such as autistic children and those with language disorders.

Provision for the education of children with disabilities was published by the Commonwealth Office of Education in 1961. The figures were collated from statistical returns from the various State Ministers' annual reports dating back to 1950. For example, the New South Wales government placed 850 'educable mentally handicapped' pupils in 'opportunity classes'. Voluntary organizations in 19 metropolitan and country areas also provided teachers and places for students with moderate intellectual disability.

The contribution of Fred and Eleanor Schonell to special education in the United Kingdom and Australia is a most noteworthy one (Andrews, 1982, 1983).

In Australia an extensive network of special education facilities had grown up. In the Eastern states this development was particularly active and the voluntary agencies were operating a number of special schools and training centres. While the Federal and State governments were providing education for disabled pupils, the services were uneven and not always appropriate.

A major influence on the pattern and philosophy of special education in Australia was the Schools Commission. This body recognized that no clear picture of the nature and extent of educational services for children with disabilities was readily available in Australia. It commissioned a national study to remedy this situation. Over the past 15 years the commission has urged that the regular and special education sectors merge their efforts to deliver a better service for pupils with disabilities (Andrews *et al.*, 1979).

During the latter part of the nineteenth century, State health departments began to take responsibility for the care of moderate to severely intellectually disabled people, usually in large institutions based on a medical–hospital model. Before this, they had been catered for in lunatic asylums.

In the last 30 years, State education departments have gradually accepted responsibility for the educational components of the programs, leaving the voluntary bodies and, to a lesser degree, the health departments to provide the ancillary services.

It is against this background that the major issues of the 1990s have emerged as one further step in an evolutionary process.

The contribution of the charitable bodies, while of inestimable value in promoting and developing the system to its present level, has been perceived to carry with it connotations of charity as opposed to rights. Critics of the system argued that every child has the right to appropriate education and ancillary services and that these services should be provided by the State. To the credit of the charitable societies, they have been most responsive to this argument.

There is also continuing concern about providing service to intellectually disabled people in large, hospital-style, residential institutions. It is argued that, while large institutions provide care and protection for these people, they segregate them from the outside world. The operational systems of a large institution, with roots in the hospital system, impose an abnormal lifestyle, as any non-disabled patient can attest. Accommodation is generally in wards, meal times are regulated by staff rosters, dependency is encouraged, initiative discouraged, and residents are segregated and denied access to the specialized educational programs which would enable them to operate outside the institution.

The State health department are aware of these concerns and in many cases have been the major initiators of change. In Victoria, the former Mental Retardation Division of the Health Department has been transferred to the Department of Community Services, thus breaking the nexus between mental retardation and sickness. The renamed Office of Intellectual Disability Services has established over 200 community residential units (houses in the suburbs and rural towns) as alternative accommodation, and has undertaken an extensive staff retraining program to prepare direct care staff to carry out an educative role. Similar initiatives are in train in other States.

Another major issue is the practice of segregating disabled children in highly specialized school settings. Critics of this practice argue that this denies children access to the normal company of their peers, and indeed denies non-disabled children experience of their disabled peers. It is argued that much of the discomfort which non-disabled people feel in the presence of a disabled person stems from their lack of experience of disability. Non-disabled children are being denied opportunities to learn the virtues of simple respect for, and acceptance of, differences.

Central to the argument for integrating disabled children in regular schools is the belief that they are members of the community and have the right to grow and develop inside that community.

In Australia a fairly strong move was made to integrate the disabled and non-disabled pupil (Schonell *et al.*, 1962). This development began in the 1960s in Brisbane. Unfortunately, the experiment foundered when the young people with special needs were unable to make the transition to 'normal' adult and working life. It became apparent that no adequate preparation was undertaken to equip the disabled adolescent to cope with the demands of the regular community.

It should be observed that in some instances in Queensland, 60% of spina bifida children were 'integrated' into the regular schools without any special provision (Andrews and Elkins, 1981). The integration of pupils with cerebral palsy and sensory disorders has not proceeded at the same pace mainly because parents and educators were happy with the superior level of services provided by the special schools. However, in Victoria following the election of a socialist government with a strong ideological commitment to 'social justice and equity', the government set about dismantling as rapidly as it could the most worthwhile features of special education. The drive to destroy the 'segregated' system has been pursued relentlessly by this narrow but powerful political group. As a result, valuable and critical aspects of education for the disabled have been destroyed systematically. Significant services such as assessment have been proscribed by the authorities; and scarce resources directed towards compliant agencies which support the socialist government.

Despite the increased fundings of the Victorian Government, the commitment to producing highly skilled teachers and associated professionals has decreased substantially.

All States, to a greater or lesser degree, have successfully introduced integration with hearing and visually impaired children, and numerous small rural communities contain outstanding examples of what can be done.

The key to further advances in integrating these children into regular schools is in the hands of legislators in each State. Although advocates and activists talk of rights, in law disabled children have no right to the education of their parents' choice.

Legislation in this area is generally outmoded in philosophy, language and intent. Such legislation allows a parent of a disabled child to absent the child from school without penalty, and most legislation empowers ministers or directors-general of education to place a child in a special setting. Nowhere is a minister obliged to provide the requisite services. The

States of South Australia and Queensland, however, have passed legislation based on the rights of disabled children.

This situation has led parents to press for rights legislation, coupled with an obligation on the part of governments to provide that requisite service. The Victorian *Ministerial Review of Services for the Disabled* (1984) has taken the strongest 'rights' position, and its guiding principles neatly summarize the concerns of the 1980s. The principles are:

1. every child has the right to be educated in a regular school;
2. non-categorization (services should be organized and distributed on the basis of need, not category of disability);
3. resources should, to the greatest extent possible, be school based;
4. there should be collaborative decision-making which allows parents a greater say in their child's placement;
5. all children can learn and be taught – in effect, no child can be denied schooling on the basis of a claimed ineducability.

However, to date, Victoria has failed to enact legislation based on its professed commitment to the right's model.

From an initial allocation of $.5 million in 1984, Victorian government resources to support its integration program have grown in 1991 to $39 million, while the special education budget has grown from $46.5 million in 1983 to $70 million in 1991. Currently, in Victoria, Ministry of Education data indicate that 4967 students with disabilities, impairments and problems in schooling receive their education in special school settings, while 4987 receive support in integrated educational settings. A particularly intriguing and ambitious recent development in Victoria is the Inclusive Schools Integration (ISI) program, which is aimed at promoting an 'inclusive' curriculum in the generic school system through reshaping syllabus content and changing teaching style and teaching strategies so that **all** students can engage in essential learning. The ISI program endeavours to generate an 'inclusive curriculum' through a variety of strategies, including team teaching, co-operative learning, peer and cross-age tutoring and teacher consultancy partnerships.

Given the amount of debate and the extraordinary number of government reviews of service provision in recent years, one could be forgiven for thinking that Australian special education is passing through a revolutionary phase, but this is not the case. Current events seem to be just one more stage in a process which began back in 1828 and which has led to visually impaired and hearing impaired children, and an unknown number of children with other types of disabilities, being integrated successfully into regular schools.

14

Sweden

Historical background

As in most western countries, the traditional schooling arrangements for pupils with disabilities has been in special schools, if the regular school was unable to meet their special educational needs. Sweden has been a pioneer in reforming the segregated system of education. In 1967 the Swedish Government enacted legislative changes whereby the vast majority of pupils with disabilities now receive their schooling side-by-side with their non-disabled peers. In order to make such a bold departure in service delivery meaningful, the government has injected substantial resources to support pupils and teachers in regular schools. The commitment to the principle of integration in Sweden has therefore been a firm and long standing one.

It would be helpful to consider the organization of special education in Sweden against the wider background of the country's education system. The general features of its provision are as follows:

Ages	**Grades**		
Below 7 years	Pre-school		
7–10 years	1–3	Lower level	Compulsory comprehensive
13–16 years	7–9	Medium level	
16–19 years	Upper secondary	Higher level	
Above 19 years	Higher or adult education		

Pre-school education for children under the age of seven years is not compulsory, though municipalities (local education authorities) are legally empowered to provide such education for six-year-olds.

All children must attend the comprehensive school for at least nine years. The school years are divided into three grades, corresponding to age groups.

Junior	(1–3)	–	lagstadium
Intermediate	(4–6)	–	mellanstadium
Senior	(7–9)	–	hogstadium

Attendance at upper secondary school (gymnasieskola), is optional, but about 90% of this age group enrol. The curriculum is based on academic or practical subjects.

Higher education is generally offered at universities. Other forms of adult education are available to individuals without university entrance qualifications, who wish to pursue vocational, industrial and job-retraining courses. Such courses, with appropriate modification, can be undertaken by disabled individuals as well.

Administrative responsibility for providing compulsory comprehensive and upper secondary schools rests with the municipalities, while financial control is vested in the State. This policy aims to ensure equal education opportunity and financial support throughout the country. In addition, it is claimed that a large measure of regional participation and decision-making in policy matters affecting educational planning and provision is encouraged by such arrangements.

A particular feature of the Swedish educational system is the major influence exercised by the Parliament (Riksdagen) in planning the overall structure and content of the national curriculum. The local authority itself has jurisdiction over planning in such matters as the provision of school meals and transport for pupils. It is allowed some latitude in the design of curriculum, subject to the strict guidelines limits laid down by the central government. The general administrative organization and relevant responsible authorities are set out below.

A modified curriculum is provided for a child with special needs.

The Ministry of Education is responsible for such general policy issues as those relating to initiating reforms, dealing with applications for grants, etc. The National Board of

Education (NBE) is responsible for long-term planning and initiation and support of research and development. It also issues curriculum guides and comments to these guides. The county (regional) authorities have co-ordinating functions and they also stimulate and support research and development. The central administration is represented at the regional level by administration and supervision and inspection of schools, the promotion of in-service teacher training and the disbursement of State grants is exercised. At the local level, the municipal education authority (LEA) with local representation including local politicians, is empowered to translate and implement state policy and to ensure that schools' premises comply with current regulations. Opportunities to consult with community leaders and parents, and respond according to local needs are freely available to this body. Some of these responsibilities are delegated to head teachers. (Figure 13.1)

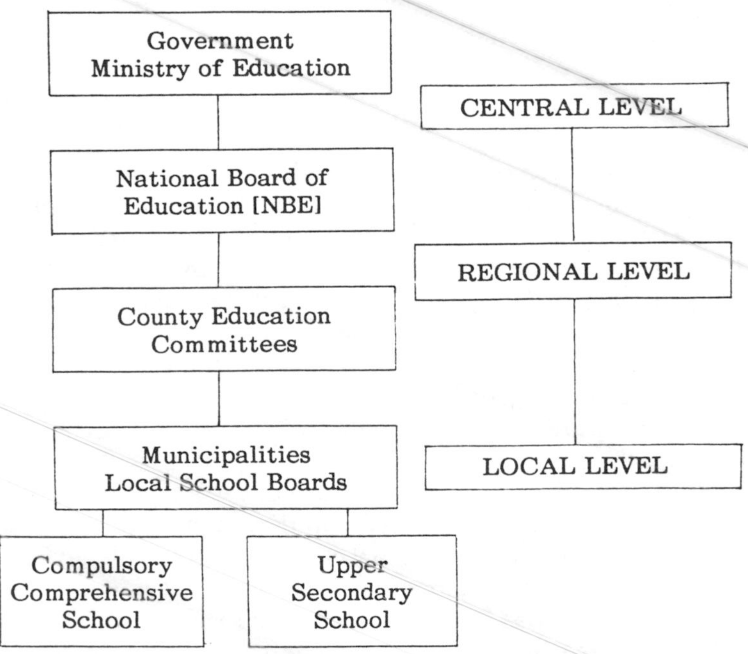

Figure 13.1 General features of administrative structure for primary and secondary education.

Financial responsibilities

Public education for all Swedes is free and as indicated earlier, a policy of devolution is pursued by the central government.

The central government meets the costs of teachers' salaries and support services, while the local authorities defray the cost of non-teaching activities. On the whole, these expenses are borne equally between the two agencies.

Recent changes have resulted in some adjustment to the grant distribution, whereby the central government not only meets the costs of teachers' salaries, but can make specific grants for particular local needs, out of funds earmarked for such purposes. The policy aims at responding in more flexible ways to requests from municipal authorities to improve conditions for deserving pupils. Special formulae govern the allocation and disbursement of state grants to schools, within the general policy of decentralization and local accountability. The underlying principles which determine funding are responsiveness to perceived local needs and flexibility in grant approval and regional recourse allocation.

Pupils with disabilities and special needs

As in most western countries, the traditional schooling arrangement for disabled pupils was placement within the special school system, if the regular school proved unable to cope with their special educational needs. However, Sweden has been a pioneer in reforming the segregated system of education by legislating for change, and the vast majority of disabled pupils today receive their education alongside their non-disabled peers. The admissions board of the school would decide the level and nature of support required. The official curriculum guide for the comprehensive school gives priority to the regular class or teaching team as the natural locus for handling pupils' difficulties. Only in exceptional cases are separate arrangements outside the normal class or school made. In order to make such a bold departure in service delivery meaningful, the government has injected substantial resources to support pupils and teachers in schools. There are, nevertheless, a minority of disabled pupils such as the profoundly deaf and some severely multiple disabled children who, it is argued, should attend special schools. Such an arrangement is defended on pedagogical, technological and cost–benefit grounds.

Children and teachers are assisted whenever necessary by 'pupil assistants' (teacher aides). These can be employed on the teaching side where they would assist physically disabled or sensorily impaired pupils with practical help in the classroom. They may be required to help prepare materials or equipment for lessons. 'Pupil assistants' can also be employed for 'care', when they would help with such things as toileting, dressing, meals and transport. The headteacher would decide in what capacity they should be used.

Hearing-impaired

A very small group of severely or profoundly deaf children attend special schools. The justification for this exception is the belief that 'substantial opportunities for genuine communication and comradeship cannot be provided in the normal school'. These special schools, it is claimed, with their sophisticated and generous array of technical equipment and educational material can best develop the language skills of deaf pupils in such domains as language, specially designed curriculum, modified classrooms, etc. Accordingly, five regional schools for profoundly deaf pupils with associated disabilities (mental retardation, emotional disturbance, severe central speech disorders, etc.) have been established in Sweden for approximately 700 pupils.

Moderate or partially hearing pupils attend ordinary schools, while those with associated disabilities such as mental retardation or behaviour disorders attend remedial classes on a sessional basis.

Mentally retarded (MR) children

The education of all mentally retarded children remains the responsibility of the county councils. These authorities not only provide education but medical, social, family, housing and other ancillary services. Mentally retarded children are entitled to pre-school education and almost 95% of them attend the regular pre-school. Children between the ages of seven and

17 years attend special elementary schools (for severely retarded). A good deal of 'location' integration occurs in which special schools or classes share the premises of ordinary schools. The educational needs of over 99% of mentally retarded children in Sweden are met by such an arrangement. A small but growing number of MR children are being integrated gradually into regular classes. MR pupils are entitled to vocational training up to the age of 21, and this can in some instances be extended to 23 years, and as a result an increasing number of young people is entering the work force.

Physically disabled children

Special schools for the physically disabled were abolished during the 1950s and 1960s. Today, physically disabled children attend ordinary schools administered by municipalities. These schools receive support and advice from a variety of educational specialists, including specialist visiting teachers. Of approximately 2700 pupils, 90% attend regular schools while the rest are placed in remedial teaching groups. The latter are a variant of the special class, with its emphasis on retaining the pupil with disabilities in the regular class and withdrawing that pupil only for remedial instruction in particular subjects. The municpial authorities are responsible for providing schooling and ensuring pupil attendance. The county councils provide treatment, care, transport and, when necessary, boarding accommodation for some pupils. Over the years an increasing number of ordinary schools have been modified and adapted to allow physically disabled children full access to and use of buildings, classrooms, toilets and playgrounds.

Visually impaired children

Because of the successful drive to integrate children with visual impairments into local regular schools, supported by appropriate technology and specialized teachers, only a small number of visually impaired children attend the two national special schools, of which one caters for children with visual impairments and associated disorders. Visually impaired pupils attending regular schools receive the full range of sophisticated technological and optical devices, for example, closed circuit television, magnifiers, facilities for enlarging, braille transcription and recording devices. They are also provided with sensory training and a modified curriculum, for example, mobility training, typing and braille writing. The ready help of visiting teachers for the visually impaired is also available.

Special education – other features

Other features of special education include instructional arrangements for:

1. separate teaching groups.
2. hospital- and home-based tuition.

Separate teaching groups
In the main, this provision has replaced the traditional special class. The criterion for admission to this group is non-categorical, a demonstrated weakness in particular subjects. There is flexibility in group size and retention of class membership of the pupil. Children are withdrawn for certain teaching periods for specific instruction in such things as reading and mathematics.

Hospital- and home-based tuition
Instruction is arranged for pupils admitted to hospital for long- or short-term periods. Often the program or curriculum is modified for subjects other than the basic ones. Individual teaching at home is also given to pupils who are unable to profit from ordinary instruction at school, for example, children in convalescence and school refusers.

Teacher training

All teachers must undertake special education units (areas of study) as part of their basic training program. As a consequence of the increased responsibility placed upon the regular teacher to instruct disabled pupils in an integrated school setting, special education is given considerable weight in the new teacher training program that is currently being launched. All teachers entering a special teacher training program must have a regular teacher certificate plus appropriate teaching experience. The present program ranges from one to four semesters, depending on the area the teacher elects for specialization, for example, hearing impairment – four semesters: physical disability – one semester. The government proposes a longer training program for most categories of special teachers. The program comprises a compulsory core unit of foundation subjects such as psychology and child development for all teachers, followed by speciality units.

Sweden has been foremost over the last 20 years in reorganizing its educational provision for children with disabilities. Teacher training is currently under careful scrutiny by all interested groups, such as government, teacher training institutions and teacher unions to provide the best educational system for children with special needs.

Conclusion

To enable disabled pupils to profit from integrated education, the Swedish Government has provided within the regular school system a high level of professional support (teacher aides, special educators, etc.), as well as material and social assistance.

In Sweden, the integration experiment has proved to be a successful venture. It has also helped to create more enlightened public and professional attitudes and practices in the community. Apart from a strong commitment to a policy of integration, there is also a greater willingness to experiment with alternative forms of school placement for disabled pupils.

Today, a more crucial debate taking place in Sweden is not whether disabled pupils should be integrated, but which children would prosper from remaining in the ordinary class and what strategies are likely to enhance their educational opportunities.

15

Hungary

Hungary has made a special contribution to the education of children and young adults with motor and neurological disabilities by developing a particular treatment method called conductive education. This method incorporates medical, social and educational approaches in one overall approach to the treatment of the whole child.

A former communist country, with little material wealth, Hungary provides us with an insight into what can be achieved with sound psychological precepts, a rigorous approach and with skilled human beings as the main resource.

In Hungary the education system is based on eight years' attendance at general school. Children enter school in the September following their sixth births. Every normal, healthy child then receives at least eight years' general schooling. Of all six-year-olds in Hungary, 97 to 98% enter general school. Education is compulsory until the age of 16: those who have not completed the eighth grade of general schooling (about 10% of each group, mainly the children of unskilled workers) must stay on at the general school till they are 16 years old. The remainder complete their compulsory schooling in various kinds of high schools (Cottam and Sutton, 1986). Most pre-school children attend kindergarten which actively prepares children for a general school.

Family allowance is paid until a child is three years old. If a child is disabled, it is paid until he/she is six years old.

The teaching in Hungarian schools is by corporate methods in classes, rather than by encouraging individual learning. Much emphasis is placed on musical education and, in the early stages, on singing and understanding rhythm. This follows a long tradition of musical excellence in the country. The influence of the educator and composer Kodaly in post-war years is much in evidence.

Special education in Hungary paralleled early developments in other countries; provision for deaf and blind children came first in the nineteenth century, followed by provision for mentally retarded children. Modern special education in Hungary is largely 'segregated', with separate provision in special schools for different disability groups.

The basic aim of the special education system is to enable children who are disabled to master the curriculum and syllabus of the general school (the first four grades only in the case of mild mental disability) (Vincze, 1982). More severely intellectually and/or functionally disabled children are considered merely 'trainable' and are 'trained' accordingly. Those with the lowest functional ability or who have chronic health problems are excluded altogether from the education system. They are provided for by the health service.

One important feature of the Hungarian system is that, to be enrolled at any school, either mainstream or special, children must be able to walk. Wheelchairs are allowed in school only for temporary disability. Children who cannot walk are entitled to receive home tuition only which is provided by the local school.

It must be appreciated that pupils with mobility disorders are not able to attend regular schools. The lack of access for children with motor difficulties was one of the main reasons why the conductive education system developed in Hungary. Hungary, unlike the policy and practices of western cultures such as the UK, USA and Australia, has no commitment to integrate the disabled into the ordinary community. It is against this background that we give an account of a pedagogical method for teaching children with motor disabilities which differs in a number of respects from contemporary practices in other countries.

Conductive education is an educational system developed by Professor Andras Peto in 1945. Peto studied medicine in Vienna and became director of two major hospitals and several rehabilitation institutes. He held as a central tenet that motor disorder need not result in a physical disability, but is a learning difficulty which can be overcome successfuly. His conductive education system (without recourse to artificial aids such as wheelchairs) teaches children and adults with disorders of movement how to function independently in society.

The fundamental principle is to break the association between the physical conditions and the handicap or disability. Conductive education, as devised by Peto, therefore, is not a 'cure' for such conditions, nor is it a medical treatment. Rather, it seeks to generate and establish sufficient controls so that people with movement disorders can participate in everyday life without the use of prosthetics and also can avoid many of the secondary problems of health and development that arise from an inability to use their limbs. Neither is it a form of physiotherapy. It is essentially an educational system which aims at transforming the personality, creating new skills and attitudes.

Peto's conductive education system is now taught and practised in the State-run Institute for Motor Disorders in Budapest. Most of the children who attend the Institute have cerebral palsy, although children and even adults attend with other disabilities, for example, spina bifida, muscular dystrophy, Parkinson's disease and stroke victims.

Dr Maria Hari, one of Peto's medical students, became Director of the Institute upon Peto's death in 1967. In 1968, a State decree made all district physicians throughout Hungary responsible for notifying the Institute of all children in the nation with motor disorders. Dr Hari strives for a unified approach to the treatment, education and management of children and adults with motor disorders. The Institute's program emphasizes the development of functionally useful movements to facilitate independence in feeding, dressing and personal/social skills, before formal academic learning is attempted. Children and adults are encouraged to apply their skills and abilities to the utmost limit, but within the realistic bounds set by the 'conductor'. It appears that the theoretical insights gained from neurology, psychology and pedagogy have been incorporated skilfully within this system and have been applied effectively to promote learning in children and adults with motor disabilities.

Conductive education uses a model of learning rather than traditional therapy or treatment. The aim is not to prevent or lessen spasticity but to learn movement through a series of tasks, which are used immediately and reinforced in function. For example, students are taught to bend the elbows, a skill which is then used for drinking; they learn to hold on, so that they can sit. The student carries out the movement actively, and is helped by the conductor. The conductor gives minimal physical support and/or will give detailed verbal instructions throughout the sequences of the movement. The conductor teaches rather than treats the student.

The conductor

One of the most important principles of conductive education is that students must receive their education from as few people as possible. Girls straight from high school study for four years in the 'Conductors' College' within the Institute. At the end of a rigorous training, consisting of six hours a day of theory and higher education and six hours of practical work with the children, the conductors are qualified to teach every aspect of a child's learning needs in a carefully structured system of total education. This is aimed at making a child physically and emotionally independent and integrated into normal society. The conductors work with parents' groups, training the mother and child also with outpatients and with groups of residential or 'inpatients'. The conductors work with these allocated groups of inpatients in six-hour shifts, thereby ensuring that a member of staff with identical training and responsibility is with the children 24 hours a day, giving continuity of education.

The conductors are highly trained and respected, and work with every aspect of a child's development, ensuring that there is a transfer of learning from one activity to another. In the course of her work with children a conductor gives only positive reinforcement. She is not allowed to scold or rebuke or tell their children that their effort is poor or movement is in any way bad. She can only praise and encourage. This approach is very similar to that of 'operant conditioning' – a technique devised by Skinner.

Eligibility and assessment

The major criterion for acceptance into the program is the

capacity of the child to benefit from instruction. According to the authorities in Budapest, children with severe mental retardation, visual, auditory and communication disorders are excluded.

Group work

At first child and mother attend the parents' school. Here, the mother is taught how she should manage at home with such things as the child's feeding and dressing. 'The goal is to activate the child. The mother learns what task to set the child in order to make it co-operate with her' (Hari, personal communication). The mother returns periodically for check-ups and tasks are changed according to progress made. At this early stage emphasis is placed on encouraging responses in the child, for example, to its name, its mother's approach and on increasing an interest in its surroundings. The child also learns 'to play and go on playing, building up his endurance' (Hari, personal communication).

After five or six months the child matures and so can participate in group work within the framework of the 'parents' school'. These groups work every other day for 1½ hours. The mother learns how to organize the entire daily program for her child who becomes increasingly independent. In the Institute a child has only two pieces of special equipment; a solidly built chair without arms and a wooden slatted plinth on which to exercise and to use as a table (Figure 14.1). If a child becomes an in-patient he/she sleeps on the plinth also.

All activities are those of the kindergarten and lead to formal education. The goal is to attempt by visual and auditory stimulation to make the child react to verbal demands and consequently to learn movement leading to definite goals. These goals should be reached by play. Abstract movements should not be used but a goal always set. The group activities are structured so that each game prepares for the development of self-help. In the beginning the children may feel insecure on the 'pot' because it is a new situation. To minimize the insecurity they must grasp a ladderback and the 'pot' may be of a larger size.

The children are encouraged to be more independent by executing a variety of tasks. First they have a roll-call or

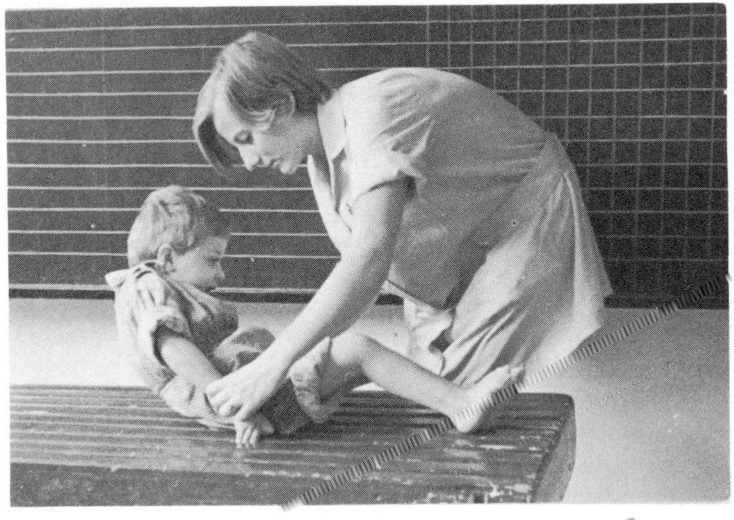

Figure 14.1 Individual exercises on plinth.

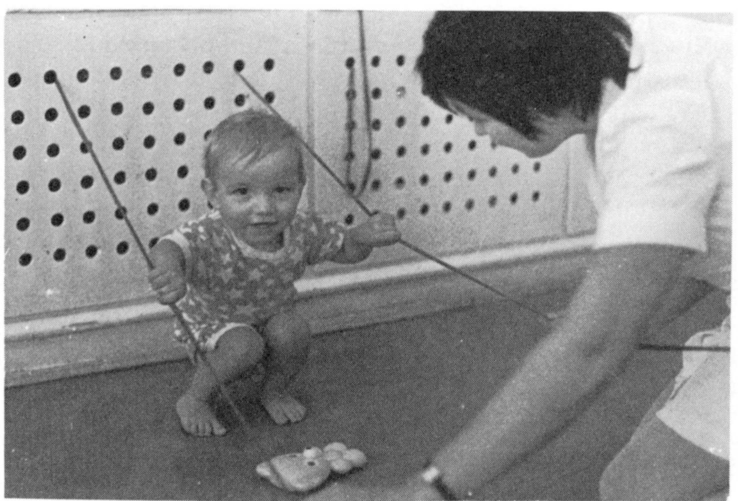

Figure 14.2 Learning to walk.

singing, then toilet training, washing and feeding. It is important that the children become noisy, lively and interested while they are eating. When they eat, they sit on small chairs in front of the plinth which is used as a table. The soles of the feet should be flat on the floor (or stool). The children eat the food they have brought. The mother is taught how she can make the child himself put the spoon, bread or mug to his mouth. The child is taught to swallow when he drinks and slowly proceeds to solid food, the child learning to chew. Swallowing and chewing prepares for speech. After the meal comes standing, walking and movement.

There must be purposeful movement, the movement having an aim. The playing finishes with going home. The individual child is not, however, forced into an unacceptable stereotyped pattern of behaviour

The common demands make it possible for children with different types of dysfunction to be grouped together. The program is common to them all. The aim is independence in feeding, toileting and mobility. The individual difficulties are different and one must find the individual means to reach a goal. Those who cannot walk may creep or crawl or roll (Some may have to learn to turn the body into prone position; others change the position of the head when crawling) Some children may temporarily have boots to prevent flexion of the knees. Others may have a raised heel to make the heel touch the ground. Every solution is acceptable temporarily. To reach the goal is the tool to further 'orthofunction'. 'Orthofunction' is the ability to function independently in the world (especially at school) without such aids as wheelchairs, ramps and care assistants. It includes the ability to walk and to use normal curricular materials. Its guiding principle is that people with disabilities should become capable of adapting themselves to 'normal' societal conditions. To be able to walk, a child must first learn to stand with support (Figure 14.2). A small ladderback chair is provided and the child learns to grasp and release it with the hands. The chair is pushed forward and the child stops at each step, learning to let go for a second. Later, hands are clasped above the head, by which the child obtains security in standing, and stretches the trunk (Hari, personal communication) (Figures 14.3 and 14.4).

Figure 14.3 Working in a group with the conductor.

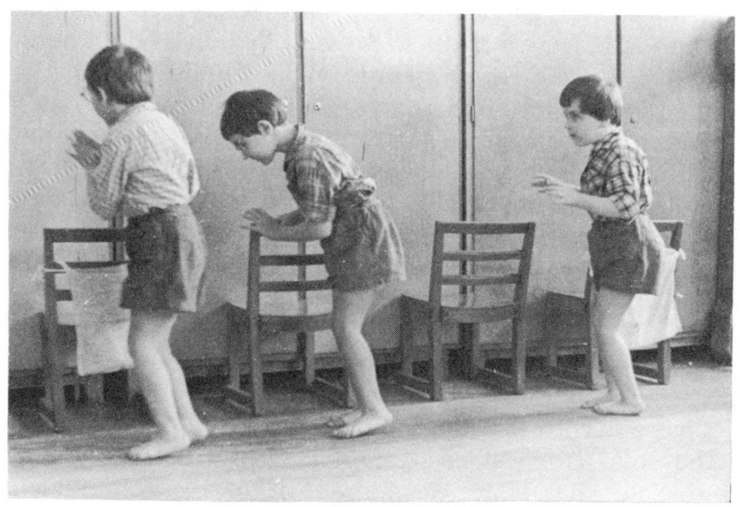

Figure 14.4 Walking unassisted in a group.

At this stage, the group work benefits the mothers almost more than the children. The mothers receive individual guidance in a relaxed atmosphere while they themselves are working with the children. Mothers become less anxious and, instead of relying on specialists, learn to become responsible for their children's education themselves. They can compare their children's progress with that of other children in the group and share the problems common to other mothers of similarly disabled children.

If a child progresses well in the parent group he/she will transfer to the outpatient group where work lasts from two to six hours a day in a group without the mother. The children attend as day patients. Some children become 'orthofunctioning' as outpatients; others may have to become inpatients. The most intense conductive education is carried out on an inpatient basis (Hari, personal communication).

These residential students are placed in groups according to their diagnoses and speed of activity. There is a range of ages in each group, providing a type of family situation and necessitating some reassortment for school work. The children benefit from being in a group as they can learn from and interact with each other instead of being 'adult dominated'. The conductor can study a child unobtrusively in a social setting. The group momentum can influence a child who is resisting. Not least, a child cannot be too dependent on the conductor in a group of 15 or more children. The group also provides security; in a group a child can learn to cope with and control his/her emotions, being part of a stable situation. Children also learn how to give and take; they can help others as others help them in giving advice or assistance in overcoming a problem of movement or posture.

The program

Daily and weekly timetables are made to fit into a definite plan by which to accomplish a definite objective. The schedule extends to every aspect of life; to movement, to seeing and hearing, speech and writing, singing, playing percussion instruments, kindergarten and school, arts and crafts, use of tools and finally work in a shop or factory. No typewriter or electronic aids are used. A child must learn to write manually.

Parnwell (1970) summarizes the program:

> At the same time that the children are learning the elements of physical control through active exercies in lying, sitting and standing and detailed hand exercises, they are putting into practice their increasing control and body awareness in active situations of everyday life. They do not wait to achieve a normal pattern of movement before using it in function; they concentrate on function from the very beginning, and so they are psychologically and emotionally prepared for functional independence as it becomes a physical possibility. The constant background of training ensures a gradual progression towards normality of motor functioning within this active and practical framework of living.

Exercises, carefully graded, are performed systematically with 'rhythmic intention' (*q.v*). 'There is no place for improvization in the conductive process. The progressive movement problems always have to be based on already existing results. Improvizations disregarding already established laws are senseless; they prevent progress' (Hari, personal communication).

Aids and devices

The Institute's policy on aids constitutes a major difference between western practice and the Hungarian system of conductive education. There is a total prohibition of devices such as wheelchairs, typewriters, computers, etc. However, the author has observed over the years some relaxation of the use of aids, e.g. children now walk with the assistance of sticks and other devices.

Rhythmic intention

Peto used the term 'rhythmic intention' to describe the way language is used during the task series. The task series is a program lasting for a specific period which encourages motor movement through tasks (physical activities) culminating in a purposeful practical movement. Rhythmic intention is a very important part of conductive education. The instruction is given by the conductor, the children repeat the instruction (the intention) all together and then they perform the movement. There are two components to rhythmic intention: an intention – a planning phase; and an execution phase – which is performed rhythmically. For example, a child might say, 'I raise my hand. I stretch my fingers. I place my hand on the plinth. One, two, three, four, five.' In the case of speech defects, substitutions are found for usual words. Peto believed that the order that would be developed in the brain by the work focused on speech and hand dexterity would be reflected in the performance of the whole body. Whether this is true or not, observers have remarked on the usefulness of the hands of children at the Institute and the fact that there is little or no gap between physiotherapy and other daily living tasks, e.g. dressing, feeding.

Family role

In the early years parents were not involved closely in the education of their children. Parents usually visited their residential children during the weekends and were merely 'onlookers'. Today, mother and baby groups thrive, and mothers in particular are encouraged to participate and become skilled co-workers. Parents are offered every opportunity to continue the program at home. Parent groups also provide effective networks of support.

A daily timetable of the most important program activities is compiled for the period following discharge and given to each student. Regular 'follow-ups' are made at the home, in school or the place of work. Social activities are also included in the program, such as signing, music, drama, sports and dancing, enabling a patient to participate in normal social life on discharge.

Psychological basis for conductive education

Peto's method and the terminology used at the Institute are always expressed in future or goal-oriented functional terms. For example, 'In order to bend down and pick up her sock, this child needs to improve her stability in sitting'. In the educational and neuropsychological field, Peto was inspired by the work of Pavlov, Luria, Vygotsky, Bernstein and others.

Conductive education is, therefore, not merely an exercise approach to learning, it is 'learning to learn'. The child with motor problems is not perceived as 'sick', but is actively engaged in self-learning and takes responsibility for his or her own life, with the guidance of conductors.

Those who attend the Institute work in groups. Adhering to a rigid timetable and a long-term program in surroundings that are free from all distraction is also a key element of conductive education. This potent teaching method is promoted by skilfully incorporating and effectively applying insights gained from neurology, psychology and pedagogy. Its main goal is to stimulate a developmental process which leads to self-care and social interaction so that children can eventually attend normal state schools and become contributing members of society. Peto's methods foster the active participation of the child (or adult) in the treatment process, whereby with guidance their own initiative can be developed.

The sound psychological and psychoneurological principles on which Peto's form of education is founded are as follows:

Motivation

Motivation has a firm neurological basis. The brain cortex of a motivated learner will arouse the reticular formation of the brain so that more information is received. Conductive education concentrates from the beginning on getting a child motivated as has been described. 'Children only cry if an activity is forced on them' (Hari, personal communication).

Conceptualizing techniques

The three types of conceptualizing techniques are used in conductive education: imagery (thinking about the movements necessary for performance); directed mental practice (directing the thinking of the performer through specific instruction) and verbalization techniques (the performer describes movements or associated feelings through the spoken or written word). These three techniques have proven value in improving motor skills in normal children.

Feedback

The learner of a motor skill can draw upon two types of feedback: internal feedback, which is related to kinaesthesis, and external feedback, which is concerned with knowledge of results. Movements of any kind provide internal feedback. Additional information which may be provided following the performance of a skill is referred to as 'knowledge of results'. Conductive education provides both internal feedback via the carefully devised exercises, and knowledge of results, which is provided by the conductor. The exercises are often repeated, providing practice.

This is an important feature of the training program – children love repeating the exercises and feel confident when rehearsing a newly learned skill like the ability to stand, or sit up. As Kay (1970) argues – 'There is a joy of repetition':

> In his strange world a child comes to love repeatable happenings; by repetition he begins to control the world around him. Eventually he will acquire such control that he will seek out the spice of life variety but for the present he has too much of it and so he pleads for the familiar story with its known ending, or the practised game which he has mastered and where he can demonstrate his proficiency. It is not surprising, therefore, that where so much is unknown a child creates its own redundancy by its love of repetition. We have to build on practised units of behaviour.

In many instances, for such children, the practice of a motor skill is interrupted, either by time between sessions, weekends, or breaks in concentration caused by various inappropriate stimuli in the environment. By the use of an integrated program taught by trained conductors, conductive education gives the maximum opportunity for retention of learned motor skills.

Summary

The systematic program laid down for conductive education applies throughout the waking period of the students, and this is held as one of the cardinal features of the method. As a result, the range of activities (movement patterns) performed by the students become severely restricted and largely predictable. Instead of having a wide range of movements, many of which are inadequately and incompletely executed, the sheer repetitive character of the teaching creates a structured framework in which there is a chance for frequent reinforcements of every aspect of motor training. In terms of simple conditioning theories, there is a greatly facilitated reinforcement of common elements of similar motor patterns and a markedly reduced interference of established movement patterns by random, chance interruptions. This in itself should enhance the motor development of children with severely disabled motor control.

A second, and probably equally important, aspect is that as a result of the speech accompaniments the student is offered a reinforcing schedule for the movements before these are undertaken, i.e. a set towards the movements develops, is reinforced by the planned utterances and maintained due to the rhythmic and practised speech content. A different feature which is associated with this, which is applicable to many children with cerebral palsy and to athetoid children in particular, is that the problems of performing two movements simultaneously are enormously greater than those of performing one at a time. By obliging the student to speak at the same time as he is executing other movements, this is achieved, and over-practised to a considerable degree. This means that the total movement pattern is broken down into its constituent elements, and that the systematic and practised element is increased still further. In summary, the Peto method for conductive education offers a means for continuous and frequent reinforcement on one hand, and for the elimination of extra, interfering movements on the other.

Peto Institute records over a 25-year span indicate that some 5500 students have been educated, with an 85% success rate for children aged six and under, 75% success in the 6–10-year group and 60–70% success above the age of 10 years. A person who becomes self-reliant and is able to integrate him- or herself into normal surroundings is considered a success.

The average conductive education term is two to three years. After leaving the institute, 90–95% of pupils are able to maintain their education level, depending upon family and local environmental support. An important principle is that children must receive their education from as few people as possible, and many other aspects of the teaching regime differ markedly from approaches developed outside Hungary.

The evidence offered by the Hungarian conductive education system is that children and adults who have sustained brain damage can be taught at an earlier age than previously suspected.

Worldwide influence

Astonishing results have been reported by visitors to Hungary and there are a growing number of attempts, in various stages of development, to replicate the conductive education system in other countries. Many children have gone to Hungary from elsewhere in Europe, notably Britain and Unified States, but also from other parts of the world: Africa, North and South America, the Gulf States, Australia and New Zealand, Asia and Oceania.

In 1991, a World Congress was held in Budapest with nearly 300 delegates attending from 31 different countries. One issue discussed was the length of time it takes to train conductors. An experimental course run by the Peto Institute lasting just two years for selected candidates was proposed in four selected centres, two in Britain, one in Vienna and one in Brussels. Also, a European network of support was inaugurated.

In Britain, the Birmingham Institute, run closely on Peto lines, is now well-established. British teachers have gone to Hungary to train as conductors and conductors have come to Britain to train students as conductors. One difficulty is that only British-trained or recognized teachers can be given teacher status in Britain, so students from other disciplines, such as physiotherapists, are not eligible for training at the Institute. Successful results are reported by the Birmingham Institute and some children have already graduated to take their place in mainstream schools in Britain. The Spastics Society has just set up an institute in London with Hungarian conductors.

Graduate conductors are practising in Hong Kong, and Hong Kong University has set up a training course for conductors. In Australia and New Zealand it is hoped to establish institutes similar to the Birmingham Institute, with Hungarian conductors working there, while Australian and New Zealanders go to Hungary for training. Brisbane and Melbourne have been suggested as possible centres for preparing conductors for future work in Australia.

Travel and communication have been made easier since the overthrow of communism in Hungary in the autumn of 1989. However, the lure of excitement and riches abroad has caused a 'brain drain' of conductors in the Peto Institute, bringing its own problems.

A major concern that has recently arisen is the evangelical zeal with which weak imitations of conductive education have been adopted in a number of countries. In some instances, caricatures of the program have been introduced into various centres and schools by poorly prepared enthusiasts. The present writer warned against such a developing trend at the International Peto Association First World Congress, held in Hungary in December 1990. He feared that the genuine method as practised in Hungary might be discredited and the hopes of parents and educators of disabled children dashed.

Epilogue

Concern for the education of children with motor and neurological disabilities can be demonstrated at a number of levels – that of the underlying medical conditions and their diagnosis and alleviation, that of the functioning impairment and ways of overcoming this and, finally, the functioning of the child in his or her social, cultural and family environment (Chauvel, 1990).

A book such as this should conclude by addressing the nature of care and development and the teacher's role in it. A wide variety of supporting professionals are involved in this care and development bringing with them a large number of disparate opinions and perspectives. Even teachers themselves vary greatly, both in interest and attitudes and consequent success. Often, graduating teachers, however excellent their training programs, find that they learn much from the job and their more experienced colleagues.

The types of teaching categories of Polloway *et al.* (1985) describing teachers who are (1) 'survivors'; (2) 'happiness specialists' and (3) 'missionaries', show that their very different foci can result in different emphases in teaching. Survivors emphasize the children rather than content and curriculum, happiness specialists emphasize some areas of curriculum, such as crafts and outings, rather than pursuing general academic growth, and missionaries deal in behaviour modification and curers of handicap.

The effectiveness of the teaching of children with motor neurological disabilities has been defined by Oliva and Henson (1980) as a function of two dimensions: (1) the amount of learning the child masters and (2) the time and effort of the teaching. The corollary here is that the more a student learns the more efficient has been the teacher. It follows then that the more effective teacher may also accelerate learning. Skinner (1968) (p. 5) stated that 'teaching is the expediting of learning; a person who is taught learns more quickly than does one who is not'. For research into teacher effectiveness, the reader is also referred to such studies as Bateman (1971), Grobman (1972), Carnine (1983) and Englert (1983).

Concerned educators and educated well-wishers should have a rational approach to student learning and be well informed and well researched. The framework for teaching comes from the philosophical perspectives of the policy documents of the agencies in which we work. This is especially relevant in the area of integration of students with disabilities in ordinary schools and classrooms. There is still debate about this policy in Australia and elsewhere, consequently special schools are still a major feature of special education provision in all States in Australia. This is true in Britain and much of the USA. This is likely to be so for the present decade. Gow (1988) found that much current Australian integration policy is unfortunately ideologically and politically based rather than based on empirical evidence related to its efficacy. However, the 'integration movement' has been expanding steadily to a point where it is the most prevalent form of special education for children with physical and sensory disabilities, and those with mild intellectual disabilities, but not for those with severe intellectual disabilities or multiple disabilities (Elkins, 1990).

Perspectives and challenges

The most important trend of the 1980s has been the increasing realization at an international level of the need for provision of comprehensive, community-based services for the disabled (Menolascimo, 1979). Professionals meet at international conferences in widely located venues considering the same issues, etc. which are affecting people in Europe, North America, Africa, Australia and most other places. These are the forums where ideas are exchanged and new methods worked out to modify and improve our approaches to and provision of effective and efficient educational supports for children with disabilities.

The message of the last decade seems to be that we must continue to write on issues and look for common purposes for all people, as is shown in the following international trends.

1. **Families of people with disabilities**
   Increasingly, the family does, and should, obtain services by right rather than through charity. People are becoming aware of their legal rights and realize they should no longer need to beg for services. Possibly the present decade will be the one in which parents will gain more power over areas of decision-making about their children.
2. **Prevention and research**
   It is probable that the dramatic increase in high technology research will decrease markedly the incidence of disabling conditions. Menolascimo (1979) has suggested that this may also come with such arrangements as:
   (a) comprehensive pre-natal care centres;
   (b) prevention of infections such as rubella and bacterial meningitis which affects the central nervous system;
   (c) early diagnostic techniques such as amniocentesis;
   (d) prevention of internal and external intoxication sources, such as toxoplasmosis, AIDS, etc.;
   (e) intervention into recurring sets of early childhood experiences which adversely affect developmental potential, by providing infants with appropriately stimulating environments.

In future we should see quicker international dissemination of information and treatment programs.

3. **The social role valorization principle**
   Wolfensberger's (1983) principle relates to a philosophical position and an associated methodology for maximizing culturally valued behaviour and lifestyle. For example, people with disabilities, no matter how severe, should be treated in ways which promote their value in society. The idea of integration follows from this and will continue to produce significant policy changes.
4. **Community-based service systems**
   Since the United Nations General Assembly adopted its Declaration of Rights of Disabled Persons in 1975, many nations have commenced development of effective community-based service systems. These should help

prepare the individual for his or her community modes of living, schools, vocation and recreation. There are a great many issues involving the variety of specific disabilities which relate to the sort of communities in which we would wish children with physical and neurological disabilities to live wordwide. Changes in this highly complex human service field will take place in proportion to the extent to which professional advocacy and family groups can make themselves heard. The international activities now going on appear to promise an immense potential for amalgamating current and future educational services to children with physical or neurological disabilities.

Further reading

Beech, J.R. (1985) *Learning to Read: A Cognitive Approach to Reading and Poor Reading*. London: Croom Helm.

Bloom, B.A. amd Seljeskog, E. (198) *A Parents' Guide to Spina Bifida*. Minneapolis: University of Minnesota Press.

Bryant, P. and Bradley, L. (1985) *Children's Reading Problems: Psychology and Education*. Oxford: Basil Blackwell.

Cameron, N. (1984) *The Measurement of Human Growth*. Beckenham: Croom Helm.

Copeland, M.E. and Kimmel, J.R. (1989) *Evaluation and Management of Infants and Young Children with Developmental Disabilities*. Baltimore: Paul H. Brookes Publishing.

Faerber, E.N. (1986) Cranial Computed Tomography in Infants and Children. *Clinics in Developmental Medicine, No. 93*. Oxford: Blackwell Scientific Publications.

Hanson, M.J. and Harris, S.R. (1986) *Teaching the Young Child with Motor Delays*. Austin: Pro-Ed.

Heilman, K.M. and Valenstein, E. (eds) (1985) *Clinical Neuropsychology*, 2nd edn. New York: Oxford University Press.

Hermann, B.P. and Seidenberg, M. (eds) (1989) *Childhood Epilepsies: Neuropsychological, Psychosocial and Intervention Aspects*. Chichester: John Wiley.

Illingworth, R.S. (1990) *The Development of the Infant and Young Child*, 9th edn. Edinburgh: Churchill Livingstone.

Kameenui, E.J. and Simmons, D.C. (1990) *Designing Instructional Strategies: The Prevention of Academic Learning Problems*. Columbus: Merrill Publishing.

Rentel, V.M., Corson, S.A. and Dunn, R.A. (eds) (1985) *Psychophysiological Aspects of Reading and Learning*. New York: Gordon and Breach Science Publishers.

Ross, E., Chadwick, D. and Crawford, R. (eds) (1988) *Epilepsy in Young People*. Chichester: John Wiley.

Smith, S.D. (1986) *Genetics and Learning Disabilities*. San Diego: College-Hill Press.

Springer, S. and Deutch, G. (1981) *Left Brain, Right Brain*. San Francisco: Freeman Press.

Stephens, D. (1990) *What Matters?: A Primer for Teaching Reading*. Portsmouth: Heinemann Educational Books.

Tinkelman, D.G., Falliers, C.J. and Naspitz, C.K. (eds) (1987) *Childhood Asthma: Pathophysiology and Treatment*. New York: Marcel Dekker.

References

Abercrombie, M.L.J. (1960) Perception and eye movements: Some speculations on disorders in cerebral palsy. *Cerebral Palsy Bulletin,* **2**, 142–8.

Abercrombie, M.L.J. (1963) Eye movements perception and learning, *Visual Disorders in Cerebral Palsy* (ed. V.H. Smith). London. Spastics Society/Heinemann.

Abercrombie, M.L.J. (1964) Perceptual and visuomotor disorders in cerebral palsy. *Clinics in Developmental Medicine,* **11**. London: Heinemann.

Albrow, K. (1974) The nature of the writing system and its relation to speech, in *Spelling: Task and Learner* (eds B. Wade and K. Wedell). Educational Review Occasional Publications, No. 5.

Alston, J. and Taylor, J. (1987) *Handwriting: Theory, Research and Practice*. London: Croom Helm.

Anderson, E. (1975) Unpublished Ph.D. thesis. University of London.

Andrews, R.J. (1982) A happy venture, Part 2. *The Exceptional Child,* **30**, 3–56.

Andrews, R.J. (1983) A happy venture, Part 1. *The Exceptional Child,* **29**, 155–90.

Andrews, R.J. and Elkins, J. (1981) *The Management and Education of Children with Spina Bifida and Hydrocephalus*. ERDC Report No. 32. Canberra: Australian Government Printing Office.

Andrews, R.J., Elkins, J., Berry, P.B. and Burge, J.A. (1979) *A Survey of Special Education in Australia; Provision, Needs and Priorities in the Education of Children with Handicaps and Learning Difficulties*. Brisbane: University of Queensland.

Ansell, B. (1976) *The Arthritis and Rheumatism Council Leaflet No. 35,* Summer 1976.

Aston Index – A classroom test for screening and diagnosing language difficulties age from 5–14 years. Newton, M. and Thomson, M. Cambridge LDA.

Bateman, B.D. (1971) *The Essentials of Teaching*. Sioux Falls, SD: Dimensions Publishing.

Bax, M.C.O. (1964) Terminology and classification of cerebral palsy. *Developmental Medicine and Child Neurology*, **6**, 295–7.

Beaumont, J.G. (1983) *Introduction to Neuropsychology*. Oxford: Blackwell Scientific Publications, pp. 249–52.

Benton, A.L. (1969) Disorders of spatial orientation. In P.J. Vinken and G.W. Bruyn (eds) *Handbook of Clinical Neurology*. Amsterdam: North-Holland Publishing Company, pp. 212–28.

Benton, A.L., Hutcheon, J.F. and Seymour, E. (1951) Arithmetic ability, finger-localization capacity and right–left hand discrimination in normal and defective children. *American Journal of Orthopsychiatry*, **21**, 756–66.

Biggs, J.B. (1959) The development of number concepts in young children. *Educational Research*, **1**, 17–34.

Binet, A. and Henri, V. (1896) La psychologie individuelle. *Annee Psychologique*, **2**, 411–65.

Birch, H.G. (1956) Theoretical aspects of psychological behaviour in the brain damaged, in *Psychological Services for the Cerebral Palsied*, (ed. M. Goldstein). United Cerebral Palsy Association, p. 56.

Birch, H.G. (1964) The problem of 'brain damage' in children. In H.G. Birch (ed.) *Brain Damage in Children: The Biological and Social Aspects*. Baltimore: Williams and Wilkins, pp. 3–12.

Birch, H.G. and Bortner, M. (1966) Stimulus competition and category usage in normal children. *Journal of Genetic Psychology*, **109**, 195–204.

Birch, H.G. and Bornter, M. (1967) Cognitive capacity and cognitive competence, in *Annual Progress in Child Psychiatry and Child Development* (eds S. Chess and A. Thomas). New York: Bruner/Mazel.

Bobath, K. (1966) *The Motor Deficit in Patients with Cerebral Palsy*. London: Heinemann Medical Books.

Bobath, B. (1971) *Abnormal Postural Reflex Activity Caused by Brain Lesions*. London: Heinemann Medical Books.

Boring, E.G. (1957) *A History of Experimental Psychology*, 2nd edn. New York: Appleton–Century–Crofts.

Bornter, M. and Birch, H.G. (1971) Cognitive capacity and cognitive competence, in *Annual Progress in Child Psychiatry and Child Development* (eds S. Chess and A. Thomas). New York, Bruner/Mazel. London: Butterworth.

Bourne, G.H. and Golarz, M.N. (1963) *Muscular Dystrophy in Man and Animals*. Basel: S. Karger.

Bowey, J.A., Tunmer, W.E. and Pratt, C. (1984) Development of children's understanding of the metalinguistic term word. *Journal of Educational Psychology*, **76**, 500–12.

Bradley, L. and Bryant, P.E. (1978) Difficulties in auditory organsiation as a possible cause of reading backwardness. *Nature*, **271**, 746–47.

Bradley, L. and Bryant, P.E. (1985) *Rhyme and Reason in Reading and Spelling*. International Academy for Research in Learning Disabilities Monograph Series 2, Ann Arbor: University of Michigan Press.

Brain, W.R. (1941) Visual disorientation with special reference to lesions of the right cerebral hemisphere. *Brain*, **64**, 244–72.

Brownell, W.A. (1941) *Arithmetic in Grades I and II – A Critical Summary and Previously Reported Research*. Durham, North Carolina: Duke University Press.

Buchtel, H.A. (1984) *The Conceptual Nervous System*. Oxford: Pergamon Press.

Buffery, A.W.H. (1970) Sex differences in the development of hand preference, cerebral dominance for speech and cognitive skill. *Bulletin of British Psychological Society*, **23**, 233.

Buffery, A.W.H. (1971) Sex differences in the development of hemispheric asymmetry of function in the human brain. *Brain Research*, **31**, 364–5.

Buffery, A.W.H. (1976) Sex differences in the neuropsychological development of verbal and spatial skills, in *The Neuropsychology of Learning Disorders, Theoretical Approaches* (eds R.M. Knights and D.J. Bakker). Baltimore: University Park Press, pp. 187–205.

Buffery, A.W.H. and Gray, J.A. (1972) Sex differences in the development of spatial and linguistic skills, in *Gender Differences: Their Ontogeny and Significance* (eds C. Ounsted and D.C. Taylor). London; Churchill and Livingstone.

Bullock, N. (1975) *A Language of Life*. London: HMSO.

Burt, C. (1940) *Factors of the Mind*. London: University of London Press.

Burt, C. (1955) The evidence for the concept of intelligence. *British Journal of Education Psychology*, **25**, 158–77.

Caldwell, E.M. (1956) *A Case of Spatial Inability in a Cerebral Palsied Child*. London: British Council for the Welfare of Spastics.

Calvin, W.H, and Ojemann, G.A. (1980). *Inside the Brain*. New York: Mentor Books

Cambridge, J. and Weddell, K. (1972). When handwriting is a handicap. *Special Education*, 1, pp. 23–6.

Carmon, A. (1970) Impaired utilization of kinesthetic feedback in right hemisphere lesions. Possible implications for the pathophysiology of 'motor impersistence'. *Neurology*, **20**, 1033–38.

Carnine, D. (1983) Direct instruction: In search of instructional solutions for educational problems. *Interdisciplinary Voices In Learning Disabilities and Remediation*. Anstn, TX, Pro. Ed., 1–60.

Carter, C.O. (1974) Clues to the aetiology of neural tube malformations. *Developmental Medicine and Child Neurology*, **16**, 3–15.

Cattell, R.B. (1965) *The Scientific Analysis of Personality*. Harmondsworth: Penguin.

Caveness, W. (1976) Epilepsy. A product of trauma in our time. *Epilepsia*, **17**, 207–15.

Chapman, J., Lewis, A. and Wedell, K. (1970) A note on reversals in the writing of 8-year-old children. *Remedial Education*, **5**, 91–4.

Chapman, J., Lewis, A. and Wedell, K. (1972) Perceptuo–motor abilities and reversal errors in children's handwriting. *Journal of Learning Disabilities*, **5**, 321–5.

Chauvel, P.J. (1990) Physical disability: Overview. In S R. Butler, *The Exceptional Child*. Marrickville, N.S.W.: Harcourt Brace Jovanovitch.

Chazan, M. (1973) *Compensatory Education*. London: Butterworth.

Clarke, M.M. (1974) *Teaching Left-Handed Children*. London: University of London Press.

Clarke, M.M. (1975) *Left Handedness*. Oxford: Oxford University Press.

Clearview Programme (1987) Andover, Hampshire: Philip and Tacey.

Cohen, J. and Clark, J.H. (1979) *Medicine, Mind and Man*. Oxford: W H. Freeman and Company.

Cole, L. (1939) Instruction in penmanship for the left-handed child. *Elementary School Journal*, **39**, 436–48.

Cole, R.A. (1977) Invariant features and feature detection: Some developmental implications, in *Language Development and Neurological Theory* (eds S.J. Segalowitz and F.A. Gruber). New York: Academic Press.

Connolly, K. (ed.) (1970) *Mechanisms of Motor Skill Development*. London and New York: Academic Press, pp. 359–360.

Cotham, P.J. and Sutton, A. (eds) (1986) *Conductive Education: A System for Overcoming Motor Disorder*. London: Croom Helm.

Cotterell, G. (1974) A remedial aproach to spelling disability. In B. Wade and K. Wedell (eds) *Spelling: Task and Learner*. Birmingham: University of Birmingham.

Cox, B. (1984) *The Law of Special Educational Needs: A Guide to the 1981 Education Act*. London: Croom Helm.

Craft, A.W., Eastham, E.J., Bell, J.I., Brigham, K. (1977) *Annals of the Rheumatic Diseases*, **36**, 271.

Cratty, B.J. (1972) *Physical Expressions of Intelligence*. New Jersey: Prentice-Hall.

Critchley, M. (1953) *The Parietal Lobes*. London: Arnold.

Critchley, M. (1964) *Developmental Dyslexia*. London: Heinemann.

Critchley, M. (1965) Acquired anomalies of colour. *Brain*, **88**, 71.

Cromer, R.F. (1980) Spontaneous spelling by language disordered children, in *Cognitive Process in Spelling* (ed. U. Frith). London: Academic Press.

Crosby, R.M.N. and Liston, R.A. (1968) *Reading and the Dyslexic Child*. London: Souvenir Press.

Cruickshank, W.M., Bice, H.V. and Wallen, N.E. (1957) *Perception and Cerebral Palsy*. New York: Syracuse University Press.

Cruickshank, W.M.A. (1961) *A Teaching Method for Brain-Injured and Hyperactive Children*. Syracuse: Syracuse University Press.

Cruickshank, W.M. (ed.) (1976) *Cerebral Palsy: A Developmental Disability* (3rd edn). Syracuse: Syracuse University Press.

Cummins, R.A. (1988) *The Neurologically Impaired Child: Doman–Delacato Techniques Reappraised*. London: Croom Helm.

Daniels, J.C. and Diack, H. (1964) *The Standard Reading Tests*. London: Chatto and Windus.

Dean, J. (1968) *Reading, Writing and Talking*. London: Blackwell.

Department of Education and Science (1975) *A Language for Life*. (The Bullock Report.) London: HMSO.

Deutsch, M. (1966) Nursery education, The influence of social programming on early development, in *The Disadvantaged Child: Issues and Innovations* (eds J.L. Frost and G.R. Hawkes). Boston: Houghton Mifflin.

Dodd, B. and Hermelin, B. (1977) Phonological coding by the pre-linguistically deaf. *Perception and Psychophysics*, **21**, 413–17.,

Doman, G. (1974) *What to do about your Brain-injured Child*. London: Jonathon Cape.

Douglas, J.W.B. (1964) *The Home and the School*. London: MacGibbon and Kee.

Downing, J. (1978) Linguistic awareness, English orthography and reading instruction. *Journal of Reading Behaviour*, **10**, 103–14.

Drummond, N.W. (1978) *Special Education in Australia*. Sydney: Torron Press.

Dunsdon, M.L. (1952) *The Educability of Cerebral Palsied Children*. London: Newnes Educational.

Dutton, W.H. (1964) *Evaluating Pupils' Understanding of Arithmetic*. Englewood Cliffs, New Jersey: Prentice–Hall.

Elkins, J. (1990) Introduction to exceptionality, in *The Exceptional Child* (ed. S.R. Butler). Marrickville, N.S.W.: Harcourt Brace Jovanovich.

Englert, C.S. (1983) Measuring special education teacher effectiveness. *Exceptional Children*, **50**, 247–54.

Eysenck, H.G. and Eysenck, S.B.G. (1964) *Manual of the Eysenck Personality Inventory*. London: University of London Press.

Fairweather, H. (1982) Sex difference: Little reason for females to play midfield, in *Divided Visual Field Studies of Cerebral Organization* (ed. J.G. Beaumont). London: Academic Press.

Fernald, G.M. (1943) *Remedial Techniques in Basic School Subjects*. New York: Random House.

Fernald, W.E. (1893) The history of treatment of the feebleminded. Proceedings of the National Conference of Charities and Correction. Boston: George H. Ellis.

Ferrier, D. (1876) *The Function of the Brain*. London: Smith Elder.

Fiorentino, M.R. (1981) *A Basis for Sensorimotor Development – Normal and Abnormal*. Springfield, Illinois: Charles Thomas Publishing.

Flexner, J.B., Flexner, L.B. and Stellar, E. (1963) Memory in mice as affected by intracerebral puromycin. *Science*, **141**, pp. 57–9.

Flourens, M.J.P. (1824) *Recherches experimentales sur les proprietes et les fonctions du systeme nerveux dans les animaux vertebres*. Paris: Crevot.

Fox, B. and Routh, D.K. (1980) Phoneme analysis and severe reading disability. *Journal of Psycholinguistic Research*. pp. 115–19.

Frith, U. (1980) *Cognitive Processes in Spelling*. London: Academic Press.

Fritsch, G.T. and Hitzig, F. (1870) Uber die elektrische Erregbarkeit des Grosshirns. *Archives of Anatomy and Physiology Wiss. Med. Leipzig*, **37**, 300.

Gaddes, W.H. (1985) *Learning Disabilities and Brain Function: A Neuropsychological Approach*, 2nd edn. New York: Springer–Verlag.

Galton, F. (1869) *Hereditary Genius*. London: Macmillan.

Gazzaniga, M.S. and Sperry, R.W. (1967) Language after section of the cerebral commissures. *Brain*, **90**, 131–48.

Gewanter, H.L. and Roghmann, K.J. (1983) *Arthritis and Rheumatism*, **26**, 25.

Gillette, H. (1969) *Systems of Therapy in Cerebral Palsy*. Springfield, Ill.: Charles C. Thomas.

Glavin, J.P. and de Girolamo, G. (1970) Spelling errors of withdrawn and conduct problem children. *Journal of Special Education*, **4**, 2.

Goldstein, K. (1942) *After Effects of Brain-Injuries in War*. New York: Grune and Stratton.

Goodacre, E.J. (1971) *Children and Learning to Read*. London: Routledge and Kegan Paul.

Goodman, K.S. (ed.) (1968) *The Psycholinguistic Nature of the Reading Process*. Detroit: Wayne State University.

Goody, W. (1969) Disorders of the time sense, in *Handbook of Clinical Neurology* (eds P.J. Vinken and G.W. Bruyn). Amsterdam: North Holland Publishing Company, **3**, pp. 229–50.

Gough, P.B. (1972) One second of reading, in *Language by Ear and Eye* (eds J.F. Kavanagh and I.G. Mattingly). Cambridge, MA: MIT Press, pp. 331–58.

Gow, L. (1988) Integration in Australia. *European Journal of Special Needs Education*, **3**, 1–12.

Gregory, R.E. (1965) Unsettledness, maladjustment and reading failure: a village study. *British Journal of Educational Psychology*, **35**, 63–8.

Grewel, F. (1969) The Acalculias, in *Disorders of Speech Perception and Symbolic Behaviour* (eds P.J. Vinken and G.W. Bruyn). Amsterdam: North-Holland Publishing Company, **4**, pp. 187–94.

Grobman, H. (1972) *Accountability for What?* Nations Schools.

Hagberg, B., Hagberg, G. and Olow, I. (1975) The changing pattern of cerebral palsy in Sweden. *Acta Paediatrica Scandinavica*, **64**, 187–92.

Hall, D.M.B. (1984) *The Child with a Handicap*. Oxford: Blackwell Scientific Publications.

Harlow, H.F. (1949). The formation of learning sets. *Psychological Review*, **56**, 51–65.

Harris, T.L. and Rarick, G.L. (1959) Relationship between legibility and handwriting pressure of children and adolescents. *Journal of Experimental Education*, **28**, 65–84.

Harrison, A. and Connolly, K. (1971) The conscious control of fine levels of neuromuscular activity in spastic and normal subjects. *Developmental Medicine and Child Neurology*, **13**, 762–71.

Hart, N.W.M. (1973) The differential diagnosis of the psycho-linguistic abilities of the cerebral palsied child and effective remedial procedures. *Special Schools Bulletin No. 2*, Brisbane, Australia.

Harvey, B. (1982) Cystic fibrosis, in *Physically Handicapped Children: A Medical Atlas for Teachers* (eds E. Bleck and D.A. Nagel) (2nd edn) New York: Grune and Stratton.

Haskell, S.H. (1972) Visuo-perceptual, visuo-motor and scholastic skills of alternating and uniocular squinting children. *Journal of Special Education*, **6**, 3–8.

Haskell, S.H. (1973) *Arithmetical Disabilities in Cerebral Palsied Children. Programmed Instruction. A Remedial Approach*. Illinois: Charles C. Thomas.

Haskell, S.H. and Hughes, V.A. (1965) Some observations on the performance of squinters and non-squinters on the Wechsler Intelligence Scale for children. *Perceptual and Motor Skills*, **21**, 107–12.

Haskell, S.H. and Paull, M.E. (1973a) *Training in Basic Cognitive Skills*. Harlow: ESA Creative Learning.

Haskell, S.H. and Paull, M.E. (1973b) *Training in Motor Skills*. Harlow: ESA Creative Learning.

Hebb, D.O. (1942) The effect of early and late brain injury on test scores and the nature of normal adult intelligence. *Proceedings of American Philosophical Society*, **85**, pp. 275–92.

Haecaen, H. (1972) *Introduction a la Neuropsychologie*. Paris: Larousse.

Hacaen, H. and Albert, M.L. (1978) *Human Neuropsychology,*. New York: John Wiley.

Hegarty, S. (1987) *Meeting Special Needs in Ordinary Schools: An Overview*. Cassell, in Series Special Needs in Ordinary Schools.

Held, R. and Hein, A. (1963) Movement produced stimulation in the development of visually guided behaviour. *Journal of Physiological Psychology*, **56**, 872–6.

Held, R. and Bauer, J.A. (1967) Visually guided reaching in infant monkeys after restricted rearing. *Science* **155**, 718–20.

Henderson, J.L. (1961) *Cerebral Palsy in Childhood and Adolescence*. Edinburgh and London: Churchill and Livingstone.

Herbert, M. (1964) The concept and testing of brain damage in children: a review. *Journal of Child Psychology and Psychiatry*, **5**, 197–216.

Hermelin, B. and O'Connor, N. (1970) *Psychological Experiments with Autistic Children*. Oxford: Pergamon Press.

Hildreth, G. (1945) Comparative speed of joined and unjoined writing strokes. *Journal of Educational Psychology*, **36**, 91–102.

Hobbs, M.S.T., Carney, A., Field, B., Simpson, D. and Kerr, C. (1974) Incidence of anencephalus and spina bifida and variation in risks according to parental birthplaces in three Australian states. *British Journal of Preventive and Social Medicine*, **28**, 67.

Hodgson, A., Clunies-Ross, L. and Hegarty, S. (1984) *Learning Together: Teaching Pupils with Special Educational Needs in Ordinary School*. Slough: NFER-Nelson.

Hooton, M. (1975) *The First Reading and Writing Book*. London: Shepheard–Walwyn.

Hooton, M. (1976) Personal Communication.

Hyden, H. (1958) Biochemical changes in glial cells and nerve cells at varying activity. *Proceedings of 4th International Congress of Biochemistry*, Vienna, pp. 64–8.

Integration in Victorian Education: Report of the Ministerial Review of Educational Services for the Disabled (1984). Education Department: Melbourne.

Itard, J. (1962). *The Wild Boy of Aveyron*. (trans. George and Muriel Humphrey) New York: Appleton–Century–Crofts.

Jackson, J.H. (1874) *Evolution and Dissolution of the Nervous System;*

Speech; Various Papers, Addresses and Lectures. Vol. 2. London: Hodder and Stoughton.

Jeffs, A. (1985) *Children and Parents and Spelling*. Home and School Council.

Jones, M.H., Barrett, M.L., Olonoff, C. and Anderson, E. (1969) Two experiments in training handicapped children at nursery school in *Planning for Better Living* (eds P. Wolff and R. Mackeith). Clinics in Developmental Medicine. London: Spastics Society: Heinemann Medical Books.

Jorm, A.F. (1983) *The Psychology of Reading and Spelling Disabilities*. International Library of Psychology. London: Routledge and Kegan Paul.

Jorm, A.F. and Share, D.L. (1983) Phonological recoding and reading acquisition. *Applied Psycholinguistics*, **4**, 103–47.

Kanski, J.J. (1977) *Archives of Opthalmology*, **95**, 271.

Kay, H. (1970) Analysing Motor Skill Performance, in *Mechanisms of Motor Skill Development* (ed. K. Connolly). London and New York: Academic Press.

Kephart, N.C. (1960) *The Slow Learner in the Classroom*. Columbus: Charles E. Merrill.

Kinsbourne, M. (1966) Backward readers – but why? *Special Education*, **55**, 23–4.

Kinsbourne, M. (1972) *The Neuropsychology of Learning Disabilities*. Paper presented at Seventh Annual Neuropsychology Workshop, University of Victoria, Victoria, B.C., Canada.

Kinsbourne, M. and Warrington, E.K. (1962a) A disorder of simultaenous form perception. *Brain*, **85**, 461–86.

Kinsbourne, M. and Warrington, E.K. (1962b) A variety of reading disability associated with right hemisphere lesions. *Journal of Neurology, Neurosurgery and Psychiatry*, **25**, 339–44.

Kinsbourne, M. and Warrington, E.K. (1962c) A study of finger agnosia. *Brain*, **85**, 47–66.

Kinsbourne, M. and Warrington, E.K. (1963a) Developmental factors in reading and writing backwardness. *British Journal of Psychology*, **54**, 145–56.

Kinsbourne, M. and Warrington, E.K.(1963b) The development c finger differentiation. *Queensland Journal of Experimental Psycholog* XV, 132–7.

Kinsbourne, M. and Warrington, E.K. (1964) Disorders in spelling *Journal of Neurosurgical Psychiatry*, **27**, 224–8.

Kirk, S.A., Kirk, W.D. and McCarthy, J.J. (1968) *Examiner's Manua Illinois Test of Psycholinguistic Abilities*, revised ed. Urbana: Unive sity of Illinois.

Kraemer, M.J. and Bierman, C.W. (1983) Asthma, in *Physic*

Disabilities and Health Impairments (ed. J. Umbreit). Columbus: Charles E. Merrill, pp. 157–66.

Lagergren, J. (1981) Children with motor handicaps. *Acta Paediatrica Scandinavica*, **289**, 1–7.

Lashley, K. (1929) *Brain Mechanisms and Intelligence*. Chicago: University of Chicago Press.

Lee, W.R. (1972) *Spelling Irregularity and Reading Difficulty in England*. Windsor: NFER Publishing Company.

Lefford, A. (1970) Sensory, perceptual and cognitive factors in the development of voluntary actions, in *Mechanisms of Motor Skill Development* (ed. K. Conolly). London and New York: Academic Press, pp. 215–17.

Lennenberg, E. (1967) *Biological Foundations of Language*. New York: John Wiley.

Levin, H.S. (1979) The acalculias, in *Clinical Neuropsychology* (eds K.M. Heilan and E. Valenstein). Oxford: Oxford University Press.

Levitt, S. (1977) *Treatment of Cerebral Palsy and Motor Delay*. Oxford: Blackwell Scientific Publications.

Liberman, A.M. (1975) The specialization of the language hemisphere. In *Hemispheric Specialization and Interaction* (ed B. Milner). Cambridge: MIT Press.

Liberman, I.Y. and Shankweiler, D. (1985) Phonology and the problems of learning to read and write. *Remedial and Special Education*, **6**, 8–17.

Liepmann, H. (1900) Das Krankheitsbild der Apraxie (Motorischen Asymbolie), Mtschr. Psychiat, in *Human Neuropsychology* (eds H. Hecaen and M., Albert). New York: John Wiley, pp. 90–127.

Livingston, A. (1961) A study of spelling errors. *Studies in Spelling*. Scottish Council for Research in Education. London: University of London Press.

Locke, J. (1960) *An Essay Concerning Human Understanding*, London: Holt.

Lovell, K. and Woolsey, M.E. (1964) Reading disability, non-verbal reasoning and social class. *Educational Research*, **6**, 226–9.

Luria, R. (1966) *Higher Cortical Functions in Man*. New York: Basic Books.

Luria, A.R. (1970) *Traumatic Aphasia, its Syndromes, Psychology and Treatment*. The Hague: Morton.

Lynn, R. (1957) Temperamental characteristics related to disparity of attainment in reading. *British Journal of Education Psychology*, **27**, 62–7.

McFie, J., Piercy, M.F. and Zangwill, O.L. (1950) Visuo-spatial agnosia associated with lesions of the right cerebral hemisphere. *Brain*, **73**, 167–90.

McGlone, J. (1980) Sex differences in human brain asymmetry. *Behavioural and Brain Sciences*, **3**, 215–63.

Mangos, J.A. (1983) Cystic fibrosis, in *Physical Disabilities and Health Impairments* (ed. J. Umbreit). Columbus: Charles E. Merrill, pp. 206–13.

Marcel, T. (1980) Phonological awareness and phonological representation investigation of a specific spelling problem. In *Cognitive Process in Spelling* (ed. U. Frith). London: Academic Press.

Marchbanks, G. and Levin, H. (1965) Cues by which children recognize words. *Journal of Educational Psychology*, **56**, 57–61.

Mattingly, L.G. (1972) Reading, the linguistic process and linguistic awareness, in *Language by Ear and Eye* (eds J.F. Kavanagh and I.G. Mattingly) Cambridge, MA: MIT Press, pp. 133–47.

Mehler, J. and Bever, T.G. (1967) Cognitive capacity of very young children. *Science*, **158**, 141–2.

Menolascimo, F.K. (1979) Handicapped children and youth: Current-future international perspectives and challenges. *Exceptional Children*, **46**, 168–174.

Miller, N. (1987) *Dyspraxia and its Management*. London: Croom Helm.

Milner, B. (1954) The intellectual functions of the temporal lobes. *Psychology Bulletin*, **51**, 42–62.

Milner, B. (1958) Psychological defects produced by temporal lobe excision. *Research Publication Association of Nervous Mental Diseases*, **36**, 244–57.

Milner, B. (1962) Laterality effects in audition, in *Interhemispheric Relations and Cerebral Dominance* (ed. V.B. Mountcastle). Baltimore: Johns Hopkins Press.

Milner, B. (1971) Interhemispheric differences and psychological processes. *British Medical Bulletin*, **27**, 272–7.

Morgan, C.L. (1984) *Introduction to Comparative Psychology*. London: Edward Arnold.

Morgenstern, M., Low-Beer, H. and Morgenstern, F. (1966) *Practical Training for the Severely Handicapped Child*. London: William Heinemann.

Moseley, D. (1974) Some cognitive and perceptual correlates of spelling ability, in *Spelling: Task and Learner* (eds B. Wade and K. Wedell). Educational Review Occasional Publications, No. 5.

Mullins, J., Turner, J.F., Zawadski, R. and Saltman, L. (1972) A handwriting model for children with learning disabilities. *Journal of Learning Disabilities*, **5**, 306–11.

Munro, J.K. (1986) Teaching disabled children how to learn mathematics. *Success in Learning Mathematics*, **1**, 15–27.

National Curriculum – From Policy to Practice. Department of Education and Science 1989.

Neale, M.D. (1966) *Neale Analysis of Reading Ability*, 2nd edn. London, Macmillan.
Nelson, H.E. (1974) The aetiology of specific spelling disabilities, in *Spelling: Task and Learner* (eds B. Wade and K. Wedell). Educational Review Occasional Publications, No. 5.
Nichols, R. (1980) *Helping Your Child to Spell*. Centre for Teaching of Reading: University of Reading.
Nolan, C. (1987) *Under the Eye of the Clock*. London: Weidenfeld.
Norwich, B. (190) *Reappraising Special Needs Education*. In Special needs in ordinary schools series. London: Cassell Education.
O'Donohoe, N.V. (1979) *Epilepsies of Childhood*. London: Butterworth.
Ojemann, G.A. (1974) Mental arithmetic during human thalamic stimulation. *Neuropsychologia*, **12**, 1–10.
Oliva, P.F. and Henson, K.T. (1980) What are the essential generic teaching competencies? *Theory into Practice*, **19**, 117–21.
Parnwell, M. (1970) Conductive education of the cerebral palsied child. *Proceedings 5th International Congress WFOT*, pp. 166–70.
Paull, M.E. and Haskell, S.H. (1977a) *Let's Have Fun with Shapes*. Harlow: ESA Creative Learning.
Paull, M.E. and Haskell, S.H. (1977b) *My First Writing Books*. Harlow: ESA Creative Learning.
Penfield, W. and Roberts, L. (1959) *Speech and Brain Mechanisms*. Princeton: Princeton University Press.
Personke, C. and Yee, A.H. (1971) *Comprehensive Spelling Instruction: Theory, Research and Application*. Scranton: Intext Educational.
Peters, M.L. (1970) *Success in Spelling*. Cambridge: Cambridge Institute of Education.
Peters, M.L. (1975) *Diagnostic and Remedial Spelling Manual*. London and Basingstoke: Macmillan Education.
Philip and Tacey (1987) *Clearview Programme*. Andover: Hampshire.
Phillips, C.J. and White, R.R. (1964) The prediction of educational progress among cerebral palsied children. *Developmental Medicine and Child Neurology*, **6**, 167–74.
Piaget, J. (1950) *The Psychology of Intelligence*. London: Routledge and Kegan Paul.
Piaget, J. (1952) *The Child's Conception of Number*. London: Routledge and Kegan Paul.
Piaget, J. (1953) How chldren form mathematical concepts. *Scientific American*, **189**, 74–9.
Polloway, E.A., Payne, J.S., Patton, J.R. and Payne, R.A. (1985) *Strategies for Teaching Retarded and Special Needs Learners*. Sydney: Charles E. Merrill.
Pribram, K.H. (1976) Hemispheric specialization: evolution or revolution? in *Origins and Evolution of Language and Speech* (eds

S.R. Harnad, H.D. Steklis and J. Lancaster. New York: New York Academy of Sciences.

Quest-Screening, Diagnostic and Remediation Kit. Arnold-Wheaton.

Rangaswamy, L. (1983) Curvatures of the spine, in *Physical Disabilities and Health Impairments* (ed. J. Umbreit). Columbus: Charles E. Merrill, pp. 59–73.

Read, C. (1986) *Children's Creative Spelling*. London: Routledge and Kegan Paul.

Rentel, V.M., Pappas, C. and Pettegrew, B. (1985) The utility of psychophysiological measures for reading research, in *Psychophysiological Aspects of Reading and Learning* (eds V.M. Rentel, S.A. Corson and B. Dunn. New York: Gordon and Breach Science Publishers, pp. 123–55.

Richardson, M. (1935) *Writing and Writing Patterns Teacher's Book*. London: Hodder and Stoughton. Tenth Impression 1975.

Riddick, B. (1982) *Toys and Play for the Handicapped Child*. London: Croom Helm.

Rourke, P. and Strang, J.B. (1983) Subtypes of reading and arithmetical disablities: a neuropsychological analysis, in *Developmental Neuropsychiatry*, (ed. M. Rutter). New York: The Guildford Press, pp. 473–88.

Rudel, R.G. (1978) Neuroplasticity: implications for development and education, in *Education and the Brain* (eds J.S. Chall and A.F. Mirsky) Chicago: University of Chicago Press.

Rutter, M. (1966) Brain-damaged Children. *New Education*, **3**, 10–13.

Rutter, M., Graham, P. and Yule, W. (1970a) *A Neuropsychiatric Study in Childhood*. Philadelphia: Lippincott.

Rutter, M. and Yule, W. (1973) Specific reading retardation, in *The First Review of Special Education* (eds L. Mann and D. Sabatino). USA: Battonwood Farms.

Schmidt, R.A. (1982) *Motor Control and Learning: A Behavioural Emphasis:* Illinois: Human Kinetics Publishers, p. 438.

Schonell, F.J. (1948) *Backwardness in Basic Subjects*. Edinburgh: Oliver and Boyd.

Schonell, F.J. and Schonell, E.F. (1957) *Diagnosis and Remedial Teaching in Arithmetic*. Edinburgh: Oliver and Boyd.

Schonell, F.J., McLeod, J. and Cochrane, R.G. (eds) (1962) *The Slow Learner: Segregation or Integration*. St Lucia: University of Queensland Press.

Simpson, H. (1973) Asthma, in *Textbook of Paediatrics* (eds J.O. Forfar and G.C. Arnell). Edinburgh and London: Churchill and Livingstone).

Skinner, B.F. (1968) *The Technology of Teaching*. New York: Appleton-Century-Crofts.

Smilansky, M. and Smilansky, S. (1967) Intellectual advancement of culturally disadvantaged children: an Israeli approach for research and action. *International Review of Education*, **13**, 410–13.

Smith, F. (1969) The use of featural dependencies across letters in the visual identification of words. *Journal of Verbal Learning and Verbal Behaviour*, **8**, 215–18.

Smith, F. (1973) *Psycholinguistics and Reading*. New York: Holt, Rinehart and Winston.

Smith, F. (1978a) *Understanding Reading*, 2nd edn. New York: Holt, Rinehart and Winston.

Smith, F. (1978b) *Reading*. Cambridge: Cambridge University Press.

Smith, F. and Miller, G.A. (eds) (1966) *The Genesis of Language*. Cambridge, Mass: M.I.T. Press.

Smith, V.H. (ed.) (1963) *Visual Disorders in Cerebral Palsy*. London: Spastics Society/Heinemann.

Spearman, C.E. (1927) *The Abilities of Man: Their Nature and Measurement*. London: Macmillan.

Spencer, H. (1904) *An Autobiography*. London: Williams and Norgate.

Sperry, R.W. (1963) In *The Mind of Man* (ed. N. Calder) London: British Broadcasting Corporation (1970), pp. 143–5.

Strauss, A. and Werner, H. (1938) Deficiency in the finger schema in relation to arithmetic disability (finger agnosia and acalculia). *American Journal of Orthopsychiatry*, **8** 719–25.

Strauss, A.A. and Lehtinen, L.E. (1947) *Psychopathology and Education of the Brain-Injured Child*. New York: Grune and Stratton.

Terman, L.M. and Merrill, M.A. (1937) *Measuring Intelligence*. London: George Harrap.

Terman, L.M. and Merrill, M.A. (1960) *Stanford Binet Intelligence Scale. Manual for the Third Revision*. London: Harrap.

The 1944 Education Act. London: HMSO.

The Handicapped Pupil and Special School Regulations 1959. London: HMSO. *Amending Regulations to The Handicapped Pupil and Special School Regulations*. (1962). London: HMSO.

Tizard, J.P., Paine, R.S. and Crothers, B. (1954) Disturbances of sensation in children with hemiplegia. *Journal of the American Medical Assocation*, **155**, 628–32.

Todd, J. (1982) *Learning to Spell. A Resource Book for Teachers*. London: Blackwell.

Umbreit, J. (1983) *Physical Disabilities and Health Impairments: An Introduction*. Columbus: Charles E. Merrill.

Uzgiris, I.C. and Hunt, J. McV. (1971) Ordinal scales of psychological development in infancy, in *Socio–Cultural Aspects of Mental Retardation* (ed. H. Carl Haywood). Proceedings Peabody–NIMH Conference. New York: Appleton–Century–Crofts.

Vernon, M.D. (1961) *The Psychology of Perception*. Harmondsworth: Penguin.

Vernon, M.D. (1970) (Ch. 1.) *Assessment and Teaching of Dyslexic Children*, Invalid Children's Aid Association.

Vincze, E. (1982) Special Education in Hungary. Proceedings of the International Conference on the Education of the Retarded, London, April 1962. *Forward Trends, Summer/Autumn 1962*, pp. 28–30.

Wada, J.A. (1969) Interhemispheric sharing and shift of cerebral function. 9th International Congress of Neurology Abstract: *Excerpta Medica, International Congress Series*, **193**, pp. 296–7.

Wade, M .G. and Davis, W.E. (1982) Motor skill development in young children: current views on assessment and programming, in *Current Topics in Early Childhood Education* (ed. L.G. Katz). New Jersey: Ablex Publishing Corporation (4), pp. 55–70.

Warburton, F.W. and Southgate, V. (1969) *i.t.a. An Independent Evaluation*. London: John Murray and W.R. Chambers.

Warrington, E.K. and James, M. (1967) Disorders of visual perception in patients with localized cerebral lesions. *Neuropsychologia*, **5**, 253–66.

Wechsler, D. (1949) *Wechsler Intelligence Scale for Children*. New York: The Psychological Corporation.

Wedell, K. (1973) *Learning and Perceptuo–Motor Disabilities in Children*. London: John Wiley.

Weikart, D.P. and Lambie, B.Z. (1970) Early enrichment in infants. In *Education of the Infant and Young Children* (ed. V.H. Deneberg). New York: Academic Press.

Werner, H. and Carrison, D. (1942) Measurement and development of the finger schema in mentally retarded children: relation of arithmetic achievement to performance on the finger schema test. *Journal of Educational Psychology*, **33**, 252–64.

White, B.L. and Held, R. (1966) Plasticity of sensorimotor development in the human infant, in *The Causes of Behaviour: Readings in Child Development and Education Psychology* (eds J.F. Rosenblith and W. Allinsmith). Boston: Allyn and Bacon.

Witelson, S.F. and Pallie, W. (1973) Left-hemisphere specialization for language in the human newborn: neuroanatomical evidence of asymmetry. *Brain*, **96**, 641–6.

Wolfensberger, W. (1983) A proposed new term for the principle of normalization. *Mental Retardation*, **2**, 234–9.

Zangwill, O.L. (1975) The ontogeny of cerebral dominance in man, in *Foundations of Language Development* (eds E.H. Lenneberg and E. Lenneberg). New York: Academic Press.

Glossary

Acalculia: An inability to carry out simple arithmetical calculations.

Afferent-nerve: Incoming sensory in-flow to central nervous system.

Agnosia: Inability to recognize objects, events, sounds, etc., even though the sense organ is not basically defective. A subject receives information but is unable to comprehend or interpret it. Usually a specific rather than general agnosia as in:

- Auditory agnosia: inability to differentiate between various common sounds.
- Form agnosia: form discrimination difficulty, for example, geometric forms.
- Tactile agnosia: inability to recognize common objects by touch alone.
- Visual agnosia: difficulty in recognition of objects or people, even though they should be easily recognized (old acquaintances, etc.).

Agraphia: Inability to relate kinaesthetic pattern (required motor movements) to visual image of a word or letter.

AIDS (acquired immune deficiency syndrome): A condition that affects the body's auto-immune system.

Alphafeto protein (AFP): A blood test offered at about 16 weeks to mothers with a family history of spina bifida giving a higher than average risk to the baby.

Allergy: A specific and hypersensitive reaction to a particular substance to which most people show a normal reaction.

Amnesia: The partial or total loss of memory for past

experiences (long-term memory). The memories lost in amnesia have not been completely destroyed for the forgotten events may again be remembered without relearning when the person recovers from amnesia.

Amniocentesis: A medical procedure that allows examination of the amniotic fluid around the foetus; sometimes recommended to determine the presence of abnormality.

Anencephaly: The absence of the brain.

Angiogram: X-ray studies of the cerebral blood vessel system following injection of radio-opaque material into the arterial system.

Angiography: The practice of studying the circulatory system with angiograms.

Anoxia: Deficiency in oxygen carried by the bloodstream, resulting in lack of available oxygen to any particular part of the body so affected.

Aphasia: Loss or impairment of the ability to use words as symbols or ideas due to lesions in the cortex and associated nerve pathways in the brain.

Apraxia: A defective ability in the absence of severe sensory or motor loss for carrying out neuromuscular acts normally, even though the patient understands what is expected of him.

Arnold–Chiari malformation: A specific malformation of the cerebellum frequently associated with spina bifida.

Arthritis: From Greek 'arthron' – joint, and 'itis' – inflammation – literally 'an inflamed joint'. Although arthritis is used popularly nowadays to describe any ache or pain in the entire skeleton, it should be reserved for cases of true joint involvement.

Associated movements: Unintentional movements accompany motor functions.

Asthma: A disease due to spasmodic contraction of the bronchi because of allergies or other irritations, resulting in wheezing, coughing and paroxysmal panting.

Ataxia: A condition characterized by awkwardness of fine and gross motor movements, especially those involved with balance, posture, and orientation in space; a type of cerebral palsy.

Athetosis: A condition in which there are sudden, involuntary, jerky, writhing movements, especially of the fingers and wrists; a type of cerebral palsy.

Aura: A sensation, such as the perception of certain

odours, sounds, images, etc., sometimes experienced just before a seizure.

Autonomic nervous system: Part of the nervous system which regulates the functions of some of the internal organs independent of the conscious mind.

Basal ganglia (or striatum): A cluster of nuclei located in the brainstem near the thalamus and concerned with various motor activities.

Brain damage: Any actual structural (tissue) damage due to any cause or causes. This means verifiable damage, not neurological performance that is indicative of damage.

Brainstem: The structure at the base of the brain connecting the upper end of the spinal cord with the cerebral hemispheres. The cerebral cortex and the cerebellum and their dependent parts are excluded from the brainstem.

Broca's speech area: A portion of the left cerebral hemisphere said to control motor speech.

Central nervous system: In vertebrates, the brain and spinal cord, as distinct from the nerve trunks and their peripheral connections (cf. autonomic nervous system).

Cerebellum: This structure consists of two hemispheres and each hemisphere has three lobes. The lobes differ in function, but together they control posture and balance. Disturbances of function lead to unco-ordinated movements, staggering gait (ataxia) or dizziness if the vestibular pathways are affected. The 'little brain' or inferior part of the brain lying below the cerebrum and above the pons and medulla; concerned with the co-ordination of movements.

Cerebral cortex: The surface layer of the cerebral hemispheres in higher animals, including humans. It is commonly called 'grey matter' because its many cells give it a grey appearance in cross-section, in contrast with the nerve fibres that make up the white matter.

Cerebral dominance: Relates to the theory (originated by Orton) that one hemisphere of the brain is dominant in controlling various body functions. Important to many perceptual–motor theorists and the basis for the ideas of mixed dominance.

Cerebral hemispheres: Two large masses of nerve cells and fibres constituting the bulk of the brain in humans and other higher animals. The hemispheres are separated by a deep fissure, but connected by a broad band of fibres, the corpus callosum.

Cerebral palsy (Little's disease, congenital spastic paralysis): A condition characterized by paralysis, weakness, uncoordination, and/or other motor dysfunction due to brain damage.

Cerebrospinal fluid (CNS): A fluid secreted chiefly by the choroid plexuses of the lateral ventricles of the brain, filling the ventricles and the subarachnoid cavities of the brain and the spinal cord.

Chorionic villus sampling (CVS): A newer technique for screening older mothers for inherited diseases. A sample of the developing placenta is extracted either by inserting a small tube through the abdomen into the womb or through the cervix.

Chromosomes: Small particles found in all the cells of the body, carrying the genetic determiners (genes) that are transmitted from parent to offspring. A human cell has 46 chromosomes, arranged in 23 pairs, one member of each pair deriving from the mother, one from the father (cf. gene).

Clonic phase: A sensation felt during an epileptic attack in which contractions and relaxations of a muscle occur in rapid succession.

Clubbing: Broadening or thickening of the ends of fingers.

CNS: Abbreviation for central nervous system.

Congenital: Means present at birth and does not carry the connotation of hereditary or genetic.

Cordeocentesis: A recent technique for identifying rhesus babies requiring a blood transfusion at birth.

Contracture: A permanent muscular contraction or shortening.

Corpus callosum: A large band of fibres (white matter) connecting the two cerebral hemispheres.

Cortex: The convoluted outer layer of grey neural tissue that covers the brain. For convenience it is divided in frontal, parietal, temporal, and occipital lobes by the fissure of Rolando and the fissure of Sylvius. Both the left and right cerebral hemispheres are similarly divided.

Cystic fibrosis: A hereditary disease of children involving defective production of enzymes in the pancreas, with disturbances throughout the body and usually with pulmonary involvement.

Deformity Refers to that part of the body already formed which has been distorted. Neither malformation nor deformity necessarily implies impairment of function.

Deoxyribonucleic acid (DNA): Large molecules found in the cell nucleus and primarily responsible for genetic inheritance. These molecules manufacture various forms of RNA which are thought by some to be the chemical basis of memory (cf. ribonucleic acid).

Diabetes mellitus: A metabolic disorder of the islets of Langerhans of the pancreas in which there is faulty production of insulin leading to high blood sugar levels, weight loss, and coma.

Disability: Refers to an abnormality which interferes with function to a significant degree.

Duchenne muscular dystrophy: A type of muscular dystrophy characterized by progressive weakness of the limbs and trunk.

Dysarthria: Difficulty in articulation.

Efferent nerve: A bundle of nerve fibres transmitting impulses from the central nervous system in the direction of the peripheral organs. Efferent nerve tracts commonly end in muscles or glands (usually synonymous with motor nerve).

Electroencephalogram (EEG): A record obtained by attaching electrodes to the scalp (or occasionally to the exposed brain) and amplifying the spontaneous electrical activity of the brain. The EEG is useful in studying some forms of mental disturbances (e.g. epilepsy) and in research on brain dysfunction.

Encephalitis: Infection or inflammation of brain tissues.

Encephalograph: An apparatus which by means of electrodes placed on the scalp records the alternating currents of the brain. It helps to find the locality of intracranial lesions.

Endogenous: A term used to refer to mental retardation caused by social or genetic factors; infrequently used today.

Engram: The hypothesized neural trace; the concept that neural tissue manifests permanent change following learning.

Epilepsy: A disorder of the central nervous system marked by transient periods of unconsciousness or psychic disturbance, twitching, delirium, or convulsive movements.

Equipotentiality: The idea that within large areas of the cerebral cortex one part is equally as potent as another part for determining a particular type of behaviour, e.g. Lashley's theory of mass action.

Exocrine: External secretion (e.g. a gland).

Exogenous: A term used to refer to mental retardation caused by brain damage: infrequently used today.

Extension: Straightening of any part of the body.

Extra-pyramidal: The descending nerve tracts which do not enter into the formation of the pyramids of the medulla (bone marrow, spinal cord).

Facilitation: Making it possible to move.

Facioscapulohumeral A form of muscular dystrophy affecting the face, the shoulder blade and the upper arm.

Fibrosis: The pathological formation of fibrous tissue in the body.

Flaccid paralysis: Paralysis in which the muscles become weak, soft, or loose.

Flexion: Bending of any part of the body.

Forebrain: The portion of the brain evolved from the foremost of the three enlargements of the neural tube, consisting of the cerebrum, thalamus, hypothalamus, and related structures (cf. hindbrain, midbrain).

Frontal lobe: A portion of each cerebral hemisphere, in front of the central tissue (cf. occipital lobe, temporal lobe).

Gene: The unit of hereditary transmission, localized within the chromosomes. Each chromosome contains many genes. Genes are typically in pairs, one member of the pair being found in the chromosome from the father, the other in the corresponding chromosome from the mother (cf chromosome, recessive gene).

Genetics: The biological study of heredity.

Genito-urinary system: The organs relating to the functions of reproduction and urination.

German measles (rubella): A serious viral disease which, if it occurs during the first trimester of pregnancy, is likely to cause a deformity in the foetus. German measles is accompanied by sore throat and fever, and is associated with enlargement of the lymph nodes.

Gerstmann syndrome: A configuration of behavioural symptoms stated by Gerstmann, a German neurologist, to result from a lesion of the parietal lobe on the dominant side.

The syndrome includes finger agnosia, defective right-left orientation, agraphia, and acalculia.

Glial cells: Supporting cells (not neurons) composing a substantial portion of brain tissue; recent speculation suggests that they may play a role in the storage of memory.

Grand mal: A complete epileptic seizure, including sudden loss of consciousness, convulsion, spasm, incontinence, and frothing at the mouth.

Gyrus: A convolution of convex fold of tissue.

Haemophilia: A serious hereditary disorder in which the blood fails to clot and in which deep tissue bleeding occurs following injury or bruising. Occurs almost exclusively in males and is transmitted through a recessive gene carried by the mother.

Haemorrhage: Bleeding.

Handicap: Relates to a disability which hinders or prevents what is expected or required of the child in his particular environment.

Hemianopia: A half visual field defect; blindness or impaired vision in the left or right visual field.

Hemiplegia: A condition in which one half (right or left side) of the body is paralyzed.

Hydrocephalus: A condition, usually congenital, marked by excessive accumulation of fluid in the cerebral ventricles, dilating these cavities, thinning the brain, and causing a separation of the cranial bones.

Hyperactivity: Overactivity.

Hypertonicity: Hypertonia or extreme tension of the muscles or arteries.

Hyper ventilation: Deep breathing.

Hypotonia: Floppiness, decreased muscle tension, preventing maintenance of posture against gravity; also difficulty in starting a movement due lack of fixation.

Idiopathic: This generally refers to a primary condition and is not the result of anything else.

Inhibition: A technical term used in treatment. Special techniques of handling are aimed at stopping the spastic or athetoid patterns which prevent or interfere with normal activity.

Insult: In neurology, refers to a lesion or neurological tissue damage.

Intracranial: Within the skull.

IQ (intelligence quotient): A measure of intellectual functioning; determined by dividing mental age (the age level at which the person is functioning) by chronological age and multiplying by 100.

Jaundice: A disorder in which bile pigment is deposited in the skin and mucous membranes, giving a yellow appearance.

Kernicterus: A condition in which there are excessive serum levels of bilirubin, resulting in brain damage. (Bilirubin: bile pigment formed by the disintegration of red blood cells.)

Kinaesthesis: Awareness of the body and body parts in space; it includes awareness of balance and motion.

Kyphosis: A posterior curvature of the spine when viewed from the side; humpback, hunchback.

Learning: A relatively permanent change in behaviour that occurs as the result of practice. Behaviour changes due to maturation or temporary conditions of the organism (e.g. fatigue, the influence of drugs, adaptation) are not included.

Lesion: A wound or injuiry. Or a more or less circumscribed pathological change in the body tissues.

Limbic system: A set of structures in and around the midbrain, forming a functional unit regulating motivational emotional types of behavour, such as waking and sleeping, excitement and quiescence, feeding and mating.

Locomotion: Movement from one location to another (walking, crawling, rolling).

Lordosis: An abnormally increased forward curvature of the lower spine (swayback).

Lumbar: Pertaining to the loins, or to the lower back in the area of the kidneys.

Lumbar puncture The insertion of a needle through the back and into the the spinal canal, permitting withdrawal of the spinal fluid (the water-like fluid that bathes the brain and spinal cord); also used to inject drugs into the spinal fluid.

Magnetic resonance imaging (MRI): An advanced diagnostic procedure for detecting a variety of diseases. The machine uses a large magnet, radiowaves and a computer but not X-rays.

Malformation: An abnormality of formation of part of the body.

Malocclusion: Poor closure of the teeth.

Maturation: Growth processes in the individual that result in orderly changes in behaviour, whose timing and patterning are relatively independent of exercise or experience, though they may require a normal environment.

Maxilla: Irregularly shaped bone which forms part of the upper jaw.

Medulla: The central portion of an organ as distinguished from its outer layer or cortex. Sometimes used to refer to the medulla oblongata – the part of the brainstem where the spinal cord fuses with the brain itself.

Meninges: The membranous envelope of the brain and the spinal cord.

Meningitis: An infection of the brain and its covering membranes.

Meningocele: A protrusion of the membranes of the brain or spinal cord through a defect in the skull or the spinal column.

Meningo-myelocele: A protrusion of the membranes and the cord through a defect in the vertebral column.

Minimal brain dysfunction (MBD): A term used to describe a child who shows behavioural but not neurological signs of brain injury; the term is not as popular as it once was primarily because of its lack of diagnostic utility, i.e. some children who learn normally show signs indicative of MBD.

Modality: Aspect of specific sense experience – for example, hearing, seeing.

Moro: The Moro reflex, first described by Moro in 1918, is elicited by sudden movement of the head and neck in relation to the spine. It can be produced by raising the infant's head slightly and then withdrawing support suddenly. This results in the extension of the arms, abduction and a subsequent movement towards the midline in the form of a clasp or embrace.

Motor area: A projection area in the brain lying in front of the fissure of Rolando. Electrical stimulation commonly results in motor responses.

Muscle tone: The state of tension in muscles at rest and when we move – regulated under normal circumstances subconsciously in such a way that the tension is sufficiently high to withstand the pull of gravity, i.e.

to keep us upright, but it is never too strong to interfere with voluntary movements.

Muscular dystrophy: A hereditary disease, marked by progressive shrinking and wasting of skeletal muscle with no apparent lesion of the spinal cord, the symptoms usually manifesting themselves in early childhood or adolescence.

Myoclonic: Characterized by spasmodic muscular contractions.

Myopathy: A weakening and wasting away of muscular tissue in which there is no evidence of neurological disease or impairment.

Neural tube: The tubular structure formed from the neural plate by the closure of the neural folds; the brain develops from its cephalic (head) portion and the spinal cord from its more caudal (tail) portions.

Neuron: The nerve cell; the unit of a synaptic nervous system. The human brain contains billions of neurons.

Nystagmus: A condition in which there are involuntary movements of the eyes, sometimes indicates brain malfunction and/or inner ear problems.

Occipital lobe: A portion of the cerebral hemisphere behind the parietal and temporal lobes (cf. frontal lobe, temporal lobe).

Occlusion: The state of closure, e.g. blood flow through an artery might be obstructed or occluded.

Ontogeny: How an individual organism develops – its developmental history.

Operant: This gets its name from the fact that in order to obtain a reward the organism does something to its environment. As Skinner puts it, the term 'operant' emphasizes the fact that the behaviour operates upon the environment to generate sequences.

Operant behaviour: Behaviour defined by the stimulus to which it leads rather than by the stimulus that elicits it, such as behaviour leading to reward (emitted behaviour, instrumental behaviour; cf. respondent behaviour, voluntary action).

Operant conditioning: The strengthening of an operant response, by presenting a reinforcing stimulis if, and only if, the response occurs (instrumental conditioning, reward learning).

Organic: Inherent, inborn; involving known neurological or structural abnormality.

Parachute reaction: The automatic placing of hands on floor when an infant is suddenly lowered from the prone position (supported face down and horizontal).

Paraplegia: A condition in which both legs are paralyzed.

Passive: That which is done to the child without his help or co-operation.

Peritoneal cavity: The interior of the sac formed by the parietal layer of the peritoneum, containing all the abdominal organs except the kidneys.

Perseveration: Continuing with a particular response after it is no longer appropriate. Inability to shift from one centre of focus to another.

Petit mal seizure: A mild convulsive disorder related to epilepsy characterized by sudden brief blackouts of consciousness followed by immediate recovery.

Photic: Photic-stimulated seizures provoked by blinking lights, sunlight dancing on water, strobe or malfunctioning fluorescent lights, etc.

Physiotherapy: The treatment of disorders of movement by means of physical exercises.

PL94–142: Refers to the Education for All Handicapped Children Act, which contains a mandatory provision stating that beginning in September 1978, in order to receive funds under the Act, every school system in the nation must make provision for a free, appropriate public education for every child between the ages of 3 and 18 (ages 3 to 21 by 1980) regardless of how, or how seriously, he/she may be handicapped.

Polyarticular rheumatoid arthritis: Rheumatoid arthritis affecting all or most of the joints of the body.

Pons: A connecting centre of the brain stem for sensory and motor nerves.

Postural drainage: The drawing off of fluid by alteration of the posture or position of the body.

Posture: Position from which the child starts a movement.

Prognosis: A forecast as to the recovery or outcome of an attack of disease, based on the symptoms and the current knowledge of the disease.

Prone: Lying face downwards.

Proprioceptor: A sense organ in the tissues of the body providing information about body functions or kinaesthesia.

Pseudohypertrophy muscular dystrophy: The form of muscular dystrophy in which there is an increase in size of the affected part due to fatty or fibrous tissue.

Recessive gene: The trait expressed only when the defective form of the gene alone is present.

Reflex: A reaction; an involuntary movement or exercise of function in a part, excited in response to a stimulus applied to the periphery and transmitted to the nervous centres in the brain or spinal cord.

Rh factor: An agglutinogen first found in the red blood cells of rhesus monkeys, which affects transfusion reaction through antibody formation. Rh factor can produce antibody formation only in Rh-negative blood, i.e. blood in which this factor is absent. About 15% of individuals are Rh-negative and thus will have transfusion reactions from Rh-positive blood.

Rhesus incompatibility: That state which arises when the blood of a Rhesus negative mother becomes sensitized by pregnancy to the Rhesus positive factor in the father's cells.

Rheumatoid arthritis (Still's disease): A chronic disease characterized by inflammation of the joints, usually accompanied by marked deformities, inflammatory changes in the synovial membranes and joints, and wasting away of the bones.

Ribonucleic acid (RNA): A material similar to DNA of which the genes are composed and which carries the 'written' messages of heredity.

Rigidity: Very still posture and movements.

Scoliosis: Curvature of the spine, either congenital or acquired from poor posture, disease, or muscular weakness due to certain conditions such as cerebral palsy or muscular dystrophy.

Seizure (fit, convulsion): A sudden alteration of consciousness, usually accompanied by motor activity and/or sensory phenomena; caused by an abnormal discharge of electrical energy in the brain.

Sex-linked inheritance: Inheritance of a trait in which the responsible gene is located on the X (female sex) chromosome. Dominant if only one gene need be present for the trait to be expressed: recessive if the trait is expressed only when no other form of the gene is present.

Shunt: The bypassing of an obstacle in the brain by redirecting the cerebrospinal fluid through a plastic tube into another area of the body.

Sickle cell anaemia: An autosomal recessive genetic disease, characterized by elongated cells, resulting in defective haemoglobin synthesis, causing anaemia and jaundice. It generally affects Mediterranean, Middle Eastern and African people.

Spasm: Sudden tightening of muscles.

Spasticity: A condition in which there are sudden, involuntary contractions of the muscles, causing voluntary movements to be difficult and inaccurate; a type of cerebral palsy.

Sphincters: Muscles which open and close the orifices of the body.

Spina bifida: A congenital cleft in the bony encasement of the spinal cord, with meningeal protrusion. If the meninges do not protrude, it is called 'spina bifida occulta'.

Spinal cord: That part of the central nervous system contained within the vertebral column.

Spino–peritoneal: As in hydrocephalus.

Status epilepticus: A condition in which an individual has continuous seizures.

Steroids: Complex chemical substances, some of which are prominent in the secretions of the adrenal cortex and may be related to some forms of mental illness (cf. adrenal gland). Used in treatment of some diseases when other drugs have failed, e.g. Still's disease.

Still's disease: Chronic polyarthritis of childhood, with enlargement of spleen and lymph nodes, and irregular fever (after George Frederick Still).

Strabismus: Failure of the eyes to converge properly on an image, leading to a squint, cross-eye or wall-eye.

Stupor (in epilepsy): A state of lethargy or unconsciousness.

Sub-cortical: Beneath the cerebral cortex.

Subdural: Situated below the dura mater which covers the brain and spinal cord.

Sulcus: A fissure or depression.

Systemic: Throughout the whole body.

Talipes: Club-foot.

Teaching machine: A device to provide self-instruction by means of a programme proceeding in steps at a rate determined by the learner; the machine is arranged to provide knowledge of the correctness or incorrectness of each reply (cf. programming).

Temporal lobe: A portion of the cerebral hemisphere, at the side below the fissure of Sylvius and in front of the occipital lobe (cf. frontal lobe, occipital lobe, parietal lobe).

Thorax: The chest.

Tonic phase: In epilepsy: unremitting muscular contraction.

Toxaemia: (Of pregnancy) - blood poisoning, high blood pressure with kidney or liver complications in pregnancy.

Toxoplasmosis: A condition that can cause blindness and brain injury in infants. The disease can be transmitted through cat faeces and ingesting undercooked meats.

Trauma: A wound or injury (suddenly inflicted).

Tremor: Shaking, shivering, trembling.

Upper respiratory tracts: The air passages from the nose to the lungs, through the pharynx, larynx, trachea and bronchi.

Valgus: Out-turned clubfoot.

Ventricle: A small cavity of the heart or brain.

Ventriculo–atrial: Referring to the operation used in cases of hydrocephalus where cerebrospinal fluid is passed from the ventricles to the atrium of the heart by a small tube.

Ventriculo–peritoneal: Referring to the operation used in cases of hydrocephalus where cerebrospinal fluid is passed from the ventricles to the peritoneal cavity (the space surrounding the intestines).

Viscid mucus: Sticky or glutinous mucus.

Voluntary movements: Movements done with intention and with concentration.

Index

Authors' names appear in *italics*.

SPACE PENGUINS

COSMIC CRASH!

For Zac, with love ~ **L A C**

For Dom ~ **J D**

STRIPES PUBLISHING
An imprint of Little Tiger Press
1 The Coda Centre, 189 Munster Road,
London SW6 6AW

A paperback original
First published in Great Britain in 2013

ISBN: 978-1-84715-250-3

A CIP catalogue record for this book is available from the British Library.

Printed and bound in the UK.

10 9 8 7 6 5 4 3 2 1

COSMIC CRASH!

L A COURTENAY

ILLUSTRATED BY
JAMES DAVIES

MEET THE SPACE PENGUINS...

CAPTAIN:
Captain T. Krill
Emperor penguin
Height: 1.10m
Looks: yellow ear patches and noble bearing
Likes: swordfish minus the sword
Lab tests: showed leadership qualities in fish challenge
Guaranteed to: keep calm in a crisis

FIRST MATE:
Beaky Wader, now known as Dark Wader
Emperor penguin
Height: 1.22m
Looks: yellow ear patches and evil laugh
Likes: prawn pizzas
Lab tests: cheated at every challenge
Guaranteed to: cause trouble

PILOT (WITH NO SENSE OF DIRECTION):
Rocky Waddle
Rockhopper penguin
Height: 45cm
Looks: long yellow eyebrows
Likes: mackerel ice cream
Lab tests: fastest slider in toboggan challenge
Guaranteed to: speed through an asteroid belt while reading charts upside-down

SECURITY OFFICER AND HEAD CHEF:
Fuzz Allgrin
Little Blue penguin
Height: 33cm
Looks: small with fuzzy blue feathers
Likes: fishfingers in cream and truffle sauce
Lab tests: showed creativity and aggression in ice-carving challenge
Guaranteed to: defend ship, crew and kitchen with his life

SHIP'S ENGINEER:
Splash Gordon
King penguin
Height: 95cm
Looks: orange ears and chest markings
Likes: squid
Lab tests: solved ice-cube challenge in under four seconds
Guaranteed to: fix anything

LOADING...

LOADING...

LOADING...

Welcome aboard the Spaceship *Tunafish*, home to my crew, the Space Penguins. I am ICEcube, the super-brainy computer aboard this spacecraft. I can take you anywhere you want to go.

Except Earth. Sorry. We lost Earth five years ago on the penguins' first space mission. My database says: eek! What was NASA thinking? Penguins in space was never going to work. They may be small and cheap to train, but they aren't the best astronauts in the world.

However, it's not all bad news. Since we lost Earth, the Space Penguins have become intergalactic heroes.

Fuzz Allgrin, the Chef and Security Officer, brought peace between the planets Burga and Chipz by introducing them to ketchup.

Splash Gordon, the Ship's Engineer, stopped the black hole named Hoova from sucking up Planet Sok by showing them where the "off" button was.

And even Rocky Waddle, the pilot with no sense of direction, flew quickly through the millions of aisles on planet Supamarkit, although he got lost on its moon, Supamarkit Ka-park.

What about Captain T. Krill? Well, he captained them in every one of their incredible missions. His bravery in space is legendary.

Right now, the main problem the Space Penguins face is their former first mate – Beaky Wader. He's turned into their mortal enemy. In fact, he's just sent a fleet of Squid-G fighter spacecraft to teach them a lesson after they managed to escape his Death Starfish. I'd better let Captain Krill know.

Buckle up. It's going to be a bumpy ride.

WARNING

BATTLE STATIONS!

WHEEP! WHEEP! WHEEP!

The alarms aboard the Spaceship *Tunafish* were going crazy. Lights were flashing everywhere.

"What's going on, ICEcube?" said Captain Krill, waddling out of his ice bath.

"Nothing too serious, Captain," said ICEcube. "Just fifty Squid-G fighters approaching at five hundred thousand light years per hour."

"Fifty Squid-G fighters and you say it's

nothing serious?" gasped the captain as he dried his yellow ear patches with a towel. "Beaky Wader's the only guy in space who owns Squid-Gs. But we're three million light years away from his space station!"

Splash Gordon looked up from tinkering with his latest invention – a long, tube-like thing with a trigger. "Then Beaky must be tracking us somehow," he said.

"I'd say that was pretty serious," said Rocky Waddle from his pilot's chair.

Fuzz Allgrin came out of the kitchen. "Too right it's serious," he said. "The alarm system has shut down my oven. It's cold mackerel for us today."

"Yum!" said Rocky, cheering up. "I never liked hot food."

"So how long have we got until they attack, ICEcube?" Captain Krill asked.

"Ten seconds, Captain. Nine … eight …"

"Into your seats, crew," Captain Krill

ordered. "Rocky? Warp speed away. We can't fight fifty of them. We'll just have to run."

"Fuzz Allgrin never runs from anyone!" said Fuzz.

"Seven ... six ... five ..."

"That's because you're a Little Blue penguin. Your legs are too short," said Rocky.

"Four ... three ... two ... one..."

ZZZZOOOOMMMM! The *Tunafish* whippod away at full throttle. The penguins were flattened to their seats.

"Yahoo!" Rocky yelled, his yellow eyebrows whistling behind him like ribbons. "Bring it on!"

As the *Tunafish* whizzed past planets and asteroids, comets and meteors, the silver Squid-Gs spread out behind them across the black sky.

"More speed, Rocky," Captain Krill ordered from his seat. "They're gaining on us."

"How fast are they going, ICEcube?" asked Splash.

"Five hundred thousand and three light years exactly..."

The *Tunafish* dived and swerved, hurtling between moons and looping-the-loop around comets.

But still the Squid-Gs gave chase through the Milky Way.

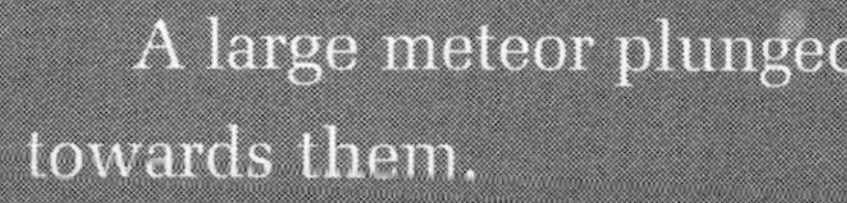

A large meteor plunged towards them.

"Rocky!" cried Fuzz. "You're steering straight towards that meteor!"

"Yeah, and isn't it fun?" said Rocky happily. "Hold on tight!"

He pulled the joystick with one flipper and the brake with the other. The *Tunafish* spun like a ballerina on ice, zooming up and sideways all at the same time. But was it too late?

"Holy mackerel!" cried Fuzz. "We're going to crash!"

The *Tunafish* leaped upwards at the very last second … and the meteor zoomed harmlessly underneath it. Now the giant space rock was heading for the Squid-Gs at thousands of kilometres per second.

"I hate to say it, but don't look now!" cried Splash as…

BANG! BOOM!

Behind them, Squid-Gs collided head-on with the meteor.

"I feel sick," moaned Fuzz as the *Tunafish* pelted on. "When is this going-fast thing going to stop?"

On they raced.

Rocky's flippers were a blur at the controls. The *Tunafish* jumped like a gazelle, thundered like a waterfall, twisted like a disco dancer. Stars blurred into streaks of light. Planets whizzed by like brightly coloured bouncy balls.

"We must have lost them by now," said Captain Krill.

Rocky pulled the joystick towards his beak and the whole spaceship rocketed upwards. The universe turned sideways for several sickening seconds. "Nope," he gasped, glancing at his screen. "They're still with us."

"Squid-Gs closing faster than ever," said ICEcube. "Five seconds until impact. Four. Three…"

A space cannonball was speeding towards them.

BOOOOM!

The *Tunafish* turned upside-down as the cannonball blasted past and exploded. The air rippled and shook.

BOOOOM! BOOOOM!

Two more cannonballs. Rocky swung the joystick so sharply that the whole spaceship did a somersault. Fuzz groaned.

BOOOOOOM!

Even Rocky was starting to sweat now.

"I don't think I can keep this up, Captain," he gasped. "There are just too many of them!"

The *Tunafish*'s engine suddenly stalled. There was a ghastly silence. Then the spacecraft started spinning uncontrollably.

"AAARRGGH!" the penguins screamed as they plunged.

They fell and fell until they couldn't see the Squid-Gs any more. A planet of some kind seemed to be appearing beneath them.

"The engine's completely dead, Captain," cried Rocky as they plummeted. "All we can do now is hope to come out of this alive."

"ICEcube?" gasped Captain Krill. "What are our chances?"

"Zero, Captain."

"Comforting," said Splash.

"I don't care," Fuzz croaked. "I just want this to stop!"

The planet was getting closer. It was wide and purple and completely flat.

"Coming in to land!" shouted Rocky.

The Space Penguins braced themselves for impact.

They skidded and swerved before plunging into something. The *Tunafish* ploughed along, sending up sheets of purple liquid. At last it came to a stop. Silence fell.

"Your chances of survival just improved," said ICEcube. "This planet appears to be made of water!"

CHAPTER TWO

ICE RAYS AND COCONUT FISH

"I think you can safely say we just splash-landed," said Rocky, looking all around him.

"Big wow," said Fuzz weakly.

A purple-coloured ocean stretched away in all directions. Little lilac waves lapped against the sides of the *Tunafish* as it bobbed around. Two yellow suns bathed the surface of the water.

"Where are we?" said Captain Krill. "I can't see any land." He peered through the windscreen. "Do you think this place is just one big purple ocean?"

"I didn't know you could get planets just made out of water," said Splash. "But it certainly looks that way."

"Thank goodness we aren't sinking," said Fuzz. "We'd be in a whole LOT of trouble then."

At that moment, everyone felt the *Tunafish* shudder. The nose of the spaceship tilted. Water started rising towards the windscreen.

"Yikes!" Rocky cried. "We *are* sinking!"

"We have to leave!" said Captain Krill. "Now!"

"Never!" shouted Fuzz. "I LOVE the *Tunafish*. Plus I've got mackerel in the freezer!"

"That's an order, Fuzz," said Captain.

There was nothing else that they could do. The *Tunafish* was sliding – smoothly, slowly, and definitely deeper – down into the purple sea. It slid faster as the water began to seep through the doors and windows. Then faster still.

"We have to get out of here!" cried Splash.

"But we can't turn our backs on ICEcube!" protested Rocky.

"Don't worry. We'll return," said Captain Krill.

"Promise?" said Fuzz.

"I promise," said Captain Krill.

"Abandon ship, crew!"

"The Fuzzmeister lives to fight another day!" shouted Fuzz as the Space Penguins raced to escape. "Open the door, Rocky. Quick!"

"It's stuck!" yelled Rocky, heaving at the door of the *Tunafish*. The water was rising all the time. "We can't get out! We're doomed!"

"You're turning the handle the wrong way!" said Splash.

"It won't work the other way either," said ICEcube. "The water pressure is too strong. You have precisely 3.4 seconds left to escape. You need to think of something."

"Let's kick down the door!" commanded Captain Krill. "On the count of three. One … two … THREE!"

The four Space Penguins flung themselves at the exit hatch. It burst open and water gushed inside in a great purple waterfall. The penguins surfed out of the cabin with their flippers close to their bodies and their feet paddling like crazy. Freedom!

"We'll be back, ICEcube," cried Rocky over his shoulder. "This isn't the end! Believe in the penguins!"

As the water carried them away, the *Tunafish* sank further into the cool depths. It spiralled away beneath the swimming penguins, down and down and down into the murky depths.

"Did you see how deep it was under there?" Captain Krill gasped as he and Splash bobbed up to the surface. "If the *Tunafish* sinks right to the bottom, we'll never raise her up again!"

"Then we'll be stuck on this planet forever," said Splash.

"Any bright ideas?" said Captain Krill.

"We could build a winch to pull the *Tunafish* up," said Splash, as Rocky and Fuzz burst out of the water beside them. "I have all the equipment I need, right here on..."

He stopped.

"Were you going to say, 'the *Tunafish*'?" said Captain Krill.

Splash nodded. All four penguins looked gloomily down into the waves below.

"Ah," said Captain Krill.

"It could be a problem," agreed Splash.

"There is some good news, though," said Fuzz.

"Is the *Tunafish* floating up again?" asked the Captain hopefully.

"Nope." Fuzz waved a fish over his head. "But I have dinner. A mackerel. It escaped from the sinking ship with me."

A few more things bobbed up beside the Space Penguins. A couple of bazooka-blammers. Some string. A balloon left over from a birthday party. Another mackerel and a pair of Splash's welding goggles.

"Can you build anything with this lot, Splash?" asked the Captain.

"A heavily armed flying fish?" Splash suggested.

"What good would that be?" said Rocky.

"Er ... none at all," said Splash.

The Space Penguins zoomed under the water again to see where the *Tunafish* had ended up. The deeper they swam, the darker it became. Captain Krill was right. This purple alien ocean was very deep indeed.

What was that? Suddenly Captain Krill glimpsed the silvery tail fin of something. Was it their spaceship? His heart soared as he darted towards it and the others followed.

Sure enough, it was the *Tunafish*, resting on a stony ridge about fifty metres below the surface. Around it, the water dropped away into deep blackness. If the spacecraft had sunk just a little to the left or the right, she would have been lost forever! It was a horrible thought.

Back at the surface, the penguins exchanged high-flippers.

"We'll have to go back down, get inside the *Tunafish* and fetch Splash's equipment," said Captain Krill. "You said you could build a winch, didn't you, Splash?"

Splash nodded.

"I knew this story wasn't over yet," said Rocky.

As the Space Penguins zigzagged back down through the purple ocean, a shoal of brightly coloured alien fish with big blue eyes appeared, following them curiously. It was the first sign of life that the penguins had seen.

When they found the *Tunafish* again, the penguins collected everything they could lay their flippers on. There were blue-eyed fish everywhere now, swimming around the penguins in brightly coloured clouds.

"What did you get?" Splash asked as they finally reached the surface.

"Four spanners and a welding torch," said Captain Krill.

"Three coils of steel rope and a mouthful of alien fish," said Fuzz.

"Did they taste nice?" asked the captain.

"Kind of. If you like coconut," said Fuzz.

A fluffy toy bear in a large block of ice bobbed up beside Rocky.

"That's Dave, my favourite teddy!" Rocky said. He didn't look happy. "What's he doing inside a block of ice?"

"Maybe he's a polar bear," suggested Fuzz.

"Ha ha, NOT," said Rocky crossly.

Fuzz handed over a long tube thing with a trigger. "Maybe it's something to do with this? I found it on your workbench, Splash."

"My new ice ray!" said Splash. "I tested it on Dave this morning."

Rocky was horrified. "You did?"

The Space Penguins looked at the iced-up Dave.

"I did," said Splash happily. "And it worked brilliantly."

"You…! I can't BELIEVE you ice-rayed Dave!" said Rocky.

"You have to make sacrifices for science, Rocky," said Splash. "While the rest of you head back to the *Tunafish* to get more equipment, I'll stay here and make us an ice floe. We need somewhere to live."

"Good plan," said Captain Krill.

Rocky, Captain Krill and Fuzz darted back to the *Tunafish* through a vast shoal of the blue-eyed alien fish. It was easier working on a full stomach, so they ate while they were there.

"Those fish are very easy to catch," said the captain as they bobbed up again. "It's just a shame they taste of coconut."

"I quite like it," said Rocky. "There's lots of them swimming around those big vents in the ridge. I'm going to catch some more."

He swam down again. Moments later, a blast of boiling hot water exploded from one of the vents and burned him on the bottom.

"Flipping flounders!" Rocky yelled, whooshing out of the water like a rocket. "Those fish must be fireproof! Where's Dave? I need to sit on him for a bit!"

CHAPTER THREE

SQUID FIGHT

On their third trip down to fetch equipment from the *Tunafish*, the Space Penguins noticed something strange. There were thousands of alien fish one minute, but then there were hardly any the next. It was as if someone had clicked their fingers and made them vanish.

Then they saw why.

Something huge … something white … something VERY scary was swimming towards them. It had more tentacles than they could count. Its belly pulsed and glowed. Its tiny purple piggy eyes boggled. It was hideous, and it was moving at high speed. It looked like a giant squid!

The penguins watched with horror as the squid monster blasted out a long tentacle and grabbed at a fleeing fish.

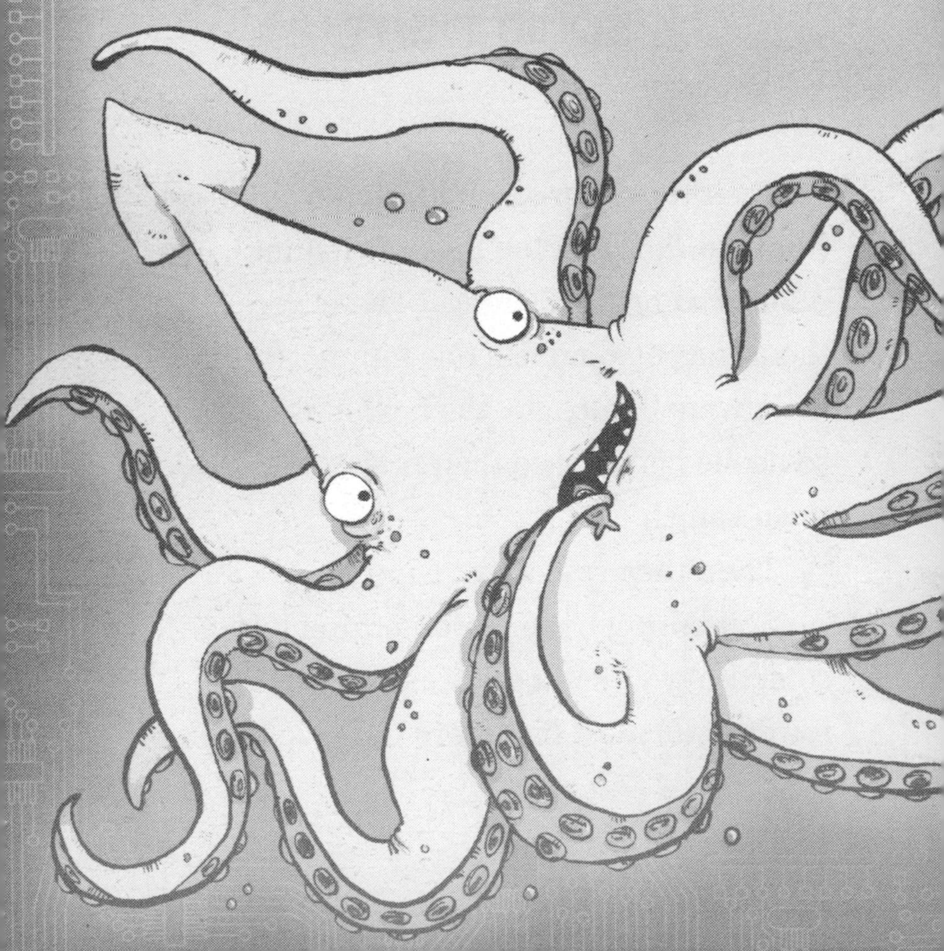

Popping the little creature into its mouth, it chomped down with evil green teeth. Then it turned its hungry eyes on the Space Penguins.

It was time to fight or be eaten. Or maybe swim away.

They decided to fight.

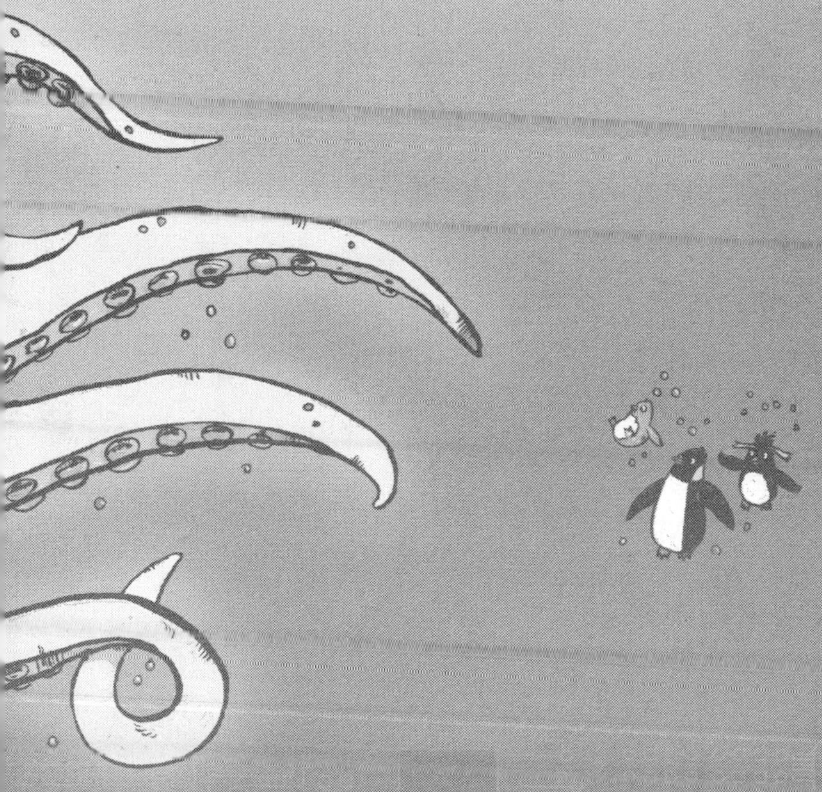

Fuzz attacked first, speeding at the monster's belly with his beak outstretched.

BOING!

The squid's skin was tough and rubbery, and Fuzz bounced right off again.

Rocky tried another tactic. WHAM! BAM! He pummelled the squid with his flippers. Like Fuzz, he bounced straight off the monster's skin. There were tentacles everywhere. The penguins felt like mice, in the power of a cat with too many paws. And now its mouth was getting closer. Closer and closer…

The penguins were running out of air. They had to get back to the surface!

In desperation, Captain Krill charged at the monster's ugly face and smashed his feet into its nose.

"WAWAWA!"

The purple ocean boomed with the monster squid's howl of pain. It pulled back its tentacles and fled into the deep darkness, trailing its rubbery limbs behind it.

The Space Penguins were safe – for now.

As the three penguins got to the surface, they found Splash sitting on top of a large purple ice floe.

Captain Krill, Rocky and Fuzz leaped aboard, their lungs burning for air.

"The fish aren't the only inhabitants on this planet, Splash," gasped Rocky. "There's a monster squid down there … and it's ten times bigger than the *Tunafish*!"

“Ten times!” gasped Splash, his eyes bobbling with fright.

“Yes, we almost got eaten!” said Fuzz with excitement. “It was wicked!”

“We can’t fetch anything else from the *Tunafish*,” said the captain. “It’s too risky. Do you have what you need to build this winch, Splash?”

Splash looked at the pile of nuts, bolts, tools, wheels, explosives and sticky tape that they had collected. “I think so,” he said. “It won’t be perfect, but I’ll manage.”

“Then do it!” commanded Captain Krill. “The quicker you make that winch, the quicker we can pull up the *Tunafish* and get out of here! Penguin power!”

“Penguin power!” the others shouted back.

So what if there was a big squid monster underneath them? They weren’t intergalactic heroes for nothing.

"We're the Space Penguins!" roared Fuzz. "Hear us flap!"

The penguins got busy. Banging and hammering filled the wide purple horizon as far as the ear could hear. Every now and again, a blue-eyed fish popped its head above the water to see what was going on. When Splash put on his goggles and fired up his welding torch, Rocky backed away. He didn't want anything else to be burnt.

"Pass me the sticky tape," Splash said as the two suns began to set.

Rocky handed it over.

Splash wiped his forehead with his flipper.

"Spanner," he said next. "Not that spanner, Rocky, THAT spanner."

Tinker. Hammer. Tinker.

The instructions went on. "I need a screwdriver! The measuring tape! A cup of tea! That little thingy with the pointy bit on the end!"

By the time the winch was finished, the two yellow suns were sinking. Fifty metres of steel rope and a heavy steel hook hung off the ice floe down into the purple water. The other end looped around a complicated set of wheels with three turning handles.

"Now that's what I call a winch," said Rocky approvingly.

"Excellent work, Splash," said the captain.

Fuzz was too busy practising anti-squid moves further back on the ice floe to say anything.

Splash preened his feathers and looked pleased with himself. "I'm glad you like it," he said. "Let's just hope it works."

The Space Penguins paddled the ice floe along. Splash lay flat on his belly, peering into the water with a pair of waterproof binoculars to see if he could spot the *Tunafish* below.

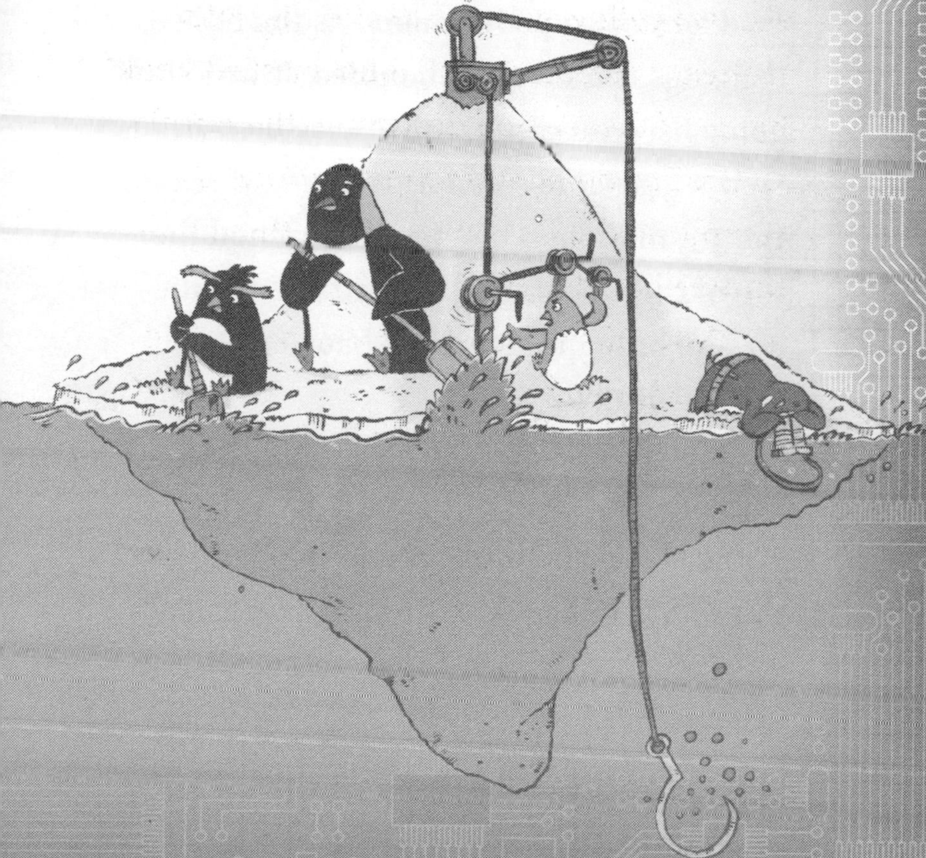

"Left a bit!" he shouted. "Right a bit! That's it! You've got it! The *Tunafish* is directly beneath us! Slowly now..."

The penguins felt the steel rope shudder, as if it had hit something.

"Yes!" said Splash. "You've hooked it! Start winding it up!"

"Here we go!" shouted Rocky.

The steel rope tightened as the Space Penguins turned their handles. It was slow going because the *Tunafish* was heavy. Fuzz's legs were so short that he lifted off the ground when his handle reached the top of the wheel. He paddled hard at the air and brought his wheel back to the ground again.

Slowly the spaceship started lifting off the ridge. Its nose came first. Then its belly. Soon the *Tunafish* was dangling from the rope like a massive – well, a massive tunafish.

"Yes!" Splash shouted. "Yes! Ye— No! NO!"

The rope suddenly went slack. The penguins tumbled backwards as the steel rope flew out of the water. The empty hook crashed into the purple ice floe, just missing Rocky's head.

"We dropped it!" said Splash in dismay. "The *Tunafish* is gone!"

THE HUNT

The two yellow suns disappeared into the purple sea. Two green moons rose in their place. It was too dark, even in the bright green moonlight, for the Space Penguins to try and find the *Tunafish* now. Who knew where she had ended up?

"We'd better get some sleep, crew," said Captain Krill.

"My mother sang me a lullaby when I was a chick," said Splash as the penguins settled down and tried to get comfortable.

Rocky cuddled Dave, who had defrosted. "It helped me to drop off."

"I never knew you had a mother, Splash," said Fuzz.

"Everyone has a mother, Fuzz," said Captain Krill, staring up at the green night sky. "No matter how far away she might be. Will you sing it for us, Splash?"

Splash cleared his throat.

"Hush little penguin, don't lose your fluff,

"Mummy's going to catch you some fishy stuff,

"When the snow storms freeze your feet,

"Mummy's going to warm them with her body heat,

"When you're feeling really bored,

"Mummy's going to build you an ice-cube sword,

"Nights will como and seals will snore,

"Mummy's going to love you forever more."

It was a lovely song. But in spite of Splash's best efforts, no one slept a wink. They lay on their backs on the ice floe, staring at the green-looking moons and feeling terrible. Here they were, four intergalactic heroes, who now needed rescuing themselves! The winch, the rope and the empty steel hook lay beside them. Would they ever get off this planet?

"Poor *Tunafish*," said Fuzz.

"Poor ICEcube!" wailed Rocky. "I promised we'd be back to rescue the ship."

"Poor us," said Splash. "Staying here forever and eating nothing but coconut-flavoured fish."

"Stay positive, crew," said Captain Krill. "I'm sure that everything will look better in the morning."

"Let's face it," Rocky said glumly. "It

can't look any worse."

Morning came ten minutes later. The planet was clearly very small, with short days and even shorter nights.

"Right," said the captain. He stood up on the ice floe and smoothed his yellow ear patches. "Let's go down there and find out exactly where the *Tunafish* is."

"What about the monster squid?" asked Splash.

"I'm not afraid of that tentacled trampoline," said Fuzz.

"We can use the fish," said Rocky.

"In what way?" said Fuzz. "A coconut casserole?"

"No, you dim dogfish," said Rocky. "Remember how the fish swam away when the squid appeared? Well, how about we swim with them, and use them as a warning system? If they disappear again, it means that the squid is coming.

Then we can disappear too."

"The Fuzzmeister never disappears," said Fuzz. He struck a ninja pose. "He fights to the death!"

"He follows orders," Captain Krill reminded Fuzz. "And I order you to swim away this time – as soon as you see the squid. Now let's go."

Thousands of alien fish glided around the penguins as they went in search of the *Tunafish* once again. The spacecraft wasn't

on the ridge where it had been before. Either it had landed further along when it fell off the winch hook, or it had vanished into the bottomless ocean forever.

A vent in the ridge exploded with boiling hot water as Fuzz swam over it.

"Yow!" he yelled, shooting to the surface.

"I feel your pain, Fuzz," said Rocky, shooting up beside him. "Actually, no, I don't. HA HA HA HA!"

They swam on cautiously, following the ridge the whole way. There were fewer alien fish the further they went. Things were looking bad.

"The emptiness down there is making me nervous," said Rocky the next time they rose to the surface to catch their breath. "The squid could be just around the corner. What if he's hiding in the shadows?"

"Then we'll end up as fish food," Splash said.

"No one makes fish food out of Fuzz Allgrin!" said Fuzz.

"Keep looking, crew," said Captain Krill.

On they went. They had no choice.

This part of the deep purple ocean was completely still and silent. Now there were no alien fish at all. The penguins had lost the only warning they had.

Suddenly, Rocky spotted something silvery lying on a steep part of the ridge. He clapped Captain Krill on the shoulder and pointed.

The *Tunafish* was in a funny position with its nose pointing downwards, but at least they hadn't lost it completely. A big black cave yawned beside it like a hungry mouth.

"Great!" said Fuzz as they surfaced. "Now we've found it, all we have to do is winch it up again!"

"I didn't like the look of that cave, though," said Splash. "What if the squid monster's in there? Or more hot vents?"

"Only one way to find out," said Fuzz, ducking under the water again.

"What's he doing?" said Rocky.

"I think he's going to swim inside the cave and check it out," said Splash.

"He'll be boiled alive!" Rocky gasped. "Or eaten! Or both!"

"Follow him, crew!" said the captain. "He may need our help!"

They pelted after their space-mate, reaching the *Tunafish* and the cave just as Fuzz shot inside. The Space Penguins would have held their breath if they hadn't been holding it already.

Moments later, Fuzz shot out again. His

eyes were wide with terror.

An impossibly large tentacle whipped out of the cave mouth. It was the size of an express train and was dotted with suction pads like giant satellite dishes. It made the tentacles on the first alien squid look like skinny spaghetti.

Captain Krill was right when he said that everyone had a mother. The Space Penguins had just found the squid monster's mummy!

CHAPTER FIVE

CHASE THROUGH THE WAVES

"Swim for your lives!" cried Fuzz.

The Space Penguins turned and fled.

The gigantic tentacle was still unrolling from the cave mouth. It whipped from side to side, churning up the purple water so that it fizzed and bubbled.

More tentacles burst out of the cave. There were tentacles everywhere the penguins looked. A sea of tentacles. An ocean of tentacles. An entire PLANET of tentacles! How many more tentacles were there? The baby squid had had loads. Did the mother squid have even more? It was too scary to think about.

The penguins tried whooshing to the surface but their path was blocked by the biggest tentacle of all. They squeezed past its groping suction cups with millimetres to spare.

"We need to get to the ice floe!" shouted Rocky, bursting from the water. "Where is it?"

"Over there!" shouted Captain Krill, pointing to a pale purple dot on the horizon.

The monster tentacle reared out of the water and thudded down on them.

SMASH!

Purple water exploded in all directions. The penguins dived and twisted. Their flippers were a blur. Their feet were like whirling propellers.

SMASH! SMASH! SMASH!

More huge tentacles whipped and thumped into the sea. Waves crashed over the penguins' heads as they sped away. Nearly there… Nearly…

Leaping from the water, they skidded into the middle of the ice floe. The sea rocked violently.

"Now that's what I call a monster squid!" gasped Rocky. He smoothed his shaking eyebrows away from his face. "It makes the other one look like a bath toy!"

"I can't believe I swam away," Fuzz said. "I never swim away from ANYTHING."

"But that thing was the size of an iceberg," Splash soothed.

"I want to go back and fight it!" said Fuzz. "Now I know what I'm dealing with, I'll beat it flippers down! I have this BRILLIANT ninja penguin move—"

"No," ordered Captain Krill.

The ice floe lurched from side to side as the monster's tentacles smashed at the water around them, over and over again.

SMASH! SMASH!

It wasn't giving up.

"There's only one thing for it," Captain Krill shouted above the crashing waves. "We have to go back down, lure the monster inside the cave again and block the mouth. Otherwise we'll never be able to hook up the *Tunafish*. It's too close to the beast's lair."

"How?" said Rocky.

BLAM! went the tentacles.

"I could make a swimming clockwork bomb," Splash said. He seized some sheet metal, a couple of blue glass marbles and a bundle of explosives from the pile of spare equipment which hadn't been used to make the winch. "The explosion will cause a rock fall and block the cave mouth. It will give us just enough time to hook up the *Tunafish* and winch it to safety. I can make it look like one of those coconut fish, so that the monster isn't suspicious when it swims into the cave."

SMASH!

A tentacle came down so close that the ice floe tipped sideways. The Space Penguins grabbed at the equipment and the winch to stop them sliding into the churning sea. Splash gave the winch a blast with the ice ray to freeze it to the floe. They couldn't afford to lose anything now.

"The squid might even eat the fish-bomb," said Rocky hopefully.

"Then I hope it likes food with an explosive flavour," said Fuzz.

Splash fired up his welding torch and set to work. The ice floe stopped rocking as the monster got bored of smashing at the surface of the sea. But the penguins knew that it was still gliding around underneath them, waiting for its chance...

"Nearly there!" shouted Splash, welding bits of metal and blue marbles together at top speed. "I've packed it with explosives. It's going to make a mighty bang!"

BANG!

A gigantic tentacle split the penguins' ice floe in half. They clung on to what was left.

"Finished!" Splash held up the little bomb triumphantly. It looked just like an alien fish, complete with blue marbles for its eyes. "Now all we have to do is lure the monster back inside that cave! Who wants to be bait?"

"Me!" shouted Fuzz.

"You're a brave penguin but we almost lost you last time," said the captain. "Your legs and flippers aren't long enough for speed swimming. You'd be eaten in moments. Rocky? You're fast. Are you up to the job? You'll have to swim into the cave with the monster and then swim out again before Splash sets off the bomb."

Rocky smoothed his eyebrows away from his face. "Aye aye, Captain!" he said, standing to attention on the broken ice floe. "Just leave it to Rocky Waddle!" He leaped into the stormy purple water.

"Rocky!" called Captain Krill.

Rocky bobbed up. "What?"

"You're going the wrong way," said the captain. He pointed. "The cave and the *Tunafish* are over there."

"Oh … OK!" Rocky ducked beneath the waves again … just as the squid pulled its tentacles back under the water and started to chase him.

The rest of the penguins leaped in after the squid.

"Good luck!" shouted Splash as their space-mate zoomed out of sight ahead of them. "You're going to need it!"

UH-OH!

The penguins swam deeper and deeper, following Rocky and the squid monster. The monster filled the ocean. Its tentacles went on forever. It seemed almost as big as the watery planet itself. And it was fast. Very fast. Rocky twisted his flippers into crazy shapes to send himself zigzagging through the water. As he swam like mad towards the *Tunafish* and the cave, he used every penguin trick he could think of to avoid being caught.

THE FLAMINGO

THE ROCKET SPLIT

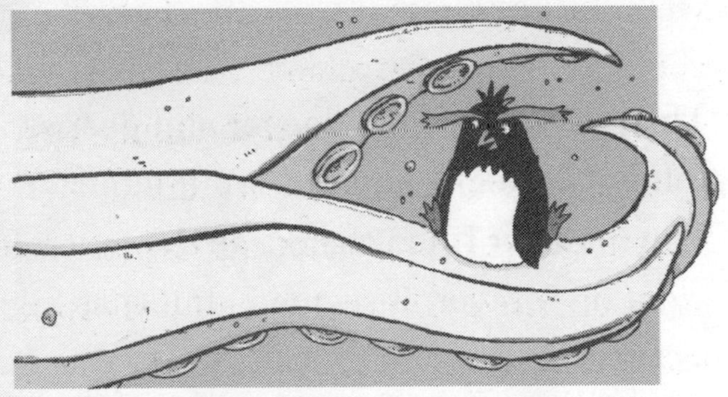

THE SKULL

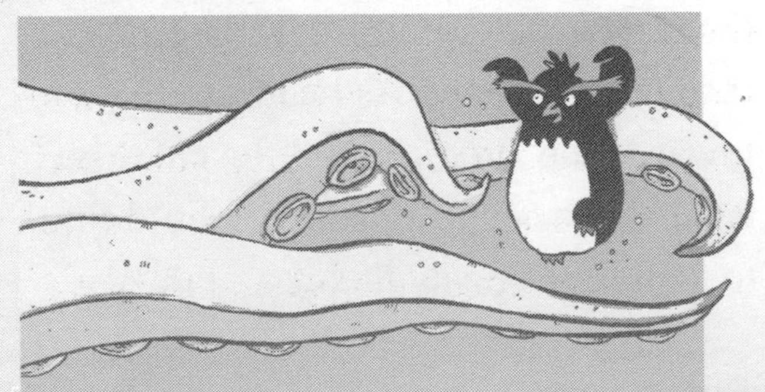

Nothing helped. The squid was gaining on him.

He burst back up and out of the water to take a breath, just as the other Space Penguins sprang up behind him to breathe as well. PING! PING! PING! Then they all dived back down.

A cloud of alien fish pelted through the water beside them for a while, before veering off into the gloom. The squid was getting closer to Rocky all the time. The other penguins stayed on its tail.

"Keep up, crew!" shouted Captain Krill as he arrowed into the air and back into the water again. "Not much further!"

"Don't drop the bomb before we get there, Splash!" yelled Fuzz. He surfed along on his belly for a bit, steering with his flippers. "Walloping whale-blubber! What a chase!"

The teetering *Tunafish* and the cave

mouth loomed into view. Rocky sped through the hole into the blackness. The gigantic squid monster followed him in and vanished like a snail curling back into its shell.

The rest of the Space Penguins screeched to a halt, back-paddling to slow themselves down. Splash wound up the clockwork fish-bomb and got ready to release it. Now all they needed was for Rocky to swim out of the cave again.

They waited. And waited. And waited.

"Where is he?" said Captain Krill, as they zoomed up to the surface for a much-needed breath.

"The squid monster must have caught him," said Fuzz.

"The baby could have been in there too," Splash said. "Why didn't we think of that? That would mean two monsters for Rocky to battle!"

"No way could those two jelly parachutes catch our Rocky Waddle!" said Fuzz. "He's much too quick."

"But what other explanation could there be?" said Splash.

"I'm going in to find out!" declared Fuzz.

"No," said Captain Krill before his feisty Chef and Security Officer could dip under the water again. "I'll go. It's a captain's job to look after his crew. Both of you must stay outside the cave mouth. And that's an order."

"Bo-ring," said Fuzz crossly.

Captain Krill swam as fast as a flippered torpedo to the cave, with Fuzz and Splash following behind. Clusters of alien fish glided around him, their blue eyes bright and curious. Even when he reached the cave, the fish didn't leave. They seemed to have lost their fear of the yawning black mouth. It was as if they knew the monsters might not be bothering them for much longer. Captain Krill ate a few to give himself strength.

He nodded firmly at Fuzz and Splash and turned to face the cave. It wasn't looking as black as before. Instead, it glowed with a pulsing green light. It was huge and very, very quiet. Where was Rocky? Should he go in? Or was this a stupid thing to do? He had no idea what to expect.

But then he thought of his pilot, trapped and helpless inside the cave, and he dived inside.

The water in the cave was cold. Enjoying the sudden change in temperature, Captain Krill swam as close to the walls as he could. If the monster saw him, both he and Rocky would be finished.

If Rocky wasn't finished already.

The cave floor was littered with piles of fish bones. Hundreds, thousands, MILLIONS of fish bones. No wonder the little fish had been scared. The placc was a huge fish cemetery. Everything shone with the same eerie green light.

Captain Krill stopped. There, at the back of the cave, sat the young squid with its back against the cave wall, glowing gently and looking at something in its tentacles. Something black and white with yellow eyebrows. A penguin! Rocky!

The slimy monster passed Rocky from one tentacle to the next. It turned him upside down. It shook him. It played with him like a penguin rattle.

Its enormous mother rested on the cave floor behind it, watching.

Rocky's eyes widened at the sight of Captain Krill. The captain gave him a stealthy flippers-up. If he did this right, they'd be out of the cave and back on the surface in no time. If he did it wrong…

The mother squid closed its watchful eyes. Captain Krill prepared to swim at the youngster and kick it in the nose again.

But suddenly, everything changed.

TICK. TICK. TICK.

A mechanical fish with blue marble eyes had swum into the cave. It was ticking loudly.

Oh no!

Splash had released the fish bomb too early. They were ALL going to be blown sky-high!

CHAPTER SEVEN

A VERY BIG BANG

This was a disaster!

TICK. TICK. TICK.

The mother squid still had its eyes shut. It hadn't noticed Captain Krill. But the youngster looked puzzled, twisting its blobby head back and forth. The captain could almost hear it thinking. *What's that ticking noise? Where is it coming from?*

Rocky struggled. The young squid tightened its grip and shook him a few more times. Its glowing eyes swept the cave curiously. The little fish bomb swam closer. Its metal scales gleamed in the cave's green light. Its blue marble eyes shone.

TICK. TICK. TICK.

Maybe Splash and Fuzz would be able to winch up the *Tunafish* by themselves and relaunch it? Captain Krill thought. Two Space Penguins zooming around the galaxy aboard the *Tunafish* was better than no Space Penguins at all.

TICK. TICK. TICK.

It was now or never. Captain Krill rocketed out of the shadows feet-first. If the two squid saw him before he kapowed the youngster, he was toast. If the bomb went off before he kapowed the youngster, they were ALL toast.

The young squid suddenly spotted the fish bomb. Its tiny eyes nearly popped out of its head.

They glowed extra bright and it made a snuffling sound of excitement. Rocky fell from its tentacles and bounced on the ground as the baby monster pounced after the shiny new toy that had swum into its cave.

Captain Krill raced down to Rocky and grabbed him under the flippers. Rocky moved feebly. He badly needed air. It looked like the captain would have to do most of the swimming. He kicked with all his might and dragged his pilot towards the cave mouth. It was a long swim – and it wasn't a moment too soon.

BADABOOM!

Rocks cascaded from the cave roof. The walls shuddered. The water boiled and surged. The current swept up the captain and Rocky and threw them out of the cave mouth as it crumbled.

"WAWAWA!"

"WAWAWA!"

The two squid monsters roared with rage and surprise. Their cave was collapsing! Everything was falling! Rocks were piling higher in the cave… The cave mouth was getting smaller…

Within moments, the cave was completely blocked. The plan had worked! The penguins had trapped the squid monsters! Would they have time to raise the *Tunafish* safely?

Fuzz and Splash grabbed Rocky and helped the captain to drag him upwards.

"WHEW!" gasped Rocky, breaking the surface and breathing for the first time in way too long. "I never thought air could taste so good! Thanks for getting me out, Captain. The small squid grabbed me as soon as I went in. It couldn't decide if I was a snack or a toy or both!"

"Why did you release the fish bomb so early, Splash?" demanded Captain Krill.

Splash blushed. "One of the alien fish got too close," he said. "Its tail brushed my feet and I dropped the bomb. What can I say? I'm ticklish!"

"There's a time and place for being ticklish, Splash," said Captain Krill sternly. "We were nearly roasted in there. Now get to work, crew! We have to hook up the *Tunafish* and winch her to the surface before those monsters work their way free!"

The penguins swam to the floe and scrambled aboard. Paddling it above the *Tunafish*'s latest position, they unrolled the winch's steel rope and hook.

BOOM! BOOM!

"That was one heck of a bomb, Splash," said Rocky, listening as he fed the steel rope and hook down into the water. "Things are still blowing up down there."

BOOM! BOOOM! BOOOOM!

"Impossible," said Splash. "Something else must be making that booming noise."

Something else was.

Beside the blocked-up cave mouth, the ridge was rippling up and down like someone was shaking it. BOOM! An explosion of boiling water shot out of a vent. Then another, and another.

"An earthquake!" gasped Rocky.

"It's more of a waterquake, really," said Splash.

"The fish bomb must have triggered it off!" said Captain Krill.

BOOOOM!

A huge explosion from a nearby hot water vent nearly boiled the Space Penguins' tails off. The ridge squirmed like an enormous stone snake beneath them. Shaken from its resting place, the *Tunafish* started sliding and bumping down the slope of the ridge.

BOOM! BOOOM! BOOOOOM!

The *Tunafish* was shaken up into the air. It was heading towards the abyss! And to make matters worse, three tentacles – one big and two even bigger – had started squirming out of the blocked cave mouth, furiously trying to break free.

What could they do?

THE BIG ONE

"This is not good," said Captain Krill as the Space Penguins jumped back on to the ice floe again. "It's bad. Very bad."

"We worked that out already, Captain!" said Rocky.

"Can you invent something else to get us out of this mess, Splash?" said Captain Krill.

"Sorry," said Splash. Water dripped from his orange ear markings. "I'm a genius at inventing stuff, but even I can't stop earthquakes."

BOOM! BOOOM!

With all the boiling water explosions, the sea was warming up. The edges of the ice floe started melting. Drip. Drip. Drip.

"It's over," said Rocky. "We're barbecued." His eyebrows drooped as he clutched his head with his flippers. "This floe will melt, and when it does we'll end up in the sea and be eaten by the monsters."

"It's over," Splash agreed. "Drip, plop, crunch."

BOOM! went the earthquake. BOOM! went the hot water vents. The quivering sea was starting to feel like a hot bath. The ice floe melted a little more.

Fuzz stood up. "You're a bunch of fish-livered wobble bottoms and you should be ashamed of yourselves!" he said.

Captain Krill frowned.

"Not you, Captain," said Fuzz. He turned back to Rocky and Splash. "It's only an earthquake, guys! A poxy bit of awe-inspiring nature! And what are two hideous squiddy space monsters to intergalactic penguin heroes like us?"

"Two hideous squiddy space monsters too many," said Rocky. "Face it, Fuzz. This is the end."

"Not so fast!" said Fuzz. "Not while the *Tunafish* is still down there."

He leaped off the ice floe and vanished beneath the bubbling waves.

"He's right," said Captain Krill to the others. "We have to bring up our spaceship or die trying. What are we waiting for, crew?"

The Space Penguins high-flippered each other and dived after Fuzz.

Below the surface, it felt like they were in a large purple saucepan that was reaching boiling point. They dodged from side to side as the hot water vents exploded around them.

As they neared the cave, they could see that the squid monsters had wiggled two more tentacles out of the blocked cave mouth and were lashing out at the hot sea. The penguins hopped about like flies in front of two massive rolled-up newspapers. They couldn't let themselves be beaten. Or indeed eaten. Not now. Not when they were so close to escaping!

A hundred metres from the blocked cave, the *Tunafish* see-sawed from side to side, teetering way down on the very brink of the ridge. One minute it pointed at the penguins. The next, it tipped away from them. They had to stop it from falling away to the bottom of the ocean. It was impossible to watch without gasping with terror. If it tipped over the edge, everything was well and truly lost.

The steel winch hook dangled down into the water beside the penguins. It swayed gently as the squid monsters stirred up the current. The *Tunafish* see-sawed even more violently.

Fuzz seized the hook with both flippers. Then he let go and sprang away, bringing his flippers up to his beak. The hook was burning hot.

The Space Penguins realized the awful truth.

Not only was the hook now too hot to touch, the steel rope wasn't long enough to reach the nose of the *Tunafish* any more.

At that moment…

BOOOOOOM!

A vent underneath the *Tunafish* suddenly exploded in a fountain of boiling water. The penguins somersaulted backwards. Struggling round the right way again, they stared as their ship lifted and took off through the water like – like what else? A space rocket!

WHOOOOSH!

The *Tunafish* flew towards the surface, nose-first, carried on a boiling head of steam. The Space Penguins chased after it. The seawater was nearly scalding.

"Wahoo!" shouted Fuzz, rocketing on to the surface alongside the others on a tide of hot bubbles. "My backside is barbecued like a beefburger, but who cares? We didn't need the winch after all! Here it comes!"

The *Tunafish* exploded into the air beside them.

SPLOOOOOOOSH!

It spun like a big silver ballerina on the jet of boiling water – and crash-landed on what was left of the ice-floe.

"We've got it!" cheered Rocky as boiling water splattered down and the steaming sea rocked around them. "Let's get inside. We're outta here!"

But the *Tunafish* was so hot that it was cutting through the ice floe like a silver sword. At this rate, it was going to sink all over again!

"The ice ray, Splash!" shouted Captain Krill. "Blast the *Tunafish* to cool it down!"

Splash dived for the ice ray, which had slid off the floe into the water, and fired it at the *Tunafish*. The boiling spacecraft crackled with ice for a few seconds, but showed no signs of slowing down as it sliced through the floe.

"It's not enough, Captain!" said Splash.

"All penguins on board, NOW!" Captain Krill bawled. "Your lives depend on it!"

"Dave!" shouted Rocky, grabbing his hot, wet teddy as it floated past him. "You're coming with me!"

The Space Penguins leaped on to the floe. The melting ice was lovely and cold under their feet. Splash blasted the door of the *Tunafish* with the ice ray and Fuzz grabbed the cooling door handle.

BANG! The door flew open. Purple water and lots of blue-eyed fish tumbled out. The penguins jumped inside, sloshing through the steaming water.

"OW!" roared Fuzz, hopping from foot to foot. "How hot is this floor?"

"Great to see you again, ICEcube," said Captain Krill. "Is everything operational?"

"Welcome back, Captain," said ICEcube

in a soggy-sounding voice. "Engines are wet but working. I am emptying the water as quickly as I can. We have exactly 4.1 seconds before this ice floe melts and we sink again. All I can suggest is that you cross your flippers."

As the penguins buckled themselves into their uncomfortably hot seats, they heard the ice floe cracking and creaking underneath the *Tunafish*.

Crack… Creak…

CRASH!

The mother squid had broken free from the cave. It leaped out of the water with its tentacles flailing. It was so enormous that its body blotted out both yellow suns. Its eyes were bigger than the rapidly melting ice floe.

"What are you waiting for?" shouted Captain Krill urgently. "Fly, Rocky. Fly!"

Rocky pushed in the throttle as the

squid monster lunged at them. It missed. With a roar and a blast of steam, the *Tunafish* lifted off … just as the ice gave a final creak and fizzed away to nothing.

They rocketed away, leaving the squid monster far behind them. They were free!

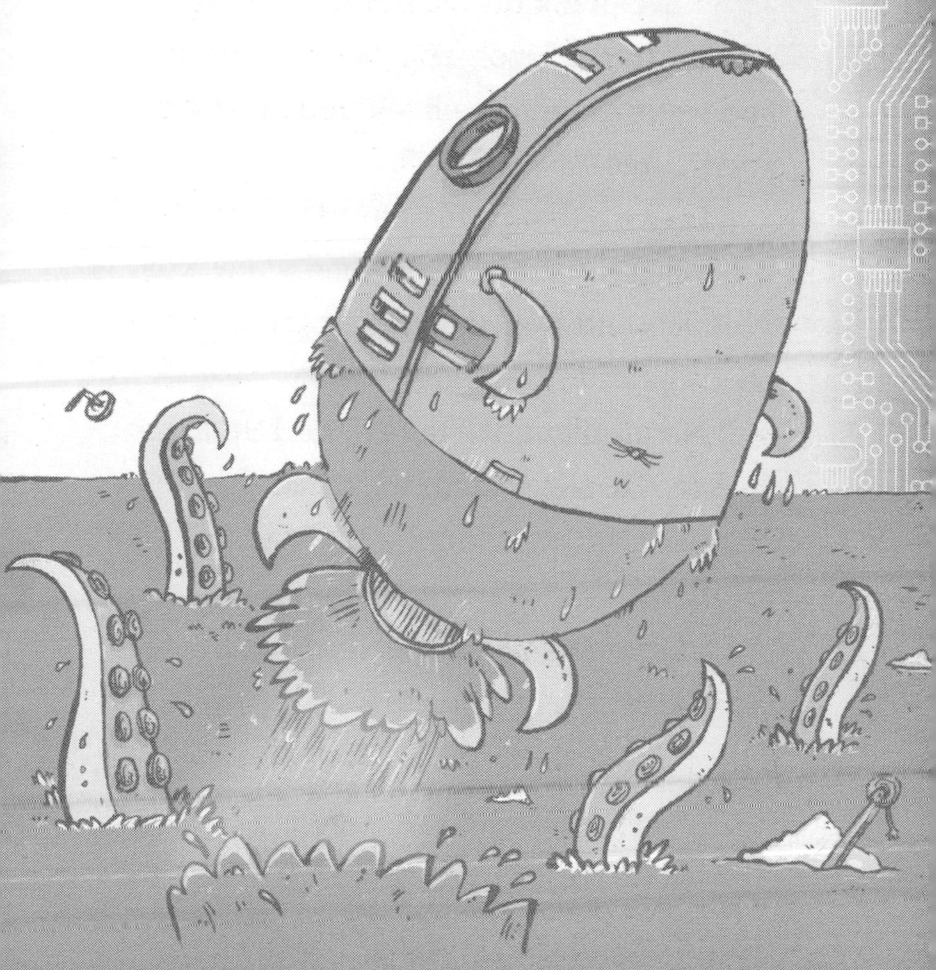

"We did it!" cheered Fuzz as they zoomed back into space. "We totally rock!"

"Head for Section F of the Universe, Rocky," said Captain Krill. "Dark Wader won't think of looking for us there. If I ever meet him again, I'll have something to say about his attack on us. But for now we need to find a nice penguin-friendly planet and settle down. I've had enough adventures for a while."

"I have a fish in my circuit boards," ICEcube said as Rocky flipped a few switches and programmed in the coordinates for Section F.

"No problem, ICEcube," said Splash. "Leave it to the Space Penguins!"

P.S.

The tiny jellyfish-shaped spy camera clinging to the bottom of the spaceship *Tunafish* coughed and woke up. Since sending information about the whereabouts of the *Tunafish* to Dark Wader for the Squid-G attack, it had been half-drowned and half-boiled, but it was still working. It started to send a new message. Back on his space station, the *Death Starfish*, Dark Wader was celebrating.

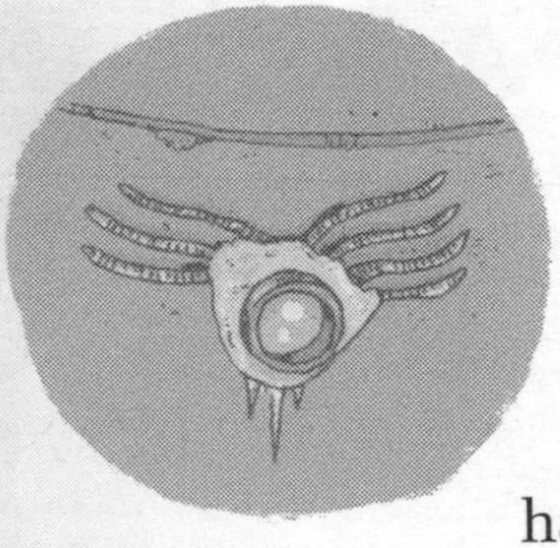

"Read me the Squid-G report again, Crabba," he chortled.

"Spaceship *Tunafish* terminated," read Crabba, Dark Wader's crusty, crab-like alien sidekick. "Your Squid-Gs blew it out of the sky. That's all the report says, boss. I've read it to you ten times already."

"Ha ha! I expect the *Tunafish* went up in a blaze of flames," Dark Wader said happily. "Those penguins must have been frazzled to cinders. I only wish I'd been there to see it! That's shown them – they should never have meddled with Dark Wader! Victory is mine!"

The jellycam's message popped up on a screen by Crabba's head.

TUNAFISH BACK IN ACTION. REPEAT, *TUNAFISH* BACK IN ACTION.

"What?" Dark Wader cried as he stared at the screen in rage and horror. "That's IMPOSSIBLE!"

But the message continued.

SPACE PENGUINS HEADING FOR SECTION F OF THE UNIVERSE. MORE MESSAGES SHORTLY.

Dark Wader thumped his armoured

flippers down on the arms of his chair.

"No one attacks me and my Death Starfish and gets away with it," he said in a dangerous voice. "I'm going to finish those Space Penguins off once and for all. Fetch me a Squid-G, Crabba. Those blubber bandits have eaten their last fish!"

Take a peek at the Space Penguins' next adventure:

GALAXY RACE!

LOADING...

FZZWZZ...

LOADING...

Welcome aboard the Spaceship Tunafish. I am ICECube, the cleverest on-board computer you will ever meet. I guide my ship and my space crew through the universe and get them out of FZZWZZ.

I mean: trouble.

My circuit boards got wet on our last mission and are still damp. I keep saying FZZWZZ for no reason. You have been warned.

You will be surprised to learn that the crew on board the Tunafish are FZZWZZ.

I mean: PENGUINS.

NASA sent me plus five penguins on a

top secret space mission five years ago, aboard a special fish-shaped spaceship called the Tunafish. Then they lost us. My database says: epic fail.

Oh well. Things could be worse. The Space Penguins have kept busy during their time up here. They are now famous across the Universe for their intergalactic exploits.

The planet Koffi changed its name to Planet T after Captain T. Krill's bravery in the famous space battle of Boyling Ketl.

Fuzz Allgrin, Chef and Security Officer, taught the planet Kungfu-BBQ the difference between a lamb chop and a karate chop.

Splash Gordon, the Ship's Engineer and inventor, introduced power showers to the pongy aliens on the Planet Smelibot.

And the Tunafish's pilot Rocky Waddle got lost on the planet Strait-Ahed, which everyone thought was impossible.

Now the Space Penguins just want to find a friendly planet where they can settle down and fish for FZZWZZ and slide around on the ice. The trouble is, they keep getting distracted. One minute they're fighting their mortal enemy Dark Wader – an evil penguin robot with plans to rule the universe. The next they're landing on wet planets, nearly drowning me and making me say FZZWZZ all the time.

Uh oh. What's this?

An enormous ball of rotting food, floating among the stars! And it's right in the Tunafish's path.

I ought to inform Captain Krill before we crash right into it. But he's busy just now, giving Rocky Waddle some bad news. And Rocky's not looking happy...

YUCK!

"The answer is NO, Rocky," said Captain Krill as the Spaceship *Tunafish* cruised through Section F of the Universe at around three hundred thousand light years an hour. "You CAN'T enter the Superchase Space Race this year."

"That's what you said last year, Captain!" complained Rocky Waddle. "And the year before. And the year before that!"

"The Superchase Space Race is the most dangerous race in the Universe," said

Captain Krill, looking down at his pilot. As an emperor penguin, the captain stood head and flippers above the rest of his crew. "Spaceships get smashed to bits every year. We can't risk losing the *Tunafish* that way. She's the only spaceship we've got."

"And the Emperor of Sossij wins every year anyway, doesn't he?" said Splash. He lifted his inventor's goggles to join in the conversation. Oil and grime streaked his face, hiding his orange ear patches. "I don't know why anyone else bothers."

"But—" began Rocky.

"Make like a sardine and can it, Rocky," said Fuzz Allgrin. He folded his little blue penguin flippers across his even littler blue penguin tummy. "When Captain Krill says no, he means no."

"Thank you, Fuzz," said Captain Krill.

Rocky slid off his pilot's chair and

glared at the other Space Penguins. He flicked his long yellow eyebrows off his face. "You know what your problem is?" he said. "None of you have any imagination. The winner of the Superchase Space Race wins the Golden Galaxy Goblet, and fame and glory for ever! I could win the Superchase Space Race with my eyes closed and my flippers tied behind my back. Everyone knows that I'm the best pilot in Outer Space—"

CRASH!

The *Tunafish* shuddered in mid-air as something smashed into it. Fuzz fell over. Rocky rushed back to his pilot's chair.

"The best pilot in Outer Space?" said Fuzz, struggling to his feet. "Then how come we just CRASHED?"

"What did we hit, Rocky?" asked Captain Krill.

"I don't know," Rocky admitted, peering

through the windscreen of the *Tunafish*. "It's gone dark out there."

"We're in Outer Space, trout brains," said Fuzz. "It's always dark out there."

"Darker than normal, I mean." Rocky pointed with one flipper. "What in the name of cod is this stuff?"

Something gloopy was covering the windscreen of the *Tunafish*, making it impossible to see out.

"It looks like a thousand mouldy squelchglub cores," said Splash.

"So it does, by halibut!" said Fuzz. He stood on his tiptoes to get a better view. "There's lots of old splattergunk peelings as well. And look! Dribblebog guts!"

The squelchglub cores were brown and mouldy. The splattergunk peelings were nearly black and the dribblebog guts were green. There was lots of other nameless mess too, smeared across the glass. It smelled terrible.

"Why have we crashed into a cosmic compost heap, ICEcube?" asked Captain Krill.

"It's not a compost heap, Captain," said ICEcube. "It's space-pig swill."

"Yuck!" gasped the Space Penguins.

"The dribblebog guts look great," said Fuzz. "I could turn them into fritters."

"Do you know why there's space-pig swill floating around here, ICEcube?" asked the captain.

"My database doesn't have that information, Captain," said ICEcube.

Captain Krill smoothed his yellow eye patches. "Rocky? Move slowly," he said. "And turn on the windscreen wipers. Best flippers forward, crew. And – go."